BLATCHFORD
BLUEPRINTS

The Art of Creating Practice Success

BY
DR. BILL BLATCHFORD
AND
CAROLYN BLATCHFORD, MST

BLATCHFORD SOLUTIONS
BEND, OREGON

ISBN: 978-0-9823836-1-2

Printed in the United States of America

Book design and photo shoot concept by
RocketDog Dental
Call for your consultation today:
1.877.869.2293
www.rocketdogdental.com

Other publications by Dr. Bill Blatchford:

Playing Your 'A' Game
Copyright © 2005

The Blatchford Dentist's Mighty Guide Book
5th printing 2000

Blatchford's Block Booking Video, 1999

For ordering:
(800) 578-9155; www.blatchford.com

BLATCHFORD SOLUTIONS
IS DEDICATING THIS BOOK TO:

Our great team of Carol Bogner, Tiffany Evans, Carol Fisher, Nanci Granahan, Nanci Huston, Debra Miller, Kaye Puccetti and Jeanne Swenson.

And to the 2000 Doctors and teams who have taken the Blatchford Coaching Program. Your commitment and dedication has given us the stimulus and enthusiasm to share with others what we have learned. Thank you for your successes and failures as we learn from it all.

PROCEEDS

Everyone should have a cause which creates a passionate commitment and involvement on your part. We encourage you to find your own.

Our passionate cause is Type 1 Insulin Dependent Diabetes Mellitus. It was a huge surprise when our youngest daughter was diagnosed with Type 1 Diabetes at age 28. Carolyn and Tiffany completed the Seattle to Portland (STP) bike race and both did not drink enough water. Tiffany, however, continued to be thirsty. Three weeks later, she was a bridesmaid in a South Bend, IN wedding we all attended. By then, she had lost 15 pounds, was eating everything, still hungry and her vision was blurred. Bill encouraged a medical visit and her Type 1 was confirmed.

Tiffany wants to be known as a friend, a sister, daughter, teacher, wife and member of the greater community who happens to have diabetes. She is taking full responsibility of herself and doing a stellar job. She is very hopeful of the stem cell research being conducted.

Nanci Granahan of Chicago, a Blatchford consultant for ten years, was diagnosed as a Type 1 diabetic at age 11. One of her passions is to reach her yearly goal of raising funds for JDRF. She is creative, relentless and committed to helping find a cure.

Why does the body attack one of its own? Medical science is still searching for a cause. Type 2, formerly known as geriatric diabetes, is arriving in epidemic proportions in America. The American Diabetes Association is an umbrella of research handling both distinct conditions. JDRF deals only with Type 1 working currently on many avenues of research including an artificial pancreas and advanced stem cell therapy. Research takes money and talent.

All profits from Blatchford BLUEPRINTS are dedicated to Juvenile Diabetic Research Foundation (JDRF). We purposely priced this book to be affordable and have included an envelope for you to make your contribution again and again.

We thank you.

IN MEMORIAM:

From *Playing Your 'A' Game—*
Inspirational Coaching to Profitability

Dr. Susan Weyers

Dr. Fred Berman

Dr. John Miner

CONTENTS

BLATCHFORD
BLUEPRINTS

The Art of Creating Practice Success

BY
DR. BILL BLATCHFORD
AND
CAROLYN BLATCHFORD, MST

WHY THIS BOOK?

Our purpose is in writing this book is to share our 38 years of business experience in dentistry. Graduating from Loyola Dental School in Chicago in 1970, I had a lot of confidence and started on my own in a university town of 40,000 with over 50 dentists. I relied on several good friends to steer me in the right direction for business success and I am grateful to them.

Along the way, I stumbled many times in between moments of success. In those low moments, I wondered, "why didn't they teach us this in dental school?" Why didn't they warn us to avoid this tunnel which has no cheese?

What I know now is the mandate of the dental school is to teach the student in four years to pass the state dental board. There is no time for business courses. Being successful in business is not the job of the professional schools. Their job is to teach the skills and science behind the skills. This holds true for medicine and veterinary practice also. Understanding that, it seems important that we share with the profession the lessons I have learned.

I have always been fascinated with business and I find dentistry to have a simple structure. However, there are some very important elements which can cause even the most brilliant science student to stumble.

- Dentists work with a small team of people who need to share a common vision (a struggle to make that happen but magic when it does)
- Dentists are full time players and do not have the luxury of full time leadership, reading, thinking and conferencing with others
- Dentistry has encouraged a quiet perfectionist personality to enter the ranks. These are not natural cheerleaders. This is,

however, changing as dental students arrive with previous careers and experiences plus, there are more right brained women.

- Dentists can feel frustrated with business and numbers as they really enjoy the doing-ness of dentistry.

Thus, I want to share with you my enthusiasm, passion and depth of concern to help keep good dentists in the game and to encourage men and women who are thinking about serving in this way to march forth with confidence and goals.

You have noticed, too, change is happening so rapidly, the curve is accelerating. The classics remain yet, as technology advances, doubling every three years and faster, we need new thinking. Einstein said, "The significant problems we face cannot be solved at the same level of thinking that we used when we created the problem."

My goal is to bring new thinking to the classics.

CHANGES IN DENTISTRY
By Bill, really!

Wow! Where does time go? My father told me that life seems to go faster as you get older. He is now 90 years old. He was right. Life is short.

It seems like yesterday I was being accepted at Loyola Dental School in Chicago. I was a wide-eyed kid from a dairy farm in Oregon. What a shock to arrive at the train station in Chicago in the fall of 1966, during a long hot summer. Chicago was having riots with buildings and cars on fire. I could constantly hear sirens and the occasional sounds of gun shots. This was a race riot, something I had never experienced.

During this emerging time of hippies, we were told on the first day of dental school as our class met in the main lecture hall to be clean shaven! That is no facial hair and no sideburns below the ala – tragus line. We were required to wear a white shirt and tie everyday to class. Our entire class or 65 students was all white males. We sat in alphabetical order everyday for four years. Our training was excellent.

Carolyn and I were married between the first and second year. The next three years went rapidly. Upon graduation, our choices were to go into the service or set up a practice. My goal was to set up a practice. We stumbled onto the university town of Corvallis, Oregon by accident. We made an emotional decision on Corvallis. We had no knowledge about demographics, how many dentists had recently set up there, or that Corvallis did not need another dentist.

I somehow expected all the dentists to welcome me with open arms. Instead, most told me to go to another town. One dentist, Dr. Charlie Stuart welcomed me and let me use his office on his day off. He told me from the start, he would not be able to refer patients to me as he was not turning anyone away. Charlie was an excellent dentist and taught me the value of complete treatment planning and allowing the patient to decide what they wanted to do.

I had no training in the business of dentistry. I knew a lot about dairy farming. Charlie was a big help. I found a small office downstairs in the same building and convinced the bank to loan me $15,000 to build out the 900 square feet and set up two chairs. There was no dental insurance. Patients had to pay cash or finance with the dentist. It did not take very long to realize that I knew very little about clinical dentistry, either. I knew just enough to pass the Oregon Board exam. Charlie helped me set a new course for education. I also worked one day a week for Dr. Phil McSorley in Eugene who introduced me to many concepts of practice management I still teach today. He also introduced me to placing implants.

In 1972, I attended the American Academy of Preventive Dentistry meeting in Chicago which was a turning point in my career. I met Dr. Robert Barkley, one of the founders of this new direction for dentistry. I had the opportunity to have lunch with Dr. Omer Reed. I decided I wanted to be like him when I grew up. I studied these leaders in our field. These mentors were all about change.

I joined an implant study club at the University of Oregon Dental School. With Charlie Stuart's

Dr. Bill Blatchford, new dentist in Corvallis, is establishing his practice at 14th and Harrison.

encouragement, I studied with Dr. Niles Guichet and the Society for Occlusal Studies.

All the while, I would attend local dental society meetings where I heard dentists arguing against any changes. They were opposed to hygienists giving local anesthetic, any marketing, denturists, composite fillings, or, it seemed anything they did not learn while in dental school. They liked the status quo. I learned early on, if you stick your head above the crowd, look out. Dr. Guichet said, "We are a profession that eats it young." I did not understand what he meant for a long time.

During the next few years, we started to deal with dental insurance. At first this was welcomed because patients could now afford better treatment. This was good. Hygienists in Oregon could give local anesthetic. This was good. Dental materials were improving rapidly. We could do things we had not imagined in dental school. I brought in a partner. We opened a satellite office in Newport, Oregon. Three weeks after we opened our doors the major employers in town offered dental insurance. No one in this small, underserved town had ever been offered complete treatment. No one had offered root canal treatment. Every adult over thirty had their lower first molars missing and had insurance with a $1,000 yearly maximum. Crown fees were under $300 per unit. It seemed they all accepted two three-unit bridges. We thought we were good at case presentation.

I started to study orthodontics with USDI in Seattle. I was also taking courses from the FACE Institute in San Francisco. I also studied neuromuscular dentistry with Dr. Barney Jankelson. I took a multi-day course on extracting wisdom teeth. Life was good. We were busy and cash flow was good. We built a vacation house in the beach community of Newport. This model continued for five years. After five years, I was out producing my partner 3:1. This was not good. We sold the satellite practice and dissolved the partnership.

I was now on my own again. I was introduced to the Quest program started by Dr. Gary McLeod and Dr. Ron McConnell. This was the first big practice management group in the country which was a major turning point for me. I started to look at the practice like a business. Their model was high production. I excelled.

I built a new building with Dr. Stuart when interest rates were 22%. I increased my staff to 16 by taking over Dr. Stuart's practice when he retired. I grew so that I was producing $1,000,000 by 1985. This was a big deal. The only problem my overhead was 80%.

I enjoyed running marathons with Carolyn. She trained and I did aerobic dentistry. I started to look at my overhead. I discovered that I was constantly chasing the overhead. I decided to lower the overhead to match my low months not the highs. The staff was reduced far lower than any of my advisors thought possible given the income we were producing. It was a gamble and it worked.

By this time, I was starting to lecture on occlusion and practice management as a hobby. I favored practice management. When I started practice management coaching in Canada, it was not legal to extend credit to patients for treatment. You could not even use a credit card. If you mentioned selling dentistry, they wanted to run you out of town on a rail. I had several dental societies tell me not to mention the "S" word at their meeting. Their message to me was, "We all want to make more money, but do not mention profit." I was the subject of discussion of several dental societies and associations. What a crazy idea, that dentists should make a reasonable living. How absurd that they should offer ideal treatment and let the patient decide what they wanted. I was presenting the idea that if you ask questions instead of lecturing to your patients, you might find out what was important to them and you should only present treatment that met that need.

In 1988, I sold my practice and started coaching full time. At that time, the business of dentistry was hardly discussed in polite company. Cosmetic dentistry was barely getting started. It was still considered heresy in many circles to remove tooth structure (the sacred enamel) just to make someone look better. Better bonding agents were coming in and cosmetic dentistry was gaining a foot hold.

Over the last twenty years, Blatchford Solutions has coached over 2000 dentists. We have experienced many changes. We have seen the advent of external marketing. Dentistry has a great product. Let's let the public know about it. The American public spends more on bottled water than on dentistry. We have seen the use of all types of media. We have seen tasteful advertising and some very distasteful advertising. Today external marketing seems to be accepted in most parts of the country.

We have seen incredible changes in restorative materials and techniques. Our profession welcomes new technology and at the same time tends to fight most change.

In the forty years, we have expanded the duties of auxiliaries. My personal belief is that we must do this even faster if we are to keep up with the growing demand for dental treatment as our population grows and ages. We only have 60% as many dentists graduating each year as we had twenty years ago. Approximately 50% of these graduates are women and only half of those are purchasing practices. Our population has grown by over 100 million people during the same time frame. My fear is that if we the profession do not address this, the federal government will. We have watched how this works in countries like the United Kingdom. After fifty years of socialized dental care, they have the highest edentulous rate in the western world.

Another positive change in dentistry is the increase in the number of women dentists. I have seen our profession move from a field dominated by white males to one that accepts women and men from diverse ethnic backgrounds. In my opinion, women are going to be the dominant force in the dentistry in the future. From my perspective, they are easier to coach. While this change is happening, our daughter found many people assumed she was studying to be a hygienist when she told them she was going to dental school.

The women who are now entering dentistry do not feel they know all the answers and are eager to seek help from the start. They actually ask for directions when lost. Men tend to keep driving in circles whether in a new city or in their practice. Women dentists seek coaching to start their practices rather than digging a few holes first. It is easier for most women to relate to the patients because of better listening skills and the ease to think more with the right side of the brain. I have noticed it is more difficult for a man to purchase a woman's practice than for a woman to purchase a man's practice. Many health care decisions are made by the women in a family as they are quicker to seek help with health care issues.

A positive change for the profession is the better dental health of our population and a better appreciation for improvement rather than remedial treatment. We have moved from just drill, fill, and bill to an age where we can really change lives by improving appearances. We can thank the early adapters of this new field of dentistry for this change. They certainly took more than a few arrows in their backs. Change comes hard to this profession. It was alright to extract four bicuspids to improve one's appearance with orthodontic treatment, but the very thought of removing enamel to make someone look better was repulsive to many. It was alright to remove the same enamel to prepare a three unit bridge, but not alright to remove healthy tooth structure for appearance sake.

The training available today has made better dentists out of the general dentist who takes advantage of all this education. Now, many cases that were at one time only for the specialists are now within the reach of the general dentist who has sought strong continuing education to learn how to successfully treat these cases. I am referring to complex restorative cases involving implants, bone grafts, sinus lifts, and the restorative stage as well. Many general dentists are also learning to do this under oral and IV sedation.

My personal prediction is that in the future we will have very well trained general dentists and fewer specialists. I also see a closer relationship with the patient's physician as we embrace the treatment of sleep apnea and continue to pursue the oral/systemic relationship of many diseases. The future of dentistry is very bright.

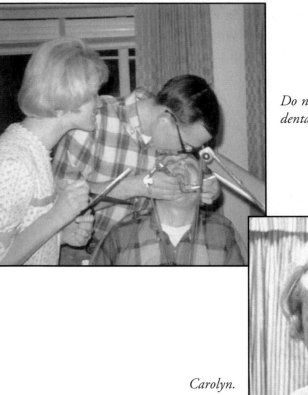

Do not hire this dental assistant.

Carolyn.

Skiing at Mt. Bachelor 43 years ago.

Enjoying Lake Michigan.

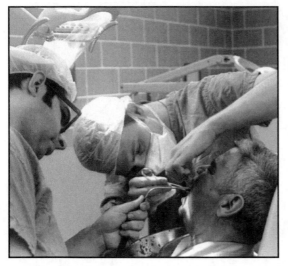

Trustworthy fourth year Loyola dental students.

DR. WILLIAM BLATCHFORD, dentist, is one of four Corvallis doctors who have opened an office at S.W. 9th and Fall Streets, Newport. The office is open on a full-time basis, with each doctor here on a part-time basis. (Staff Photo)

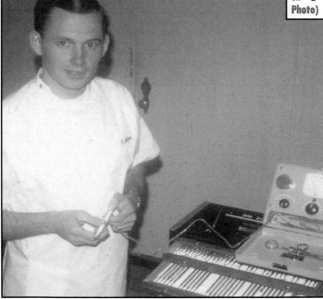

A proud new student in the clinic.

WHY DOES BILL DO WHAT HE DOES?

Why did Dr. Blatchford quit the practice of dentistry?

Some have asked why Dr. Blatchford did not continue the practice of dentistry while coaching. Here is his wife's take on the why. He enjoyed learning the business of dentistry while practicing. Always a CE student, he loved occlusion, ortho, TMJ (before it was known as "neuro-muscular") and learning sales.

He and several dentists worked for two years with a psychiatrist studying the emotional process of sales—how we make decisions. While practicing, he was asked to teach sales and occlusion with several groups, finding himself away some weekends to make it work. He loved both. He had mentored several associates, and purchased his building mate's practice of equal size just as an associate. After two years, the associate purchased the practice, leaving Bill free to pursue coaching.

Though his principles of business would be applicable in many venues, he stays only in dentistry. Others think that it is valuable to have a coach who has done the work, watched the clock, made a payroll and tried to make it more efficient.

He has audited the cosmetic and implant courses to keep current. Our oldest daughter is a fourth year dental student in Oregon. They have talked of Bill doing endo one day a week. He does miss the practice, especially the generations of patients and the business of dentistry too. Not having his own practice has allowed him the opportunity to move about and learn other successful business models rather than just coaching from his own narrow practice outlook. He enjoys the challenge of being a futurist and seeing a larger picture for dental success.

Most dentists see just their own practice and the picture is smaller. Bill has worked with 2000 practices and can see there are many models that work. The question is "what will work for you?"

COACHING AND INFORMATION WITHIN

Many doctors are looking for that one last pearl of information, hoping it will bring it all together and the puzzle will be finished. They search high and low on the Internet, talk to friends and colleagues, as well as be on a number of dental forums. They take a marketing piece from Topeka and a staff suggestion from Tuscaloosa. They are always looking for that one last piece, the one that is going to make the difference. Will they ever find that one last piece, the nugget?

What I know about myself and coaching is that I can have all the information on any given subject and still not complete the work well. Physical fitness is a good example. I belong to a gym and am fairly active in a number of activities. Yet, my results do not start to make a difference until I have a physical trainer or a steady coach to keep me accountable and on track. I have the information and the equipment. Coaching makes THE difference. A good coach directs you to the results you said you want and keeps you on the right path. It is a rare individual who is thoroughly motivated to achieve greatness in any area on their own.

Some doctors have asked why am I willing to give out so much information. I say it is not information that makes the difference. It takes action. What I know is very few will act on the information within. They will try a portion and say it didn't work. They will take baby steps and then give up, saying it is too hard. They will put it aside saying, "they really don't need it."

Yet, doctors are intrigued with Blatchford Doctors that are able to increase their net income by $100,000 or more, take six to eight weeks off to refresh (some even take a full month off at a time) and genuinely enjoy dentistry with all its challenges. How can these doctors ethically be producing those numbers on a daily basis? How can they be so efficient and still have relationships with patients?

Most people are not willing to do the work to actually change behavior and paradigms. They have fear about making the decisions they know they need to make. Dentistry can be a successful profession even with ugly pink elephants (poor communication skills) in the room or big black holes of unprofitability (could be over purchase of equipment which is never used or keeping too many unmotivated staff members) or even a total lack of decision making. If you have an inviting personality and are in a community of dental awareness or underserved, you will do just fine. You probably won't hit the big numbers but you will certainly be in the "rich" category for taxes.

This is why I only take 50 new clients a year. I love to work with doctors who want to make a difference but cannot find the path. I want to work with doctors who want the results now instead of "do it yourself-ers" who take five years and are now stuck on a new plateau.

WHAT IS COACHING?

A good coach doesn't give answers and doesn't tell you what to do. A good coach works with you to find your answer, not something he wants. A good coach frames it so you answer your question to fit your vision. A good coach holds your vision as his own. A coach gets you to do what you said you wanted to do. A good coach is not a teacher but rather a facilitator for you to find the results you want.

At a famous gathering of winning athletic coaches, this is their advice. It works in business too.

Coaches are 100% involved…Coaches make it safe to make a mistake….They do it by pointing it out, making corrections and teaching….Coaches need to be careful of their own ego by being willing to think and feel like a player….Everyday is a "game day"—you've got to feel as though something big is going to happen….Coach's word has got to be law….Obstacles become the chance to excel…..A good coach doesn't just pass information, but communicates so as to open the action….Ground rule for relationship between coach and players is "there are no problems we can't handle together"…You must have respect for your coach….Every day is important, every play is important…Treat each player as responsible…You've got to love your players and your job…This helps create respect for the coach. A coach needs to be committed to the players and want them to succeed…If you want to be a champion, acting like one and dressing like one, will help you become one…Doing something for money never works…Do what you think is right—have guts…Coaching power lies in the process of working together vs. getting the results only…Don't let bad chemistry go on for longer than one minute…You will think individually but not for yourself—think as a team…How do coaches select winning players? It is more than ability, it is someone who wants to win as much as you, sharing the same vision….Listen for "what can I do for the team?" vs. "What about me?" behavior—it is better to notice what is being perceived and change that, then the behaviors will change themselves…. Great coaches will always find a way to win, no matter what the game…Be interested in finding the best way, which may not be your way….Study players, then develop a coaching plan…Don't have a system that you make people fit into….Losing coaches don't know what is missing (they do not know what they do not know)….Coaches have the ability to communicate so that people you are coaching see your love and knowledge….Great coaches are usually unreasonable people—they make big requests—they make people stretch…..Coaches create the safety to make big requests…There is trust and love in the relationship.

1

THE STARTING LINE

MOTIVATION AND COMMITMENT
FROM THE LEADER

How committed are you to change?

Einstein said his definition of insanity is doing the same thing over and over, and expecting different results. What would cause you to want to change? What is bad enough for you to take a risk to change?

Coaching has great results when the leader makes the decision to be coached. If a spouse is all excited and eager for the dentist to sign on for coaching, the result will not be the same. If your team wants you to be coached and you are hesitant, the results will not be the same. Coaching is a leadership decision, not made by a committee.

You, you're the one who has to dig deep within and make the decision. I am inspired by this Goethe quote,

> "Until one is committed, there is hesitancy, the chance to draw back, always ineffectiveness. Concerning all acts of initiative and creation, there is one elementary truth the ignorance of which kills countless ideas and splendid plans: that the moment one definitely commits oneself then providence moves too.

All sorts of things occur to help one that would never other-wise have occurred. A whole stream of events issues from the decision, raising in one's favour all manner of unforeseen incidents and meetings and material assistance which no man could have dreamed would have come his way.

Whatever you can do or dream, you can, begin it.   Boldness has genius, power and magic in it. Begin it now."

Dr. April Ziegele was a new coaching client when one of her staff members said to her, "I have tried coaching before and I'm not sure we should do this." Dr. Ziegele's response to her was, "I have already made that decision. Your decision is whether or not you want to continue to work here."

TRUST ME, I AM A DOCTOR

The owner dentist creates the personality of the practice. There is no clear equation for great personality always equaling an outstanding and profitable practice. We have witnessed extremely quiet Doctors who do very well. We have observed very physically attractive dentists with gregarious personalities create practices which struggle. What is the key? Building trust.

Trust is built when you show your guests and your team you are interested in them. A quiet and naturally shy dentist can win people over by asking questions and showing genuine interest. One does not need to lead the conversation. Responses like, "then what?" "Wow, how did that happen?" For eight hours a day, you can ACT like you care and pretty soon, you do care.

You can be a detriment to creating trust when you talk too much, especially about yourself. Your guests really don't care about your life, even if they ask. Keep your comments short and turn the conversation around about them. Yes, you would like to tell them your uncle also has a cabin at that lake but remember, your guests are the stars and they don't really care about your stories.

People learn to trust you when you want to know about them. We joke about dentists who meet a new patient by walking into the treatment room and washing their hands with their back to the patient then continue to read the records with their back to the new guest. Could we create a different set of logistics? Most new patients would be pleased to meet in the consult room and have the dentist actually shake their hand, look them in the eye and make a real connection. At this meeting, the doctor should be dressed in a shirt, tie, dress pants and polished shoes. Female dentists should wear nice slacks, blouse and long white lab coat. The new patient conversation is so much more approachable without the scrubs, gloves, mask and surgical hat.

Patients know you can do the work or they wouldn't be there. What they want to know is, can I trust you? Do you care about me?

You also must be able to look people in the eye with kindness, warmth and confidence. Your eyes are the windows to your soul. Learn to use them well.

With your team, you must be the same person at the office as at home. Walk your talk. They count on you to be consistent and the person with whom they want to make a professional difference in their lives.

ONE OF THE FASTEST GUNS IN THE WEST

Dr. Kevin Rykard, Oklahoma City

Listen up! Dr. Rykard's overhead is at 50%. His practice has grown 33% in the last three years while working 24 less days with just three unbeatable team players.

He works just three regular days a week and uses block booking as a guide. He will gladly prep eight crowns at 3 PM if that is what the team and guest decide. And no, he doesn't visit his office on his four days off.

Kevin is efficient as is his team. With just three, there is complete accountability. There is no one else to blame. "We do quadrant dentistry when a full treatment plan cannot be accepted all at once. I am fortunate to have an assistant who has worked with me for 12 years. She knows what is going on before I do and that is the best thing going. I have always done my procedures as close to exactly the same way every time. That way, my assistant is not guessing and wasting time. We are paperless and have digital x-rays—no need to pull charts. We use Smile Reminder service (brucem@smilereminder.com), which is efficient. We all just do what is necessary to get the job done."

Last year, each of his team members earned a bonus of $25,000. "When the Blatchford BAMometer was added, the team kept track of where they were. It is much more effective when the team monitors it." Kevin gives praise to his team.

He feels the main reason he is as successful is because he has a focused and caring team. They are focused on selling dentistry. They understand they are a very important part of case acceptance success rates. "I am able to trust my team members to know what to do, which allowed me to empower them to make the best decision based on their judgment."

Kevin relates, "We had five staff members before starting Blatchford Coaching. In order to practice at the pace I do, my team must be on their game. In the past, I hired for "bubbly." Now, I look for maturity (not in age but attitude) and an ability to have a good eye to eye conversation. I have learned a successful sale is not all about me. The patients spend more time with my team and that is where the relationship is built."

Dr. Rykard and team feel Blatchford has given them the confidence to present the dentistry that is available to the patient. "I don't presume a 'no' answer. I still find a 'no' regularly, but we have offered them the best available. Though I get 'no,' I feel I get many more 'yes's" on the large cases than I did before."

The Rykard team feels their attitude is very important to their success. "I try to leave my "baggage" at the door. My team does, also. We do talk about personal things with patients, but they really don't want to hear about us, they want to talk about themselves."

Kevin's leadership is driven by his personal vision to provide for his family and have financial security. "My practice is THE integral part of my vision. I learned a long time ago investing in coaching/training was a much better investment than equipment. Equipment does not sell dentistry—no matter what the sales people say."

"I am not a quick decision maker when spending money is involved. I like to think it through. But once I make up my mind, I never second guess my decision. I have a self-motivating team and hopefully, it is because of my hiring process and leadership. They help to keep me focused when needed and they feel comfortable enough to tell me what they think without repercussions."

Kevin recently added CEREC and is in the CEREC learning curve. He has a nice web presence and is listed on a number of sites. See the YouTube video. "Marketing is a double edged sword. When it works, it is great. When it doesn't, you feel like you are wasting your kid's education fund."

www.rykarddental.com

Dr. Kevin Rykard

2

YOUR VISION

WHO ARE *YOU*?

Becoming a successful dentist requires much self discovery and introspection. To be a winner, you must feel you are on the right track for you. Very few others can tell you what that right track is or where it is located. The old adage is true:

> "If it is going to be,
> It is up to me."

Discovering your own vision and finding your own path is the most important message in this book. Most people spend far too much time worrying about the "how" and not enough thought is given to the "what." Let's focus on you.

To help you discover your own vision, there are a number of exercises to do, all work well. I think it is helpful to remember back when you were a child and think about the things you liked to do and interests which grabbed you. Perhaps a sibling or a parent could trigger these thoughts. Why as a child? As adults, we lose our childlike qualities as we gain responsibilities, worries, money issues and taxes.

As a child, did you enjoy spending time alone? Figuring out problems? Were you always with people? Are you an organizer? A self starter? There are no right or wrong answers here. You are unique and it is important to discover your passions as well as your dislikes.

Another method is to imagine your 80th birthday party and all the people in your life that would be celebrating with you, from family in earliest childhood to the present. What would you like them to be saying of you and what would they be sharing about you? Write those things down and visualize an excellent outcome.

Another exercise is to read Victor Frankl's book, *Man's Search for Meaning*. Dr. Frankl was a young Jewish psychiatrist in Austria, sent to Auschwitz. He decided to accomplish three things while in that horrendous situation. He wanted to survive. He wanted to treat his fellow man with his medical skills. And third, he wanted to learn something from the horrendous experience. Find out what he learned. When you find out the lesson he learned, this will help you discover who you are and what you have to contribute.

Your own vision statement is important in forming your own business and having like people follow you. Write it down, mull it over, rewrite and make it short, rather than an autobiography. How will a personal vision statement help you? It gives you confidence and courage. It will be communicated to your prospective clients through body language and written on brochures. A team forms when they know and buy into the leader's vision. This team eventually helps you deliver your excellent dentistry.

DREAMS

"There is nothing like a dream to create the future."
—Victor Hugo

By looking into the future, everything becomes possible because the barriers of today disappear. We need to go to that place twenty years from now to see our real hopes and dreams. What might be possible for you?

"Nothing happens unless there is a dream first."
—Carl Sandburg

When we live our life without dreams, we are stuck in today's demands and problems. Without a dream, you are wondering if you will be able to make payroll on Wednesday, did the assistant order the _____, or is the staff lounge clean as the new guest passes by at 10 AM? Dreams allow us the ability to see a larger picture and make decisions which can ease the worries of today.

"If you lose hope, somehow you lose the vitality that keeps life moving, you lose that courage to be, that quality that helps you go on in spite of it all. And so today, I still have a dream."
—Martin Luther King, Jr.

What is your dream? What would you like to happen in one year, five years, ten or twenty? Think about your personal life as well as your professional life. Dentistry is a profession with a great deal of freedom of choice. Yes, it is hard physically and mentally. Yet, in most cases, you are your own boss and you can create a life worth living. What would that be for you?

"Dreams pass into the reality of action and from the action stems the dream again; and this interdependence produces the highest form of living." —Anais Nin

Without dreams and hope, your life has fear, problems and can move geometrically into a spiral. Without dreams, you are stuck in the problems of today and fearful of taking a big step. There is no leap of faith for you because the dream is not a solid committed action. Without dreams, you are stuck!

You do however, have a choice, to continue to be stuck in today's dilemma or find yourself a dream. Let's begin to explore what is right for you.

Goethe said, "Dream no small dreams for they have no power to move the hearts of man."

In your practice in one year, five years, ten and twenty years out:

What would you like your net to be?
What are you willing to do differently to get there?
How many days a year, month, week will you see patients?
What skills will you be adding or subtracting?
What will be your percentage for staff and lab?
Who would you like to be working with?
Are you in the same location, city or state?
What is success? Are you successful? Would you like to be more successful?

FOLLOWING YOUR OWN DREAM

Dr. Tracey Hughes of Louisville, CO
in her own words—

I've always known I have a drive to be successful, but I just couldn't find the way to be a good leader to make it happen. Since I was young, I've always believed "if someone else has done it, so can I!" This drive was making me desperate to move my practice forward and I knew my actions were holding me back.

I was working with my second consultant who had me in the "adding more staff, space and equipment" mode to increase production. I thought, "What good is this when the overhead is increasing at an equivalent rate?" Staff overhead skyrocketed as a result of an out of control bonus.

I thought I was happy because I did have a happy staff who loved me and they were making a fortune! Now, I was working twice as hard to continue the same net when I had fewer staff. I was exhausted, frustrated, overwhelmed and losing my motivation. I felt I was working for the staff to bonus but I was struggling to pay the bills and taxes. The practice was growing 30% a year but the net income was not growing.

I attended the Chicago Midwinter where I heard Dr. Blatchford speak of how you could work less, have fewer team members and increase net income. I was on the edge of my seat. As I visited the booth, holding back tears, I told them of my 8 month old daughter and 2.5 year old son who would be sleeping when I left in the morning. I had just one hour a day with them because I was exhausted and had the same bedtime as my children.

I knew I needed to change but I was not good with change. I felt the staff would not be supportive of a change in practice philosophy despite the fact it was my dream to have more time away, greater net and a team which supported my goals. I bought the book, *Playing*

Your 'A' Game and placed it in a desk drawer for a year, unread. Finally, I pulled it out and first read about Dr. April Ziegele. I felt I was reading the story of my life. I thought I had goals but now realize I had no courage to make the necessary decisions to attain them. I had no vision.

Dr. Blatchford had said, "If you keep doing what you're currently doing, you'll keep getting the results you are currently getting." A light went on. There would be no growth without a change. A brighter light came on! If I wanted to be successful, I had to start acting like successful people and do what they do.

I was now very excited as my husband and I met Dr. Blatchford and Carolyn for our first meeting. They asked us a life-changing question, even before discussing numbers, staff issues and other items on my complaint list. "Are you sure Riverside, Iowa (pop. 900) is where you want to spend the rest of your lives?" What was he asking? My immediate reaction was, I can't move. I have a successful and growing sedation practice which will gross $1M next year. I was reacting without having a bigger picture—a vision of what I am, what is important to me, what gets me excited and keeps me going, what are my core values?

We left the Summit with completely different possibilities posed. My wheels were turning and my vision began to evolve. No, Riverside wasn't really where we dreamed of living. There were no mountains, not enough sun and no awesome weekend get-aways to ski, cycle and hike, creating family bonding time. We were in Riverside because it was comfortable. I discovered that emotional, lifestyle and family goals were more important than financial and practice goals. The practice was directing my life and I realized I was the creator of my own unhappiness. Good news! Change is possible.

My husband, Bill and I knew we could sell my practice, sell our home and move to our dream state of Colorado where Bill and I had met. I spent a whole month clarifying my vision, now it was crystal clear and in writing. My vision is what guided me through the process of selling my home and practice, purchasing a new practice and moving my family to another state.

Prior to having a vision, decision making was difficult for me. A staff member would ask a question of me and usually I would change my mind three times, still unsure of the right decision. I just lacked confidence. As my vision became clear, I just asked myself, "Does the result of my decision bring me closer to my goals or keep me from attaining them? This brought clarity and confidence to my decision making.

I placed my practice of seven years for sale and had a full price offer within two weeks. Now I needed to find out where we wanted to live and practice. I didn't want to settle somewhere just because there was a great practice opportunity. We wanted to live in Boulder County, Colorado. A practice broker called with an opportunity—retiring dentist of 30 years, practice not on market yet, moving downward at $480K and net of $150K with 1100 patient base. I knew I had the right tools, the right coach and the right attitude to bring this practice around.

I did begin to panic. I now had a practice closing in three months. Would our Iowa home sell in time? Could we afford a home in Boulder County? Would the cash flow pay the bills? I just decided not to panic. Dr. Blatchford helped me keep my eye on the ball—a home with a view of the Rockies, more time with my family and fun weekend get-aways.

Our home in Iowa did sell and we moved to Superior, Colorado. On that weekend, I attended a three day Millenium PerioLase LANAP certification training in Denver. Dr. Blatchford was encouraging diversity in skills and by adding new skills to my practice, I was creating a niche to set myself apart. By offering conscious sedation in combination with the ability to treat moderate to severe periodontitis with the first FDA cleared Laser procedure, LANAP, our patients are able to receive a much less invasive option with less bleeding, less swelling and much less recovery time. I discovered that the majority of fearful patients seeking sedation dentistry have untreated periodontitis due to their fear and staying away from dentistry for 10 years or longer. They are not about to readily accept their great fear of cut, flap and sew surgery. Incorporating this procedure added an additional $73K of practice revenue in the first year of my new practice which covered the cost of the technology.

I began practicing two weeks after moving. I inherited a staff of three. I shared my practice vision. They nodded and agreed it sounded good. I brought them to a Blatchford team seminar. Within six months, it became evident that their actions and attitudes did not support my practice vision. The part time hygienist whispered to another staff, "This won't work in this practice." I had the strength to let her go.

Excellence begins with the TEAM and one person can ruin the entire process. I wanted to hire a "team" of individuals who wanted my practice vision as their own. During interviews, I shared my vision and if someone didn't share the same vision, that was OK but they couldn't be part of the team.

My entire focus for the first five months was developing a team of individuals whose attitude and actions would help the practice reach its vision, not hinder it. After a few 90 day trial periods, I decided the only way to make it happen was to start completely new. Seven months into the practice, I had no team. This was probably my scariest time. What did Dr. Blatchford say, "What does water do at 211 degrees? What does it do at 212?" I said, "It produces steam which can move a locomotive." If I had kept the same staff, I wouldn't get to 212 degrees. I had to give myself a "yeah-but-ectomy" and overcome all my excuses.

My husband, Bill, was answering the phone and I hired temps until I was able to find exactly what I was expecting in an exceptional team. Temps are not a walk in the park. Positive thoughts attract positive things.

My employment process is simple, "if you aren't passionate about my practice vision, find someplace else. Life is too short!" I am looking for attitude, curiosity about my vision and where we are going, strong interest in continuing ed courses and team building. If it is all questions about salary and benefits, we are not a fit.

My first temp relieved Bill from receptionist duties, had a great attitude and was interested in hearing my practice vision. She took ownership as though it were her own and became the new Treatment Coordinator. She knew of a dental assistant with a great attitude looking for an opportunity, and incidentally, was an experienced sedation assistant. An ad on Craig's List helped me find a hygienist (Blatchford experience a plus). My hygienist has a fabulous attitude and is self-motivated about continuing education. She is laser certified and has implemented a soft tissue management program addressing disease and bleeding. She doesn't just tell people to floss better, she treats inflammation and infection. All our guests are offered Laser Bacterial Reduction Procedure at the beginning of each hygiene visit. We have informed consent and they are informed of bacteremias, cross contamination and periodontal pathogens causing inflammation. The process is painless and takes 5-10 minutes prior to probing or scaling. The fee is $30 and they are informed it is not covered by insurance. In addition to the LBR procedure, our hygienist uses her diode laser during Periodontal maintenance visits and of course, scaling and root planning of early periodontitis or moderate cases if the guest does not accept LANAP as the first treatment option.

I call my group "Team 10" because we all have terrific attitudes. With our new office agreements, we are able to hold each other accountable. These are positive agreements we wrote together. One agreement is "we arrive together and leave together." If someone breaks an agreement, I just simply ask, "Did we have an agreement?" I don't accept excuses. "Can we count on you in the future?" My team has learned to accept responsibility for their actions and move forward. There is no more pouting, whispering and negativity. It does not exist in my practice vision. The team of three has shared $3302 in the last three BAM cycles.

My team makes decisions without having to constantly place the phone on hold and ask me what they should do. The practice vision empowers them to feel like they have a choice in making our practice exceptional.

We have become completely fee for service by eliminating the five PPOs. We started the process slowly because I did not feel my relationship with the new patients was strong enough. I personally informed every guest as they visited our practice. I said, "What we have found that works well to keep billing costs down for you and our quality high is to eliminate ourselves from the middleman position with insurance companies. We will still submit your claims electronically. We just ask you pay at time of service. Your insurance company will send your benefit check to your home, typically within 7-14 business days."

We terminated our contracts with Blue Cross and Delta. It feels GREAT! Our A/R is a credit balance is $15K and we expect that to be $45K in three months due to pre-paid blocks booked. All of our crown, bridge, cosmetic, sedation and LANAP appointments are paid in full at the time of scheduling.

Dr. Blatchford has continued to encourage me to add more skills and services to separate me from being "average" and the same. You can participate in training continuums at one of the major institutes available. I am completing my LVI training and I use an exceptional lab with the best master technician to deliver restorations which reflect my fees. I have increased my marketing to cushion the loss of insurance driven patients and replace them with people who see value in what we are able to deliver. I feel blessed to finally have the exceptional, confident team who positively supports change and is trained with proper communication skills to handle questions and objections.

After obtaining my IV sedation permit, I started receiving much more complex restorative cases and began to feel my clinical skills inadequate to treat such large cases. Dr. Blatchford encouraged me to improve and advance my knowledge and skills, which was great advice. LVI's Core 7 continuum has introduced me to neuromuscular dentistry with exceptional hands on training. I realized occlusion was a huge weakness of mine. Previously, I focused on working on one tooth at a time. Now, I have knowledge and skill to actually evaluate the patient's occlusion, posture, and neuromuscular signs and symptoms of what I now refer to as "severe bite disease" to patients. This is the kind of dentistry I have always wanted to practice, as opposed to the mundane daily routine of drill and fill. LVI has provided me training in cosmetic dentistry to obtain not only beautiful results, but results that last!

I use a master ceramist at Las Vegas Esthetics laboratory for all my esthetic cases and posterior custom designed ceramic restorations. I use Bellglass composite material for inlays and onlays, Empress for esthetic crowns and Zirconia or E-max in the posterior. We are currently in a learning curve with our newest CAD/CAM technology, E4D by D4D technologies. We mill single composite and ceramic inlays, onlays and crowns using MZ100, E-max or Empress using this technology. This is a big time WOW! factor as patients are fascinated by the technology. They know they are in the right office when they see up to date, state of the art equipment.

In my first nine months of practice, we produced $762K and collected $746K working 173 days (3.5 days a week). The entire team had eight weeks of time off with pay. We have a cell phone rotation for every vacation. One team member answers the office phone forwarded to the office cell phone. With a paper print out of two weeks schedule, they receive $35 for every new patient they schedule while answering the phone. My team overhead is 22%. We want to collect nearly $900K this year and net $360K with an average of 20-25 new patients a month.

The key to lasting success is finding balance in life. I turn problems into opportunities. A vision without action is a daydream. Action without a vision is a nightmare! Never, ever give up!

www.bouldervalleydental.com

Boulder Valley Dental's Office Vision:

We are the leading team in dentistry today. We started as four individuals who have come together as a team sharing the common ideal of being genuinely concerned with your overall health and self esteem.

We will provide you with a dazzling smile using the finest materials, the very latest technology, and the most advanced skills. You will receive a truly remarkable, relaxing experience while we focus on your comfort.

We are committed to making our practice successful and sharing the rewards equally. We do all of this while having fun one hundred percent of the time!

We provide exceptional dentistry for guests who both value and appreciate the level of care we provide.

Dr. Tracey Hughes.

Hughes family, now of Colorado.

Learning to ski...

...in beautiful...

Colorado snow.

SEEING THE FUTURE—THE BLUEPRINT OF YOUR ULTIMATE ACHIEVEMENT

In our Custom Coaching Program, we spend time and emphasize the importance of personal vision. If you do not know who you are and where you are going, you waste a lot of time going down tunnels where the cheese is not to your liking.

Vision is a positive statement of what you see, how you believe and desire your life to become. Vision is seeing the future of what you hope to be.

Personal vision is not about numbers and goals. A long range goal would be WHAT you do. Discovering and acting on your values is WHY you do what you do. Personal vision is the bigger picture of you. It is the values and standards that cover you 24 hours a day. Imagine a panoramic camera lens as opposed to a close-up lens. Bring to the table those values and standards you want to share with future generations. The next generation should know and own your soul. They need to know for what you stand. What are you willing to die for?

Discover your highest priorities by imagining placing an I-Beam from one high rise to another. What things or people would be great enough for you to walk across that I-Beam?

- What activities are important to me?
- What do I really enjoy doing and sharing?
- What am I doing during the moments when I feel a complete sense of harmony and inner peace?
- To what am I willing to dedicate my life?

Dream of something you have always wanted to do but were afraid to pursue. Does it match anything from the I-Beam exercise? What are some things like mistakes, obligations or circumstances that prevent you from doing or having the things you have always wanted?

If you could be the perfect you, what would that look like?

What are some things from above that would help you to be that person?

What are some things you have identified that prevent you from reaching that level? Can you let go of those things? Are you willing to make that change?

What do you spend your time doing? Put a star by those things that line up with your values. Put an X by those things that keep you from pursuing your values.

How much of your time is spent on doing things you want to do?

"It is not enough to be industrious; so are ants. What are you industrious about?" —Henry David Thoreau

As you start to identify the important values for you, ask yourself, "what is important to you? How can you make that value or idea a reality? What can you do about it today?

For example, your value may be honesty. What would be a long-range goal for honesty? What would be an intermediate goal and what would you need to do today to start making that a reality and an integral part of your life?

Finding and owning your own personal vision takes time. Here are some helpful guidelines:

- Take time to be alone to identify your values. This is not a committee decision or a family meeting.
- Explore the yearnings of your heart, the longings of your soul
- Seek the answer to "when my life is over, what will I be glad I stood for?"
- What are the things you are good at now?
- Who are your heroes and why do you admire them?
- Seek inspiration by listening to your intuition, inner voices and spiritual sources. Ask: why am I here?
- Keep it very simple. This is not a manual but a few short sentences.

- Write your values down and why they matter to you. This will help you discover some passion about life and how to live it.
- It will take time

Confidence and satisfaction will rush in when you see the values and standards by which you want to live. A written vision creates a solid path for making plans, decisions and living your life to the fullest.

"The future belongs to those who believe in their dreams."

WOMEN CAN AND WOMEN DO

Dr. Angela Cameron of Johnson City, Tennessee

I came to the Atlanta AACD Convention looking for a new consultant. I had never heard of Dr. Blatchford when I attended his sold-out lecture, "The Leadership Challenge—Playing Your 'A' Game". I was so inspired! I told my husband at lunch I wanted to be coached by Dr. Blatchford for I was struggling as a leader in my practice. What appealed to me is Dr. Blatchford asked at the beginning of his lecture, "What is your dream?" He said "you should design life first then build your practice to support your life dream." I wanted to learn to play my 'A' game.

I was the first in my family to go to college. My mom and dad are the only siblings who graduated high school. They have always worked hard, sometimes holding three jobs just to support my sister and me. Some of my aunts and uncles have GEDs, others do not have a high school education. Most of my relatives rely on government assistance for their only financial support. Some have not had jobs in twenty years and their families live at my grandparent's home. Many have been treated for alcohol addiction and unfortunately, others are still battling those demons.

I knew from a very early age, I did not want to become part of the cycle of poverty. I saw education as a means to better myself. I was doing better scholastically than kids who came from the most privileged backgrounds. Their futures looked assured and in my mind, I knew my future would be as bright as any of my classmates.

My family is made of good-hearted people; unfortunately, many have made one poor decision after another. In the midst of all this, my parents provided a solid, loving, drug-free, smoke-free, Christian home filled with support and encouragement. Our Church family also served as a strong foundation for me to grow and flourish. My parents never forced me to participate in extra activities nor insisted I go to college. They did support my decisions. They were just as proud of my older sister who at 17 dropped out of high school and got married. A few years ago, my sister realized she wanted to better herself, finished her GED and earned an accounting degree, making her the second person in our family to graduate college.

Another motivating factor was seeing the lives of my co-workers in various jobs I held starting at age 12. I enjoyed my weekend and summer jobs and liked the people with whom I worked. I could see though, I wanted a different path.

One of the main driving forces to complete my education and ultimately become a dentist was my desire to have a better life than what my family had when I was growing up. We literally lived pay-check to paycheck. As a child, I would often worry about what would become of us if one parent became sick or had to miss work? Would we lose our home and become homeless? How would we buy grocer-ies? Many of our relatives were worse off than us and often, they would borrow money from my family and never pay them back. This made our financial situation even worse.

Now that I am a dentist and have achieved my career goals, I still want to do my best. I am in the middle of my accreditation process with AACD and working on my AGD fellowship. I was recently awarded a fellowship in DOCS. I have a long list of personal and professional goals. I often ask myself, "where does this drive to keep going come from?" Honestly, I do not have any magical answer but I am just the kind of person looking at the next goal even before the initial goal is complete. This begs the question, 'when will enough be enough?' I do not know but I will probably keep going until I can no more. I am only in competition with myself and there is always room for improvement.

I have been lucky, I have not had to face nearly as many obstacles as most people from my socio-economic background. God has always blessed me and for that I am truly grateful. He has protected me and guided me.

I have had some financial obstacles. My parents did not have the money for college tuition and I went to a very expensive school, Furman University. I had to work hard to get college scholarships and student loans for dental school. My parents helped with some living expenses. In college, I had a $12 weekly budget for groceries and entertainment. In dental school, people would pay me to be the class note taker when it was their turn to take notes for the class. Since there was no one in my family who had taken the college route, I had to find my own way and make decisions the best I could.

I literally knew no one when I entered dental school. I had only been to Memphis one time before for my interview. Adjusting was a challenge as it was so different from Furman or the eastern hills of Tennessee. During my first year, I was busy studying for block exams. I had been studying the entire weekend. I always talked to my parents on Sunday nights and in talking to my dad, I explained to him how I was just trying to survive and complaining about how much time I had spent studying for exams. He said if I was that unhappy, then he would start right now for the nine hour drive to come and get me. He told me to start packing my things. I quickly realized that as bad as I thought things were, it was worth it to complete my dental degree. I assured dad he did not have to come and get me. I never complained again. I chose instead to be thankful for being in dental school. A few years later, we talked of that phone call and my dad said he loved me and knew by saying that, I would choose to stay in school.

I graduated from dental school in June. I had signed a letter of intent to purchase a dental practice in the early spring of my senior year. I could not actually purchase the practice until I had a dental license which did not arrive until two weeks before my wedding. I signed the papers two days before the wedding and took possession when I returned from my honeymoon. No patients were scheduled but the first hygiene patient wanted to see me! I sourced eight upper veneers, she paid and scheduled to return. This set the tone for my career. The selling doctor stayed for a long three months and would be the subject for another book. Suffice it to say, the transition was rough. I kept striving to keep the main thing "the main thing"—to provide excellent care for all my patients.

My personal vision is so important. Wayne Gretzky was asked why he skates so fast and he replied he skates so fast because he skates to where the puck will be, not to where it is. Vision is the ability to see possibilities before they become obvious. I have always tried to visualize the possibilities. I chose dentistry over medicine. I saw the possibilities in dentistry and observed the negative effect of managed care in medicine. Upon my graduation, the average dentist was netting more per year than GPs while the GP was working almost double the hours of dentists. Some people questioned my choice of either medicine or dentistry.

I also chose to purchase a private practice immediately after dental school. I had the vision this would put me about five to ten years ahead of my classmates. I knew it would work. It was risky because I really did not know how I was going to do it; I just knew I would do it. I just went to where the puck would be, not where it is now.

Another example of my personal vision was when we signed up to be coached by Dr. Blatchford. Both my husband and team were less than enthusiastic. My husband was skeptical because I could not tell him how Dr. Blatchford was going to help my practice and he was concerned about the cost. My team was holding back because of the uncomfortable feeling of change and uncertainty. I did my best to keep my husband and team focused on our goals. Fourteen months later, we have had a record breaking year with two less team members.

The most impactful results in Blatchford coaching are:

- Having a TEAM of 10's
- Looking forward to going to the office
- Leader is less stressed which helps positively at home
- Leader is in better emotional and physical condition
- Record setting year
- Efficient office and happy TEAM

I have learned through Blatchford that attitude is a choice, I am part of the problem and therefore, I am part of the solution. I have learned there is no escalator to success and that energy and passion are keys.

When I met Dr. Blatchford, my practice was producing $1.2M from $750K when I purchased it five years previously. I had nine staff and thought I wanted an even larger team. The staff ruled by committee. I tried to make everyone happy. We had a great reputation but I was miserable and the stress was overwhelming. My overhead was 80%. My personal income was decreasing. I knew something was horribly wrong to be producing $1.2M and I personally had to take out a second mortgage to pay payroll. Some staff did not care for me (the new younger female professional) or respect me and would roll their eyes at a suggestion or openly question my decisions. I was anxious and depressed and started having blood pressure problems at 33. The physician suggested I sell my practice to reduce stress. I knew there must be another way.

With Dr. Blatchford's encouragement, my vision and leadership grew. Staff positions were eliminated or switched, some left for other positions and we now have a real TEAM. I now make the decisions and the team carries my vision with enthusiasm and commitment. The team is accountable, fully cross-trained and with our training meetings, morning huddles and evening huddles, we reach our goals and are having more fun.

As a leader, I have learned I need to be a 10 also. I have to make decisions and stick by them. I listen and ultimately, I must make the decision and take responsibility for it. I have learned you just cannot reach some people. A person must choose to change and I cannot change for them. I have learned I cannot be "friends" with everyone. I love my team and I know I need to keep that slight separation.

Dr. Blatchford taught me to make the decisions. I am like most dentists and I prefer to have every last piece of information to evaluate, think and rethink before making my decision because I want it to be the right decision. He helped me end the cycle of Paralysis by Analysis and keep my practice moving forward. Motivating a team to move forward is interesting. They will move forward without me but I still like to be the catalyst to make things move faster. I give them structure and they make it happen.

Systems I cannot live without are Block Booking, phone scripting, the bonus system and cross training. We implemented the assistant and hygienists collecting at the chair. It was scary at first and now they love it and feel empowered. Did I tell you I love Block Booking? Let me tell you again, I LOVE Block Booking!

Attitude is a choice. I used to tolerate a bad attitude because someone had good clinical skills but realize now, the situation was detrimental to reaching our goals. Now, my team is committed everyday to choosing to have a good attitude.

I am thrilled with how the numbers have changed. Overhead has decreased 25%. Last year's production was $1.45M. This is a $200K increase over the previous year while working fewer days and with one less hygienist. Team salaries are at 20% instead of 38% and my net has greatly increased. The bonus has been very positive and they shared $50K last year. Bonus gives them ownership mentality. Last cycle, we had our largest bonus to date and each received $1700 which is $100 per day extra salary. We love to share with each other what we are doing with our bonus money.

Dr. Blatchford coached all of us to do a task analysis. I found many things that I was doing that I was able to delegate to others (like two days a week of book work). We have also automated many systems to be more efficient.

Before I started working with Dr. Blatchford, our staff made most of our policies based upon what our worst patients did. We spent much time on the phone with a new patient explaining all the rules before they even entered our practice. When we applied the 80/20 rule to our existing patients, I was shocked to see who was in my top 20% of patients. It changed my entire perspective when I found out where to spend my energy. This has had a huge impact on the practice. I have learned if you spend your time and energy focusing on what the top 20% desire, you will attract more people who appreciate the same. I learned I am losing money on the bottom 10% and recognize I probably will never please them.

My biggest challenge is finding harmony and balance between my professional and personal life. At work, my goal is to be fully engaged with my patients and team. At home, my goal is to be a wife, mom and fully engaged with my family. I have to really work at this balance. As we speak, I am staying home for six weeks following the birth of our baby girl. My husband is a dentist, too, and he is taking my place in the practice while I am away. We are in the middle of a building project for my new office which has space leased to other professionals.

In finding balance, the life of a dentist/mom/wife/businesswoman is so dynamic that true balance on the top of a rolling ball will probably never be achieved. I can only hope to find harmony between the different roles/hats I wear. Other keys for me in finding harmony and balance, are Loehr and Schwartz' book, *The Power of Full Engagement*. It says that greater efficiency and effectiveness will only be achieved if a person is fully engaged in whatever activity they are doing. For this reason, I do not have my children at work during patient hours. At home, I do not do business or make phone calls until the children are asleep. I also take time to disengage, to be fully disengaged.

Both my parents and grandparents gave me a good foundation of strong values. I am thankful for the sacrifices they made for me. I could not be the person I am today without them. The interesting thing—they would love and support me just as much if I would have decided to choose a different career path. They just want me to be happy.

When you are a trailblazer and a pioneer, it is challenging because people outside your team will question your vision and direction. When they see the path you have created does lead to success, they try to follow you or create short cuts to reach your level. There are no short-cuts to success.

This is a wonderful time to be a dentist. As long as all dentists are not required to participate in some type of government imposed health care system, the future will belong to those who offer a better product. I plan to offer a better product.

I do not have magical answers. I do my best everyday. Abraham Lincoln was quoted, "Whatever you are, be a good one." I remind myself, whatever role I am at the moment, I should strive to be a good one.

I have to give praise and thanks to God for all the blessings he as given me. Finding that personal vision involves trusting your instincts, being willing to take risks, taking time to get information from many sources, having an awesome team of advisors, and accepting the love and support of a good family. I think creativity is important. Think like a child. Ask yourself, "What would I do if I could not fail?" Then go out and do it. Hard work, reading, growing on a spiritual, personal and professional level are keys to having a strong personal vision.

www.sophisticated-smiles.com

Dr. Angela Cameron.

THE LEADER'S PERSONAL VISION

This is undoubtedly the most important part of finding and keeping success in a dental practice. The leader needs to know the path, be passionate about life and possibilities, then communicate that vision. This is the area most dentists ignore and instead, want to know the details of block booking or a bonus. If you do not have enthusiasm and conviction on your path, no amount of information and instruction will help you reach the top.

Personal vision is most imperative for leading a group during troubled times. Vision is what you practice all the time yet, it is what you call upon during changing times that makes the difference. Vision is the strength of conviction which will carry you and your team during adversity and greatness. It is discovering who you really are and communicating it in all you do.

In Alice and Wonderland, Lewis Carroll writes, "

One day Alice came to a fork in the road and saw a Cheshire cat in the tree. "What road do I take?" she asked. His response was a question, "Where do you want to go?" "I don't know, Alice answered. "Then, said the cat, "It doesn't matter."

Uncovering your personal vision takes some soul searching. We are speaking here about your standards and values, like honesty, responsibility, or courage. Personal vision is not goals or specific skills. It is a short and passionate statement for what you want to be known. This is not an invention but a delving into yourself to discover what is already there and what you aspire to become.

Personal vision should not have to mention teeth or practice. It is about your own standards and values which are near and dear to your heart. What values are you teaching your children? If you feel you lack passion, enthusiasm and energy, write a vision of what you hope to become and then become that person.

Another approach is thinking about "what do I want to be remembered for? What is important to me? What is my legacy? Again, this has nothing to do with teeth, money or goals. Vision is the essence of YOU. It is your umbrella that covers you 24 hours a day.

Stephen Covey has some suggestions—imagine your 85th birthday party and everyone in your life is there. What accolades would they be giving? What values and standards would they say you had exhibited during your life? What would you like them to say about your life?

Here is a simple and passionate example written by one of our Doctors:

> I want without reservation to bring Glory to God, to honor others, to honor myself, to achieve my destination and enjoy the journey. I want to be a man of wisdom, a man of substantial love, a man of integrity, a man of joy.

Find your vision and communicate it in words and body language. You cannot copy someone else's vision. It must be your own. It must motivate you and bring you to your knees.

George Bernard Shaw wrote:

> This is the true joy in life: being used for a purpose recognized by yourself as a mighty one; being a force of nature instead of a feverish clod of ailments and grievances complaining that the world will not devote itself to making you happy.

> I am of the opinion that my life belongs to the whole community, and as long as I live, it is my privilege to do for it what I can.

> I want to be thoroughly used up when I die, for the harder I work, the more I live. I rejoice in life for its own sake. Life is no brief candle to me. It is a sort of splendid torch which I have got hold of for the moment and I want to make it burn as brightly as possible before handing it on to future generations.

Many people avoid this important work for a number of reasons:
- It takes too much time
- I would rather not discover now I have basically been wasting my life, going in the wrong direction.
- I can't see the value and how it will be used (see the next chapter)

One more vision example while exploring during my college days:

Greatness is born neither of ambition nor persistence nor genius nor mere strokes of luck. In fact, those we call great are those least concerned with achieving greatness, who are rather consumed by the fire of their commitments, by a passion for being alive.

You and I may not find ourselves in circumstances that call for daring bravery or heroic acts. Each day, however, presents us with a choice: an opportunity to settle for merely doing our best—or to carve out for ourselves a bold vision of what living might be, and to launch ourselves, with renewed spirit, into action that makes that possibility real.

For myself, I take Helen Keller's guidance, "Security is mostly a superstition. It does not exist in nature, nor do the children of men as a whole experience it. Avoiding danger is no safer in the long run than outright exposure. Life is either a daring adventure or nothing."

Search deep within you to find what inspires you. It is within you now. Uncover it just like an onion has layers, you have layers, too. Events have occurred in your life. You may have suppressed some segments where you once desired and displayed interest and even passion. Find those places.

WHAT IS SO IMPORTANT ABOUT VISION?

Dentistry attracts perfection, skill, and science. The dentists I know are highly skilled people who like to work on tiny white things in dark wet spaces. You know your craft. However, vision also helps you in business. A vision of not only your technical delivery but your sense of service to others and your integrity will demonstrate itself in the business side. You are highly skilled in what you do but many times, not so confident on the business side. Your personal vision marries the technical skill with your business direction. Albert Einstein said, "A perfection of means and a confusion of aims seem to be our main problem." By working on your personal vision, there will be a light at the end of the tunnel.

When your own personal vision has been uncovered by you, communicate your passion daily. Walk your talk. Passionate vision will actually attract people to you who feel the same and want to help you make your dream a reality. As a leader, you want to attract a team who is genuinely with you, who feel the same energy and passion to accomplish something special.

Without vision, you are a rudderless ship. The people who come to work with you are busy 8 to 5 doing what they have always done but there is no collective effort and support. We call this group a "staff," not a team. Like Dr. Ziegele says, "a staff is an infection." In a practice without vision, there is high staff turnover. The really great people continue to leave because they are not challenged and cannot see any long term difference they can make.

What then remains is the bottom of the barrel. Yes, without vision, direction, and energy from the leader, a staff will come to work and want to perform well, but find no central theme or reason to go beyond the norm. A staff will do what is comfortable and what they have always known from previous work experience. There is no curiosity, no accountability and little feeling for the team. Bickering continues and everyone, including the dentist, feels underappreciated.

Without vision, the staff will invent their own path and the dentist is literally working for them. What is wrong with that, you say? It is your practice, you have invested thousands. You must stand for something or anything is allowed. Your good reputation in the community is formed from your own personal vision of standards and values. What do you stand for? If you do not stand for something, you will stand for anything.

> Vision without action is a dream.
> Action without vision is just passing time.
> Vision with action can change the world.

SHARING YOUR VISION

You have done the soul searching, the introspection and espoused the standards and values that are near and dear to your heart. You have bared your soul and now have a paragraph of words uniquely yours.

Now what? Once you have actually brought to the surface a statement of your life which always was within you but never exposed, you can't help but share. There is more confidence and it shows in your body language. You stand taller plus you are stronger in your thoughts and convictions. It should be easier for you to make decisions because you have something solid on which to base your choices.

Your vision is you. It covers you 24 hours a day like a big umbrella. You walk your talk. You are the same person at home as you are at work and play. You cannot be duplicitous. Do not compromise your own personal vision. It is uniquely yours.

Share your vision with your spouse and family. The result will be valuable discussion. Do not change what you have written. It is you. Now, share it with your team. Share it every day as you write your office purpose or mission statement (next adventure). Continue to share your personal vision every week, then every month. Encourage your team members to write their own personal vision for this is a powerful exercise and helps them become stronger and yet more sensitive in understanding themselves and others.

"Where there is no vision, the people perish…" Proverbs 29:18

"When you cease to dream, you cease to live."
—Malcom Forbes

"Man's mind, stretched to a new idea, never goes back to its original dimensions." —Oliver Wendell Holmes

PARTNERS IN PRACTICE AND IN LIFE

Drs. Jim and Candace DeLapp
of Highlands Ranch, CO

The best and most unique feature of this practice is two talented Doctors who share a single practice. Married to each other, Candace and Jim each work 2.5 days with the office open Monday thru Thursday. As an added bonus, their only child, Sarah, chose dentistry and will enter their practice upon her graduation from U of CO Dental School in 2010.

"We feel very blessed that Sarah chose dentistry as her profession. Sarah has seen the lifestyle we live, comfortable and non stressful with a strong family focus," Candace reflects. Jim says, "Could we live in a larger home or have a newer car? You bet, but living nearly debt free is the key for us. Retirement is not in the picture by choice. Too many people can't wait to retire because they are tired of the routine, management or want to do something "fun." Well, why not do something fun before you retire? Both of us teach part-time at the Dental School and truly enjoy this different approach to dentistry. It is truly gratifying to have influence and mentor the next generation."

Further, Jim says, "retirement is overrated but days off are not. Working 2.5 days a week is spectacular. When Sarah enters our practice, we may take one week off a month. The intellectual challenge of staying in business keeps your mind sharp."

Dr. Candace feels the biggest impact Blatchford has made for her is "looking forward to arriving at the office! I felt before like I was pulling the boat and had to check everything. Most dentists would say their biggest frustration is management of staff. Now our team pitches in for each other as well as our patients. We see every patient on time every time and present the best dentistry has to offer. I look forward to being at my office with my team to work hard and play harder."

Dr. Jim feels two concepts are worth discussing. One is the dentist does not have to work longer and charge less to be successful and happy. "I always felt guilty charging the fees we did, but when we significantly raised our fees, the objections to the fees went down. You can't give Ritz Carlton service at Wal-Mart prices. It is much more enjoyable to see one patient at a time than run from room to room."

The other Blatchford concept is coaching. "I actually coach swimming and some of my swimmers are nationally and world ranked. Coaching is methods of mastering the everyday issues. It involves a non-biased set of eyes looking into your situation. One of the most difficult things posed to anyone is "change." In Blatchford, you are surrounded by people who are willing to change. Improvement is only seen in its constant application of the change. I have always loved dentistry and the Blatchford program takes it to a new level. Coaching is about the continual goal of excellence. Coaching is what makes it happen. The greatest athletes in the world have coaches. Once you have learned it all or you think you don't need help….it is time to quit," concludes Dr. Jim. As a coach, Jim shares, "coaching involves constant feedback on what is right or what is lagging. On Dr. Blatchford's coaching calls, experienced doctors reinforce what you are doing well and point out areas to improve. Since everyone is committed to change, the feedback and empowerment is spectacular."

Before starting Blatchford, Drs. Jim and Candace were spending 43% on staff. Now team costs are 22%. Lab is 15%, up from 6%. Overhead now is 60%. They used to alternate their workdays but they started early (6:30 AM) and ended late (9 PM) and worked Fridays and Saturdays. "We had four more staff members who literally spent all day Friday chasing down payments and insurance checks and mailing statements. This provided little or no time to build, plan or work on the business vs. working in the business. We have found that our patients like us much more when they do not owe us money. We have delayed treatment on certain patients until they felt comfortable with the financial outcome. We do not feel we are forcing or coercing patients to have treatment done. The patient is empowered to choose when and where any treatment would be accomplished."

In 2005, they felt their 'old neighborhood' was getting old. After 23 years in practice and everything paid for, they noticed their patient base was becoming more insurance driven and not open to complete care. They ended up moving their office three miles south. They studied median income, price of housing, new schools indicating area growth, travel patterns and competition of other health facilities.

The new office sits at a busy intersection of two roads and serves several housing developments. Jim's advice, "In the US, we get to choose where we practice and on what type of patient. If you think your patients will not accept certain types of treatment, consider moving to an area where they will."

In assessing important elements which have made them successful, Dr. Candace offers 'LISTENING.' "I adhere to the 80/20 rule and try to listen 80% of the time. There is much more clarity in my conversations and everyone feels rewarded in being heard. The conversation is about them. In the beginning, I had to bite my cheeks because I wanted to display my knowledge. What I didn't realize is you actually appear more intelligent by being contemplative and by listening. You don't jump to conclusions or create additional conflicts. I find I say 'yes' much more frequently and there are no problems, only challenges and solutions."

Dr. Jim says an important element he has learned is to treat their practice as a business. With all businesses having similar concerns, he and Candace have read over 100 books on business, leadership, biographies, marketing and sales since joining Blatchford. "There is a common theme in these biographies. It is not easy and it takes perseverance. A coaching program can short cut the process to implement the strategies. Understand however, the commitment and perseverance is still up to you."

"My personal vision," Dr. Candace says, 'is rooted in high integrity, honesty and to do my very best. I don't want to be the same dentist next year that I am this year. Constant improvement is a fundamental goal. One very advantageous aspect of being a Blatchford Doctor is having the support of others who believe and practice similarly. I never diagnose a patient's pocketbook or character. I always present what I feel is truly the best for their health and the best I can do for them. This may mean I refer them for treatment. We work together, the patient and me with their goals and my guidance as our primary focus.

"I want to give the best care and have fun doing it," says Dr. Jim. It is the patient that is fun and challenging. Your vision should not be a place or point but something that continually reaches higher and higher. Keep resetting the thermostat and make it harder and harder to reach that goal."

"Our team is more streamlined and efficient," Dr. Candace shares. "We have one receptionist, two part-time hygienists and one assistant. We have learned over time it is not more staff or more hours that lead to success. It's doing right by your patients and listening, doing right by your team and yourself. Additionally, we have learned to trust our team and allow them to step up and carry the ball. If you give them the vision and get out of their way, they will take you there. I'm becoming more like Ronald Reagan who had great ideas, let others pick up the reins and have systems in place to monitor the progress."

Dr. Jim asks, "Can you learn to delegate if it is not natural? You can, if you first recognize you are not good at delegating and make a decision to change. Coaching helps you make those changes. The question is 'can you apply this and make it happen?' Sometimes it takes a third party observer to recognize the issue and help you make the change. The concept of change is frustrating at times because you cannot go on autopilot and just cruise. Constant improvement, however, is exciting because something new is around the corner. Blatchford doctors are looking for change and are not satisfied with the status quo."

They both share their feelings about the importance of attitude. "We hire for attitude and train for aptitude. You can teach the skills necessary to work in a dental office but you can't teach someone to be nice!" shares Dr. Candace. "Put your team members in positions where they can use their talents best. However, don't let team members slide on doing his or her part just because someone else does it better. Bill really encourages cross training and role-playing of sales skills."

Dr. Jim calls a poor attitude "bad-ittude" and feels it is highly contagious. Don't read newspapers or watch programs on television which involve conflicts. Don't participate as it is 'third grade politics.'"

"The bonus keeps the team focused on the goal," Dr. Candace observes. "It is probably the biggest difference in having patients schedule at least a quadrant at a time rather than our old "Crown of the Year" club. Now, treatment plans are sequenced and prioritized according to the best outcome for the patient, not the insurance company. Bonus has empowered the team to look at the profitability of the practice and do what is best for the patient. Fewer appointments are a benefit to everyone, especially the patient."

Dr. Blatchford introduced the business concept of Pareto's Law, the 80/20 rule as doctors and teams apply it to their practice. The DeLapp's feel they can now better allocate their assets of time and money into the most beneficial elements of their practice. "One of the many elements we find important is patient recruitment. How did the majority of your good new patients, not just your new patients, find you? At first, you may look at what is bringing anyone in but later you may refine your evaluation to which patients are the best or most reliable. List 100 of your best patients and see what factors they share. Focus your time and effort on replicating these patients," offers Dr. Candace.

On leadership, Dr. Candace feels she walks a fine line with the team who is predominately female. "I want to be friendly yet not too friendly. Previously, there were times when team members tried to enfold me in the office politics; something they would never try with Dr. Jim. I had to learn to find the balance of maintaining a respectful relationship in the office and enjoy their company outside the office. I also learned to contemplate my decision making process, which comes quickly, permanently, and naturally for me. I learned to say, 'Let me think about that,' which leads to a much better outcome. Jim has helped me be more effective by talking about the bigger picture and letting the team develop plans to create it."

Dr. Jim feels leadership is a never-ending journey. "You need to be flexible yet consistent. Plus, motivation is an art that has never been perfected for everyone. Blatchford wants you to become the coach for your team. They will give you the skills and confidence but you have to step up."

"We follow block booking to the letter. It was difficult at first; sitting with open hours is against my basic personality. It is amazing, however, to see a very comfortable schedule with open hours and the production is great! Work smarter, not harder."

Both doctors volunteer in the community in activities and causes in which they have passion. They have taught at the U. of Colorado School of Dental Medicine for years. "Our interaction with other faculty has brought many referrals to our private practice including them. I have several dentists as patients and have done smile makeovers for colleagues. Additionally, many patients have referred others to us, seeking 'the experts,'" says Dr. Candace. "A measure of a person is not just what you do; it is what you do for another with no expectation of something in return. If you volunteer with the idea of receiving something specific from it, you are doing it for the wrong reasons. All of us can help our community in some way. Serving on a board or volunteering for a cause in which you feel passionate is very important," Dr. Jim feels.

He adds, "Volunteerism sometimes is more than giving your time or money. We all have the ability to do more. Getting on the list to give bone marrow is one of the many things you can do for your fellow man. Dr. Candace went beyond this and really does not mention this to anyone. She actually donated one of her kidneys to my brother. As I write this, a tear comes to my eye because she gave him life. He was tied to a dialysis machine and had no energy. Since the transplant, he has been able to live a full life. We named the kidney "Bessie Pearl" and my brother sends us letters from all over the world from him and Bessie Pearl. Becoming a donor is a simple thing to do. Let your wishes be known to others. If you are able, consider being a bone marrow donor. From a front row seat, I know how this can impact someone's life.

Both dentists have taken extensive study at Las Vegas Institute and through the American Academy of Cosmetic Dentistry. Dr. Jim feels, "skill acquisition is a constant and never ending process and can be defined in many ways. I take a wildlife carving class at a local wood-working store. This has improved not only my hand skill but also my perception of color, which helps my dentistry. Your skill acquisition should be varied and unique."

"Our biggest cases come from our website. Dr. Jim has become our webmaster and is quite proficient at blogging, URL's and all those web-things," says Dr. Candace. "On our website, we state, 'if cost is your biggest concern, we are not the practice for you.' Seeing one patient at a time and giving Ritz service is what we strive to do," Dr. Jim relates.

Both doctors feel the future for dentistry is very bright. They selected dentistry because of the continual learning process. Having seen the explosion of new technology and techniques over the past ten years, they feel the next ten years will be even more so. "How exciting it will be! With Sarah joining our practice, I see a real shot in the arm by having the youngster come in with fresh, new ideas," the mom says with great anticipation.

Dr. Jim feels their plan for the future is to be right sized for any economy. "I found out, I can do a root canal on my own. The doctors can pitch in to clean rooms, answer the phone, and make appointments or whatever. It is a team effort and we all can do whatever it takes," Dr. Jim concludes.

www.cottonwooddentalgroup.com
www.cosmetic-aesthetic-dentistry.com
www.dentist-denver.blogspot.com
www.denverimplantdentistry.com

Drs. Jim and Candace DeLapp.

Jeff, Sarah, Candace and Jim.

Jim at Normandy.

Broncos game:
Jim, Candace, Jeff, Sarah.

DeLapps in Long Boat Key, Florida.

3

OFFICE PURPOSE

OFFICE PURPOSE FROM 9 TO 5

What is it you do during the day? People work hard. The dentist works hard. Why isn't it more fun, rewarding and a real pleasure?

Do you have an active office purpose or mission statement which the current team collectively composed? A personal vision statement covers your whole life yet, for eight waking hours, you are deeply involved in the practice of dentistry. You and your team need a purpose!

This is not just an opportunity but a necessary part of transforming a staff (a group of people doing their own thing) into a real team, forcing all to move in the same direction. The goal of the office purpose or mission statement is several—to bring the team together for the common good and to allow your patients and potential guests to have insight about you, which allows them to make better decisions for themselves based on commonalities in your mission statement. It is an excellent form of communicating who you are and who you aspire to be.

Why do you do what you do? You don't want each year repeated with the same frustrations for 30 years. People want to make a real difference in their lives. They want to contribute to make something better. They want to feel needed, rewarded and recognized.

A step towards success is writing your office purpose—what do we do everyday? Who do we inspire? How can we make our purpose come alive?

Obviously, the leader's personal vision has great impact. The standards and values espoused by the leader are the core of how this practice will operate and succeed. The office purpose is written collectively, however, each team member must participate. Think about these questions:

Who Are We?
What Do We Do?
For Whom Do We Do It?

Think hard about the bigger purpose of your office. Is there anything about enjoyment or fun during the day? Isn't your ultimate purpose to make enough money to support the lives of the team and Doctor? How will you share the profit motive which we all like to avoid stating?

Now rewrite it with an emotional leaning. Right brained words can be used like—calm, pampering, inviting, special smile. Avoid left brained words like tooth, emergency, free of pain. Is there room in your purpose for fun, profitability, longevity, family and health? Keep it positive and move toward what you would like your office to be, perhaps what you want to become.

Encourage thoughtful contributions from all. Everyone should participate. This opportunity is not dominated by the Doctor. This is one of those moments when individuals can move from staff to a real team. Dr. April Ziegele says "staph is an infection; I want a team."

It is important to revisit your purpose and actually have a rewrite as different team members come on board. They need to be a part of rewriting the office purpose to feel included. Team reforms again.

Once the office purpose is written, it needs to be:

- used to open the morning huddle
- revisited at the weekly team meeting
- written on the back of your business cards
- shared with your guests in any literature
- framed in your welcome room for all to view
- the magnet which pulls the team together when disaster occurs or joy is felt.

We thank Dr. Steven Greenman for sharing his office purpose and how he uses it. Dr. Greenman has been a niche cosmetic practice in West Lake Village, California, and is now diversifying by adding implants and IV sedation. His purpose reflects those changes. When dentistry is complete in a few years, Dr. Greenman wants to give back by inspiring high school students to excel in math.

PURPOSE STATEMENT OF GREENMAN SMILE CENTER

WHO ARE WE?

A team of individuals, who share common values and life goals for ourselves and our families; who want to enjoy and feel passionate about how we make our livings and secure our futures.

WHAT DO WE DO?

We sell hope and happiness by providing advanced life enhancing cosmetic, implant, and sedation dental services within an environment of comfort, attractiveness, attentiveness, and enthusiastic customer service that is second to no other organization or business.

FOR WHOM DO WE DO IT?

For people who want, value and appreciate our services.

Dr. Greenman adds, "This statement has undergone at least five revisions, if not total re-writes over the past ten years. It was last revised to include the phrase *sedation dental services* at our most recent BMW 4X4. In fact, the motivation for us to earn our IV sedation permit came from the document, specifically the words *goals for ourselves and our families*, found under *Who Are We?*, and *within an environment of comfort, attractiveness, attentiveness, and enthusiastic customer service that is second to no other organization or business*, found under *What Do We Do?*.

I feel very strongly about the definition of who we are. It is the first litmus test I use when evaluating a possible new hire. Everything else in our office purpose flows from the first part.

Recently, I made the difficult and painful decision to terminate a team member of over five years. At first she began to violate our office agreements. However, when I learned that she did not *share common values and life goals* for herself and **her** family, the choice for me was clear.

After terminating her, I ran an ad for her replacement on Craig's List. Within 24 hours, I had 45 resumes. I set a date for a group interview. Eighteen candidates showed and I used our office purpose to winnow down the applicants. I feel I've made a good hire."

MAKING PURPOSE COME ALIVE

A mission statement is a dynamic and contemporary statement. As your team transforms and new members are added, rewrite your office purpose with them. Let them be an important part of forming this synergy.

Some teams have their office purpose printed on the back of their business cards. Successful offices have their office purpose nicely framed and visible to guests.

Sharing your office purpose allows new guests to find commonality and validate their choice in selecting you. Certainly, it is on your website, your e-newsletters, and possibly on your e-mail signature. Many offices start their morning huddle by reciting their office purpose on a regular basis.

Your tag line for your phone could come out of your office purpose. What is the one sentence that says who you really are?

Purpose is not just used for your office. Every organization, store, corporation and non-profit and all levels of government are finding the importance of stating their purpose. How about extending that to the purpose of your marriage, your church or prayer group, your family and even extended family?

When people know what a hospital stands for, a community organization or youth group, we can best interact with them. It also is a stand for those involved to live up to their purpose. When trouble starts, be it financial, emotional or perceived, a purpose draws you back to the basics of why am I here? What do I need to do to live my purpose?

An office purpose is not a rigid dynamic but rather a statement of what we want to accomplish in our business and with our team. When personnel friction starts and statements are made that simply do not better the team or schedules fall completely apart and goals are not being met, this is the time to regroup and pull out the office purpose. Energize it and give it life. This is your standard. A recommitment to purpose by each person will start the rebuilding process.

ARE YOU TAKING ACTION ON YOUR OFFICE PURPOSE?

Lofty right-brained words, promises of fine service and positive attitudes are beautifully calligraphied in a fancy frame. We promised we would work well together forever. Soon, the enthusiasm fades and the office purpose is a distant memory. We are back to the same ole, same ole.

Make your teamwork count by using solid systems which create **Accountability, Reliability and Efficiency,** with the acronym ARE. We ARE no longer looking for that one piece of paper, cleaning out drawers again and again or spending time after hours at the office doing chart work. Our goal is to create solid systems which have the team being accountable for actions, systems that one can count on to work and be repeated with consistent results, all of which creates efficiency. We want to be efficient for our guests, for ourselves and to create profit.

In *BluePrints*, we will share solid systems which any dental practice of any size, location or philosophy can implement to create accountability, reliability and efficiency. Our clients share how different systems have made their dental life create more time for important things like vacations, family and recreation. You will find evidence throughout this book.

Dentists do not learn systems in dental school. There, paper work still reigns supreme. In real business, each action each of us does needs to be examined and evaluated for real results vs. "busy-ness."

4

AGREEMENTS

LEAN ON ME—AGREEMENTS OR COVENANTS

Your office purpose is a nice statement of who you are, what you want to be known as and how you want to treat others. By itself, it has no action or way to move forward. Blatchford can help create the support of that office purpose with agreements or more strongly, covenants.

Without agreements as to how you will conduct yourself, a team is prevented from forming, banding together and counting on each other. We remain frustrated individuals, even though we have written the office purpose together and it is hanging on the wall.

To make these covenants stick, a strong element of trust must be developing. Leadership sets the example by encouraging everyone's participation and making each idea heard and important. The leader needs to avoid having a perceived favorite person on the staff with whom grievances are shared about others as well as "secret" plans for the practice. This is a trust breaker, for sure. If the leader is a perceived gossiper, see how quickly the others will adapt to that standard.

Allowing gossip can kill a practice. Make an agreement about gossiping of patient stories, vendors, team members and the leader.

Nip it in the bud by not starting a conversation about someone else that if they walked in the room, the conversation would stop. You can also be strong in stopping a conversation from someone which would be harmful to them if they were to enter the room. The speaker and the receiver are equally involved.

Here are some possible agreements to discuss and make specific as to your attention and conduct in the office. One of the most important items is the element of timeliness. What does "on-time" mean in your office? The discussion and agreement on these items can be a "come together moment" or a blame game for why it is happening poorly. You choose how you want to conduct this discussion.

When you hold your morning huddle, what is "on time"? Are you presently allowing your staff members to arrive and leave as they NEED? How can your staff move to become a real team when there is no direction or commitment to the group and practice?

Is some of your staff late to team meetings or choosing not to participate at all? If you agree to a certain type of behavior, everyone agrees. You make a pledge as the leader to conduct yourself so the group can count on you and form a strong team.

A good morning huddle where you are coaching to goal is so critical to your success. Everyone on your team must be there on time, ready to go. What do you need to do to make that happen every day, every time?

An on time agreement will take much discussion and decisions by the leader. If you run late with your guests, what is causing that? If the Doctor continually changes his mind once the patient is in the chair and arrangements have been made, make an agreement you will conduct yourself differently in your diagnosis and arrangements. If the leader is encouraging the appointment book to be filled on every line and is running late, create a new agreement as to what you want and stick with it.

Other agreement issues can be attitude, cooperation, completion for each patient, communication, participation and, commitment to having fun each day.

WE ARE BROKEN—WHAT TO DO

Covenants were made and agreed upon. Enthusiasm was high. Attitudes were positive. What happened? Where did it break down?

Agreements and conduct take constant vigilance. It is not like big brother is watching you. A successful dental practice is a unique business with a small number of real team to support the effort. Because the leader is a full out player, too, attitudes and conduct can break down slowly.

Let's use time as an example again. You agreed rooms would be ready to go before team meets for the morning huddle at 7:45 AM with breakfast finished, hair complete, uniforms on and information in hand. Your highly skilled hygienist who knows everyone and does a great job is five to ten minutes late at least once weekly. No one wants to say anything to her because she really does contribute when she is there. Yet, grumbling amongst the staff has started.

Doctor, nip this in the bud and recreate your agreements about time. The next late time, the Doctor needs to say "Mary, we have an agreement to be here ready for the huddle at 7:45. Can we count on you being here ready to go at 7:40 from now on?" What you want is a renewal and recommitment in front of the team. Now Mary is whole again and she can choose to keep her agreement or be one who just can't get that together. Then, you as the leader need to have a private conversation about your decision for her future employment with you.

If you openly allow an agreement to be continually broken with no consequences, you can expect undercurrents, hurt feelings, others not playing full out because Mary doesn't have to. This can cause gossiping, grumbling and be sabotaging your leadership.

5

ATTITUDE

ATTITUDE

"Everything can be taken from a man but…the last of human freedoms—to choose one's attitude in any given set of circumstances, to choose one's own way."
—Viktor Frankl in *Man's Search for Meaning*

Our attitude shows in our behavior. How you choose to conduct yourself is a reflection of your attitude. The key word here is CHOICE. Attitude is a choice. You can be:

- A giver or a taker
- A negative influence or a positive force
- A pessimist or an optimist
- A praiser or a blamer
- A worrier or a sea of calm
- Selfish or self-less
- An attention-getter or an attention giver
- Refuses change or embraces change

Your attitude is a choice and it determines everything. Dentists ask "does personality make a difference in success of a practice?" We have seen successful dentists who have such different personalities—

shy, bold, serious academics or a laugh a minute. It isn't personality. It is attitude. Everyone likes someone who is comfortable with themselves and that is a choice. No one likes a negative grump to do their dentistry. You choose your attitude.

> "Your living is determined not so much by what life brings to you as by the attitude you bring to life; not so much by what happens to you as by the way your mind looks at what happens." — John Homer Miller

Dr. Candace DeLapp of Highlands Ranch, CO says, "Attitude is everything, absolutely everything. I strongly believe you hire for attitude and train for aptitude. You can teach the skills to work in a dental office but you can't teach someone to be nice." Candace and her husband, Dr. Jim DeLapp, share a practice and a team, each working separate days.

> "Any fact facing us is not as important as our attitude toward it, for that determines our success or failure."
> — Norman Vincent Peale

Drs. Jason and Colleen Olitsky of Ponte Vedre, FL agree attitude is huge. One day, both were home arguing about nothing just after their baby arrived and the phone rang. Neither felt like answering so they didn't. It turned out it was their publicist calling for their quote to be in SHAPE magazine (a goal of theirs). When they called back 45 minutes later, the opportunity had passed to another dentist. "We finally came to realize our bad attitudes were to blame and we know attitude is a choice."

"Attitude is a choice," says Dr. David Ward of Woonsocket, R.I. "God placed us on this earth and gave each of us free will. This is a tremendous responsibility because we, as human beings, tend to blame others for our own misfortune. I have grown to understand my attitude is probably one of the few things I can control in my life."

My very wise 96 year old mother in law, Ruth Pasley, with amputated legs due to PAD, wants to share this:

"The longer I live, the more I realize the impact of attitude on life. Attitude, to me, is more important than facts. It is more important than the past, than education, than money, than circumstances, than failures, than successes, than what other people think or say or do. It is more important than appearance, giftedness or skill. It will make or break a school, a company, a church, a home. The remarkable thing is we have a choice every day regarding the attitude we embrace for that day. We cannot change our past…we cannot change the fact that people will act in a certain way. We cannot change the inevitable. The only thing we can do is play on the one string we have, and that is our attitude. I am convinced life is 10% what happens to me and 90% how I react to it. And so it is with you. We are in charge of our ATTITUDES."

Blatchford Guiding Principles

- Keep your promises
- When you arrive at work in the morning, let the first thing you say brighten everyone's day
- Never admit at work you might be tired, angry or bored
- Watch for opportunities to show praise and appreciation
- Answer the phone with enthusiasm and energy
- Look for opportunities to make people feel important
- Don't allow self-pity. The moment this hits, do something nice for someone else less fortunate than you
- Don't let someone else choose your attitude
- Never tell anyone they look tired or depressed
- Become the most positive and enthusiastic person you know
- Never deprive someone of hope; it may be all they have
- Surround yourself with positive people
- Fire the negative people in your life
- Laugh a lot. Dentistry is neither brain surgery nor a mortuary science.
- Give thanks for every day, every opportunity
- Be enthusiastic about the success of others
- Improve your performance by improving your attitude
- Take responsibility for your own actions and behaviors
- Do not share your fears and insecurities at work
- Never show anger or be upset in front of a guest
- Stop blaming others. Take responsibility for every area of your life
- Either you have your reasons or your results. It is up to you.
- The first twelve words out of your mouth should be a compliment
- A problem is a chance to do your best
- If you think you can, you can. If you think you can't, you are right, too
- A friend is a gift you give yourself
- Avoid reality shows, television news or reading pessimistic newspapers. Soon, you start believing the doom and gloom and infect your team
- While one person hesitates because he feels inferior, another person is busy making mistakes and becoming superior
- Change is good, welcome it
- You are always at choice. Situations are never forced on you. Make things happen

Dr. Ken Novak

Husband, Father, Son, Dentist, Type 1 Diabetic since age 3,
Blatchford Client

Dr. Novak's motivation in sharing his story of dentistry and diabetes is to show the consequences when you do not take care of yourself. He hopes others will be more responsible.

When Ken was diagnosed at age 3, his mother did a great job at controlling it with diet and exercise. Even at a young age, his siblings noticed the extra attention given to Ken and resented it. Ken shares that when adolescence hit, he was tired of being "a diabetic kid" and wanted to be like his friends. His rebellion was to stop watching what he ate and drank. He admits he did not get serious and accept responsibility for his health until he was midway through dental school.

His decade of rebellion had damaged his kidneys and with a diabetic diet and blood pressure control, he was able to avoid dialysis for 13 years. He had a wife, newborn son and a dental practice when he was put on a waiting list for a kidney and pancreas transplant.

Dr. Blatchford was drawn to Ken's unique situation; his struggle to keep a practice going while taking care of his health. Bill became his friend and health coach.

The next five years, Ken was on a nightmare train ride. His hospitalizations included heart concerns and three infections from his peritoneal dialysis catheter while he was waiting for dual transplants from Ohio State. His first call for available organs required a 2.5 hour drive and upon his arrival, the organs had started to deteriorate. He and his wife had a very silent drive home.

The second call a few months later resulted in a fast two hour drive to receive new organs on Independence Day. They started working well immediately. He was told to take it easy and started seeing a light schedule of dental patients after six weeks. However, he started increasing his hours and days too soon. The result was 23 transplant hospitalizations, two MRSA infections, seven cases of pneumonia, two surgeries and 14 other various hospitalizations.

Ken's overwhelming goal is to be there for his wife and son. He is in the process of rebuilding his practice from the ashes and knows he can reach his practice goals. He has never been one who desires great material things. He sees the blessings of his many medical challenges. He was able to spend much time with his son and his marriage is stronger. One suggestion he has for dentists is to befriend their patients who have conditions which need regular medical attention. Encourage those patients to take full responsibility and control of their condition.

Ken's point is, Bill has been his steady friend and if he can help Ken, imagine what he can do for your practice.

kjndds@aol.com

6

GOAL SETTING

PRACTICE SETTING GOALS

Goal setting is a powerful process for thinking about your ideal future and for motivating yourself to turn this vision of the future into reality.

Setting goals helps you choose where you want to go in life. By knowing precisely what you want to achieve, you know where to concentrate your efforts. With strong goals, you can quickly spot the distractions which could lure you from your course.

Real goal setters build their self confidence with each victory. Goal setting is used by top athletes, business people and big achievers. With goal setting, you have long-term vision and short-term motivation. Goals help you focus your knowledge and help you organize your time and your resources so that you can make the very most of your life.

By setting sharp, clearly defined goals, you can measure and take pride in accomplishing your goals. You can see progress where before you saw a long pointless grind.

A good exercise is to set goals in all areas of your life. A balance is what we want. In dentistry, it is easy to have an imbalance with work being 80% of your life, thoughts and time.

To balance your life, set goals in all areas. You must have specific physical goals, community goals, spiritual goals, professional and family goals.

Spreadsheet on all goals with timelines

> 12 month goal
> Fiscal period goal
> Daily goal
> Overhead goal
> New patient goal
> Diagnosis goal
> Long term goal
> Financial goal—savings

GOALS TAKE ACTION

Goals motivate people. We throw out numbers and it sounds so exciting. What happens when repeatedly, goals are not met? What happens to team morale? What is the reaction of your team when you want to establish more or different goals?

What does it take for a goal to turn into results?

For example, we want to increase our production to $65K a month from an average of $52K a month. How will you accomplish this increase of $13K a month?

- You need to be diagnosing at least three times the increase or nearly $40K a month additionally
- What are you offering that is different than anyone else?
- What has been your history of the value of every new patient? Let's say each have averaged $2300. How many more new patients would it take to equal $13K increase a month?
- What are you doing to promote that number of additional new patients a month?
- What is a diagnosis? Is it just the Doctor conversation? When do we count a diagnosis?

For goals to turn into action, it takes leadership and consistency. If you announce a new program, are excited about it for a few days and then drop it, become distracted or discouraged, never mentioning it again, your staff sees this clearly. Their message is "just wait a few days, the Doctor will calm down and we can go back to normal."

If this is your consistent pattern, they see it loud and clear. Team will voice enthusiasm initially, knowing full well, there will never be any follow through or change.

How do you achieve a different result with goals?
- Behavior is a choice
- Be committed to your goals
- Follow through is mandatory—ask what is working, what needs to change? And then change it so the result is there
- Compliment consistently and specifically
- Celebrate
- Keep it going, make it part of your corporate structure

SUCCESSFUL GOAL SETTING

Unless you shape your life, circumstances will shape it for you. You have to work, sacrifice, invest and persist to achieve the goals you want. Choose them well.

You are the sculptor of your own image. Are there people who have accomplished what you dream of doing? Study them and do what they did. Believe in yourself and your abilities. This is your life to live, day by day, step by step.

Write down your goals. Only 3% of people have written goals and only 1% read them daily. Visualize reaching your goals. Goals are dreams with dates attached.

BOHAG...Big Old Hairy Audacious Goals
Do you set big and unreasonable goals or safe goals?

Setting goals is an uplifting experience because you are looking into your future. There is a positive spirit which moves you to believe you will be present and achieve the target. Team members love goals as it gives them specific targets to see.

SMART goals are more than wishful thinking. Take a look at these tips:
Specific
Measurable
Action-oriented
Realistic
Timely

To be effective, goals must be positive and precise with details and prioritized. Write your goals and better yet, share them with a friend. By speaking to others, you make a commitment to achieve those goals. You want to share your goals with supportive people rather than weak people who will allow you to waffle on your goals.

The language of successful goal setting is an important factor in actually reaching your goals. Start out positively with "I will." Anything less will not do.

Cross out:
- I hope
- I wish
- I should
- Maybe
- Someday

The goal must be stated in a positive. To lose weight, say, "I will weigh 125." Avoid the negative, "I will lose 15 pounds." "I will work out at the athletic club for one hour starting at 6 AM Monday, Wednesday and Friday so I can weight 125 pounds by April 15."

PROFESSIONAL GOALS

We need to aim for a real balance in our lives with the L.D.Pankey philosophy of the Cross of Life between Love and Worship, Play and Work.

This is however, a book on exceptional dental practices and how to implement them. Continual goal setting is an integral practice in all successful businesses. Dentistry is no exception.

We have, however, noticed there is enough net in dentistry that one can skate by without setting goals. This is dangerous skating because, to quote Dr. Bill Dickerson, "you don't know what you don't know."

Guidelines for setting your goals:

Fiscal period goal—12 months divided into the number of work days scheduled for the year

Daily goal—from the fiscal period goal, divided those equal days into a daily goal—the same every day. What is the hygiene goal per day and what is the Doctor goal?

Overhead goal—no matter the swirling economics, the leader's goal is 55% and decisions need to be made to keep it at 55%.

Net goal—would be 45% take home

New patient goal—a general practice should have at least 15 adult new patients a month.

Diagnosis goal—three times your daily goal

Long term goal—be there, be successful. Days working, daily goal, net return are all part of the long term goal

Financial goal—In addition to a 401K plan or retirement savings, you can also have post tax savings. It is said if you play in the stock market or real estate personally, you need six months of expenses and net in savings as you are going up against the pros and you have no control over the market. If you are producing $100K a month, you need $600K in solid savings and then you can play.

SPECIALISTS CREATE SUCCESS
WITH BLATCHFORD, TOO

Dr. Mark Beckstead, Peninsula Periodontics, Palo Alto, CA

My goal with Blatchford was to take a successful practice to the ultra-successful level. I was impressed with the bonus system and I wanted my staff to be well compensated, motivated and meld as a team. I brought seven to the first team seminar. Some jumped at the chance, others gave lip service and we now have a real team of four plus my wife, Kevin, a CPA by training. We asked Kevin to join us when the last staff member departed. She brings a bright and positive outlook in streamlining the financial affairs of the office. The team will not let her go.

At the first team seminar, everyone wrote down their dream salaries. I asked if they were all in six figures. With a "yes" from each, it has been my goal to help them reach their dream salaries and we are almost there. Our overall team expenditures are 23% (a level we chose) with eight weeks of time off with pay scheduled this year. When I share this with others, they either think I am crazy or they want to work with us.

In our periodontal office, we have effectively implemented Block Booking, regular communication and training workshops, team member accountability, resigning from insurance assignments and deciding who we want to treat and what we want to do for them.

In April, we moved to our new office. We had known for years that our old facility was not conveying the right message of relationships and level of care. I had been working for four years as the owning partnership (LLC) of the old building and the group was not working well. With contention among the partners and dissimilar goals and interests, communication had diminished to costly and ineffective attorney conversations. I negotiated out of the partnership and created an office 4-5 miles away (a significant move) which is centrally located with easy access from a major expressway. I stretched myself financially to purchase the building, complete the build out and find a tenant to share the building.

The result is a class A building with real character and charm, spacious and decorated to provide a comfortable homey feeling. I was initially concerned about negative feedback from patients. In reality, we have enjoyed wide spread compliments and appreciation. As a team, we feel empowered to unleash the very best we have and to raise the bar in quality of services.

I like to work with "can do" people who like to move forward. I want to be willing to make decisions, stick to those decisions and require accountability from each of us. At the recommendation of our Blatchford consultant, Kaye Puccetti, we increased our hygiene fees 40%. We made that decision and stuck to it. We did have some people leave but we had some "dead wood" anyway. During the economic downturn, we made a decision to institute a minor fee decrease in hygiene. We let our patients know what we were doing and why. There has been heartfelt gratitude. The fees will slowly go back up and I think the effort will be rewarded with loyalty.

A lower overhead is a blessing. With a lean team, I feel more confident during economic changes. I believe we are more agile, responsive and can modify our practice as needed. It is very satisfying to watch team members take on responsibilities which extend beyond their normal scope of work. They have become more cross-trained and multi-dimensional.

Our niche is that we provide the latest, most up to date treatment in an efficient way to make the total experience in our office extraordinarily positive. We have adopted treatment protocols to reduce treatment time, reduce pain and down time with minimally invasive and effective techniques. Several years ago, I developed proficiency in microsurgical techniques. We have operating microscopes in our surgery ops and all procedures are done under magnification.

We have taken advantage of improvements in implant design and implant surface technology to provide better initial stability of implants and faster integration. Doing this along with the use of growth factors such Plasma Rich in Growth Factors (PRGF), Platelet Rich Plasma (PRP) or Platelet Derived Growth factor and bone graft materials allows for immediate placement of implants in extraction sites and in some cases, immediate temporization with optimal healing results.

As a periodontist, a large part of my practice is dedicated to gingival augmentation for the treatment of recession and root exposure. We now provide that treatment without harvesting tissue from the palate. We are achieving great results using Alloderm, the Tunnel Technique and PRGF. The patient experience is amazingly positive. Since there is an unlimited supply of Alloderm, all the recession defects can be treated at one appointment under IV Sedation.

Having invested much time and energy in studying the periodontal literature, I feel compelled to practice "evidence based" dentistry to be sure the treatment we recommend is supported by controlled studies published in journals. After serious consideration, we are treating moderate to advanced periodontitis with laser assisted periodontal therapy or LANAP. It has taken a while to develop dependable protocols with reproducible results with the laser. I have completed my training with the PerioLase and we are now offering minimally invasive, pain free treatment for periodontitis.

Continuing education and the adoption of new technology is inspiring and invigorating to me and the Team as it offers the patients some real advantages. Talk about avoiding burn out! I am more excited about the treatment we are providing and the results we are getting than ever before. I love to bring the Team together at a completion to see the final results and also congratulate the patient for doing something positive for themselves. Our guests go back to their general dentist raving about their experience and refer their friends. Patient referrals in a specialty practice are especially rewarding.

I love to work hard and play hard. I consider myself first a husband and father, then a periodontist, then a cyclist, skier and golfer. There is only so much time for extra-curricular activities but exercise and diversion for dentists is **critical.** I exercise six days a week and take great satisfaction in being "in-shape." It provides balance to the many hours spent indoors doing dentistry and related dental business activities. It helps me to be positive and ward off many of the physical effects of doing dental work.

I ride my bike almost everyday, including to and from work. I ride with a club on a weekly basis and as a group we have done several century rides in addition to our regular Saturday morning rides of 50-70 miles. I typically ride 6 days per week and I average 150-200 miles per week. I have developed deep friendships with my riding buddies, many of whom are dentists! The hours of training and suffering together on long tough rides has created a bond of brotherhood which has been an added benefit and greatly appreciated.

My competitive biking events include the "Death Ride, which I won first in 1995 and then each of the last four years. I have completed six double century rides as part of the California Triple Crown series. I completed three doubles in one year which is the California Triple Crown.

I make specific goals for weight, percentage of body fat and completion of specific events. Whenever possible, I include my family in my recreational pursuits which has given us many meaningful memories and developed skills we all enjoy. Dentistry is hard work and you need to be in shape to do it well! A book Mark recommends is *Younger Next Year* by Chris Crowley and Henry Lodge.

I enjoy being the leader in my practice. I have had limited success with associate doctors and partners. However, there is value in sharing skills, teaching and mentoring others. Our Seattle Study Club is set up to facilitate meaningful interaction among top level clinicians with the sharing of ideas and techniques.

I believe the future of dentistry is very bright. Technology will continue to bring advancements to improve patient care. In our busy society, there will always be a place for personal quality care and patient-centered practices. I hope to stay on top of my game to see many more advances come my way.

www.periodocs.com

Dr. Mark Beckstead.

7

LEADERSHIP

WHO IS THE LEADER?
YOU, YOU'RE THE ONE!

How would you evaluate yourself on a scale of 1 to 10 with 10 being the highest? What do you need to do to make yourself a 10?

Dentists struggle with leadership. They abdicate and abandon the station. Why such a fear? Who knows but it hurts everyone.

- Is it because I am a left brained scientist and really can't be bothered with the business of dentistry and leading a group?
- Is it my fear I might make a mistake so it is best if I don't even go to that place?
- I struggle with decisions so we move slowly on committee decisions
- I love the dentistry but dislike the leadership, so I avoid it

Can't someone else be the leader? Some consultants advocate a strong team member to lead. How I see it is you, the dentist, will be the last one to close the door at the end of your career. In your lifetime, you will see excellent team members roll through your life because of moving away, finding another career or lack of energy for what you need.

Bottom line: you cannot abdicate leadership and have a successful business career.

Being a leader is a choice, just as choosing to abandon the chair is also a choice. Choose behavior that emulates a good leader. At first, it may be an act but you will grow into the role if you give it a go.

Dr. Candace DeLapp says, "The biggest thing I have done is learn to delegate. I'm becoming more like Ronald Reagan. Ideas are great, let others pick up the reins; just have systems in place to monitor."

THE DECISION MAKER

Dr. Tara Jennings of Stevens Point, WI

Dr. Jennings has natural leadership skills to create private practice success. She finds she does not struggle with decisions when her vision is clear. Dr. Jennings looks out twenty years as Dr. Blatchford suggests and works her way back. Thus, she sees clearly what needs to be done in the short-term to make the bigger picture a long-term reality.

She is a young mother of two boys and her husband is an endodontist next door. Her greatest quest is balance and next to that is being profitable and efficient while at work.

As a young female leader of the team, just eight years into practice, and one year as an owner, Dr. Jennings realizes she may not always make the popular decisions but she is becoming more comfortable with that. Their morning huddles are organized with coaching, no gossip or non-topic discussions. They have organized trainings once a month on safety protocol and full business discussions. They all know in advance the topics so preparation is key for communication and meetings being productive.

"Success is all about attitude. Sometimes, I fake it, but when I walk in the door in the morning, having my game face on is all that matters. The team plays off me and each other. If one has a bad attitude and I see the others being brought down, I have been known to call a short pep rally together."

Efficiency is a key word for Dr. Jennings. She moved from four days to three patient contact days. The team has made bonus every cycle since starting and the bonus has made them more proactive in filling Dr. Jennings' schedule to goal. They are even more eager once they have passed the BAM level and the bonus is a reality. They absolutely follow block booking as Tara says, "I don't want to do denture adjustments all my life." She does implants which gives her the freedom to make solid case recommendations. "I keep this in house and do all from start to finish."

The Jennings' team is reading sales and marketing books as well as role-playing sales conversations. "We ask great and easy questions like, 'what are your goals and how do you see your smile years from now?'

I knew I was ready to have my own practice before I actually did. I had been looking for a building to start as there were no practices for sale. I was going to build it out when I was ready.

A doctor was off for medical reasons and I was put in touch with his staff to cover for a week. After that week, the staff approached me to buy the practice. I decided I could make it work. I was ready to do anything to move on with my career. When I purchased this practice, I had to transition out of an associateship. I worked both places for the next 30 days. I intended to keep the staff at my new office but that didn't work out.

If I had to do it again, I would have rehired them with a 60-90 day probation period. No two dentists are alike and people don't change. This is my experience with the staff I kept.

Thus, I had the building before I had the practice. I had been renting the space, but the building and set up was not of what I dreamed as it was very small and not well kept. I do prefer small. I also had minimal options for signage and wanted more control. I wanted to own versus rent because I wanted it done my way and to retain control. It has been very busy through the construction. Dr. Blatchford suggested I reduce my support square footage vs. production square footage to add tenant space. This was the right thing to do and got me very excited.

I have made some tough decisions, but only when it really counted like cabinetry, phone service, and a general contractor. It is interesting to see how different service providers are aggressive to win my account. I reinforced my ability to say 'no' and still be professional. I have tried to keep things local and reuse what I can, which gives me a good feeling.

This is a small town and people are quite impressed at my skills and ability to balance family and a profession. There are some interesting comments but I just decided that I am going to do this my way. It may not be their way, but it doesn't have to be. I wonder if the dentists working 4-5 day weeks wouldn't really love to work the 3-4 days of my week. I like to think the answer is yes.

To be visible in the community, we wear our uniforms. We were in the local Christmas Parade. We've had gift baskets at different school events. The new location is on a very heavily trafficked road. We all have business cards ready to hand out. I also like to send notes or letters to patients for any little thing. And our latest is a website, www.excellencedental.net. I am starting to send patients here more often and my web address is on my building signage and all our literature.

I was stimulated to purchase my second practice because of a teleconference call Dr. Blatchford had before I became a client. He discussed different ways to buy another dentist's practice. I thought this could be a way to grow. Brilliant! When I purchased the second office, there still wasn't enough work to hire more than the three team members. I also wanted to filter out the bottom 20% from both practices and I knew not all patients would transfer to me. I paid per chart, after I had seen the patient. I am so excited to have my own practice.

As my kids get older, I want to grow at work, too. It hasn't been easy everyday. It can be a challenge to meet eight "new" patients in a day, everyday of the week. It does create the habit of "turning on the charm."

I do rise at 5 AM, before the kids. I also go to bed about the same time as them, 8 PM. I like the quiet in the morning to get my day started and boy,' do I need my husband's and cleaning ladies' help! I just need to figure out who will get my groceries for me!

I did not even recognize or realize the work behind the scenes which my team tackled when taking over a practice and merging with another. There are claims, collecting and expectation of patients of how "it used to be." I did keep the hygienist from the first practice as she is a real leader and "gets me." My assistant is curious, willing and able. The front desk coordinator is very professional and business minded. I love the opportunity to work with these three talented ladies. Grateful is what I am!

www.excellencedental.net

Dr. Tara Jennings

IT LOOKS LIKE A LEADER

What does a leader of a small business look like and act like? You still remain who you really are. Your personality shines through. The leadership activity that is most successful is to be very clear on your bigger picture of where you are going, be able to communicate that vision, delegate and let others do the work. You make decisions. You continue to be the guiding light, finding your way.

Behavior is a choice. We observe your behavior. Choose to act like a leader. Choose effective behavior.

You are the coach for your morning huddle. You allow others to lead the weekly team meeting and organize your training sessions by having communicated the bigger picture of results.

Your team knows your values and philosophy so well, they do not need to place anyone on hold and then interrupt you to ask what they should do about the next procedure or problem on the phone. A well-led team works like Nordstrom where each member of the team is accountable and takes responsibility to complete tasks. They can do this because they believe that your path will best serve their feelings of being needed and rewarded. With your encouragement and real delegation, team members want more responsibility.

"Our chief want in life is somebody who will make us do what we can." —Ralph Waldo Emerson

You have an individual responsibility to be the best you can be. Become that leader by first acting like a leader. Soon, it will become part of you.

Making decisions is a struggle for most dentists. Our "C" personalities dictate we need ALL the facts thoroughly digested and then, maybe, we can come to a conclusion. That works well on equipment items only. Things move fast in a dental office and decisions need to be made on the spot. This is why the journey and outcome of a personal vision quest is so important.

Once you have your vision in place, you can make decisions based on that vision. Ask yourself, "Is this consistent with my vision?" If the answer is yes, move forward. Make the decision.

Johann Wolfgang von Goethe said, "Until one is committed, there is hesitancy, the chance to draw back, always ineffectiveness. Concerning all acts of initiative and creation, there is one elementary truth the ignorance of which kills countless ideas and splendid plans: that the moment one definitely commits oneself then, providence moves, too.

All sorts of things occur to help one that would never otherwise have occurred. A whole stream of events, issues from the decision, raising in one's favor all manner of unforeseen incidents and meetings and material assistance, which no man would have dreamed would come his way."

Whatever you can do or dream, you can, begin it. Boldness has genius, power and magic in it. Begin it now."

A SECOND CHANCE

Dr. Keri Chellis, West Seattle

When I was in 7th grade, I received a gift that would influence and shape my life forever; the gift of orthodontic therapy.

I was a quiet self-conscious child and daily, my Dad would poke fun by saying, "you could eat corn off the cob through a picket fence!" I was very aware my two front teeth stuck out so far they could reach through the pickets. Since we were in a lower income level and struggling to put two kids through church school, I never imagined I would have braces. There just wasn't enough money for extras.

The experience of having my smile changed at 13, radically improved my self-esteem. I smiled, was more confident and became social around others. I realized I wanted to be able to help others receive this gift. I decided right then, I wanted to be an orthodontist. The gift that had been given to me inspired and compelled me to design my future to pay it forward!

I knew I had artistic abilities, creativity and hand skills. I needed people skills and a degree to enter dental school. I chose Dental Hygiene at Loma Linda, receiving a B.S. and graduating magna cum laude. I was one of the first members of the first dental hygiene class in California with "expanded duties" included in my license. This included administering local anesthetic, nitrous, scaling and root planning.

At age 20, I just wasn't ready to go to Dental School, realizing the full responsibilities of being a dentist and taking care of someone else's life. I practiced dental hygiene for several years and my favorite experience was with Dr. Gary Gregory, then president of the American Academy of Implant Dentistry. In the 1980's, we had a "bigger is better" practice.

I did the anesthesia for two doctors and a hygienist and even had my own dental assistant. We prepared each patient for the doctors and then took over again after the doctor had prepped, possibly placing and carving amalgams, making temps and post-op instructions and dismissal. I learned the basics of removable and implant supported prostho, participated in six handed dentistry doing surgery for full sub-periosteal implants. The dental magic was giving an edentulous patient a whole new ability to smile and chew with confidence when the dentures is implant-supported.

At age 27, I still wasn't sure I was ready to be a dentist. I moved to Colorado and tried in vain to find another office like Dr. Gregory's. Finally, I was ready and was accepted at age 32 to University of Washington in my hometown. However, this time, instead of being at the top of my class, I was surrounded by 50 other top of their own class students who gave me a run for my money! All I did was study and graduated in the top 10% of my class with nine academic and clinical awards.

I was so grateful and secure after graduation knowing the world could knock me down physically but the knowledge I had inside my head could never be taken away from me.

Two years after graduation, I purchased a practice in West Seattle where the selling doctor was already a "Blatchford office." I discovered they had been happy without me and doing just fine. I was untrained in the Blatchford system and had to scramble to keep up. The staff made it absolutely crystal clear they did not want a new doctor. The selling doctor never told them he was selling and the staff was adamant they were going to drive me away and break my spirit. I was the new owner but the charismatic selling doctor stayed for seven years and never told the patients or staff.

I had a $13K a month loan payment and struggled to generate enough production to pay the bills, do office work at home and have a social life. Finally, I met Henry, my husband to be and it was wonderful except I no longer physically felt good. Things were seriously wrong with my body which created great pain. I put on a brave face and said " I am excellent," when anyone asked.

An eight doctors and ten month investigation finally determined I had Stage 4 colon cancer. At 45 years of age, my life came to a screeching halt! I thought I might be out four weeks but the cancer was much worse than I thought. I came within nanometers of dying multiple times. A deep abiding faith in God, the love of my husband, my parents, my love for dentistry and my great patients sustained me during those dark months. I knew if I made it, it would be for a reason.

Fifteen months later, still not back to normal, but for financial reasons, I dragged myself back in to pick up the practice or lose it! I was still barely able to walk up the stairs or to sit chairside for an hour at a time.

The next 2.5 years were a blur of fighting to regain my strength, madly doing dentistry and trying to replace the staff. In addition, I had to design a new space and physically move as I had been practicing without a lease for several years. This time around, I wanted better. Instead of staff, I wanted a team. I wanted a great practice instead of one that had been so hard. All this proved exhausting on my body still not recovered from it's bout with disease and chemotherapy.

I had a revolving door of staff members who just wanted more money and wanted to do less. My staff of six never felt they had enough people to do all the jobs. The joy of connection with my clients which had been the major overriding measure of happiness in the past seemed lost in the effort of rebuilding the staff. I was putting in 12-14 hour days on the practice and not taking care of my body. Aging had caught up with my post-cancer body and I was desperate to do things differently, but I didn't know how.

Out of the blue, the Blatchfords called to reconnect. I realized I needed a coach again. They gave me hope, helping me see there was a way to get my life back on track. I did not know how I was going to find the mental strength to make the difficult changes that were needed but I knew if it was working for other Blatchford Doctors, it could work for me. All I had to do was do what Bill advised me to do.

I had to change the vision of myself. I decided I couldn't completely be "Dr. Nice Boss." I realized it was not my job to "keep six women happy at the same time." The new Team truly is empowered; accountability is the biggest blessing in my life and we now have great fun! Our team costs were at 35% and now are at 17%. At the same time, we have increased our production to an all time personal best. Before working with Dr. Blatchford, I tried to see "both sides of the coin," be the peacemaker and the nice mother-figure/boss. Now I choose to say which I want and my new team looks for ways to make that happen. I no longer worry about being the "nice boss." **It's my party!**

We use "walkie-talkies" for team communication and we have great fun playing together and teasing each other. When one person starts it, everyone else gets to hear and chime in. A good attitude is infectious!

With a team of three and utilizing all our communication and training vehicles, we are honing our skills of efficiency and aligning our focus. I need to surround myself with self-motivated individuals who are willing to get the job done. When I let them work in their own way, they amaze me. I have learned to expect less of the way the team does things and to appreciate how they choose to work and their results.

The Blatchford Bonus system has been the best thing ever! The very first month, we made bonus with three team members. They realize they are in control of what we produce, collect and team salaries. They no longer want to add a team member when they feel the load getting a bit tougher. They want to keep BAM as low as possible so it is easier to bonus. They understand they have earned 20% of everything over BAM. Every time I sign a bonus check, I realize there are extra dollars in my bank account as the practice receives the other 80%. It takes the team to a whole new level of ownership!

My team is embracing the concept of asking themselves "WHY" do I/we do this? In going paperless, this is relevant as we have traditionally used the paper chart as a receptacle for all records sent by specialists. Now we scan the incoming papers and shred them. We are embracing the digital revolution. New this year, we now have our guests complete their medical/dental history and the entry form on line. We download them and store them electronically in the digital chart. At the office, we capture their signatures on forms with an electronic signature device "e-pad."

Before, we struggled to obtain our guest emails. We now say, "We confirm all appointments via email or text messages. Which would you prefer?" We now have better access to electronic communication.

In marketing, we now know who our top 20% of patients are and I focus on them. I make sure I touch base with them personally, each visit, sharing what is new in the practice and thanking them for their support over the years.

We have had a website for years. This year's marketing success has been with the social networking on sites such as Citysearch, West Seattle Blog, Yelp and Angie's List. The most bang for our buck we have ever received is a small printed glossy magazine entitled *West Seattle's Leading Ladies* put out by the local newspaper. Print media may be dying but people love this little book.

Marketing does bring in new bodies but self-selected new guests don't arrive pre-conditioned by our raving fans. We really practice our Blatchford sales skills in our training meetings. We did a West Seattle Street Fair, manning a booth 12 hours for three days, just the four of us. We met hundreds of people and have seen a good number of these for dental care.

With the Oral-systemic connection becoming clearer to me everyday, healing present disease and prevention of further disease is a huge priority for me. I am very excited about my affiliation with World Congress of Minimally Invasive Dentistry which has me focused on preventing dental disease. Whenever we restore a decayed tooth, we have a conversation about how they can prevent new decay by treating the disease process itself, not simply filling the hole that is only the symptom of the disease.

With Dr. Kim Kutsch's CareFree systems, combined with other preventive products today, we routinely test for an overload of specific bacteria that cause cavities and we prescribe products to modify the oral biofilm to change a client's predisposition to decay as well as remineralize tooth structure that has been affected.

Similarly, with the advent of DNA testing for periodontal pathogens and the host resistance to disease, we can specifically target the appropriate pathogens with systemic antibiotics and eliminate the disease processes that have not responded to traditional flossing and brushing.

I achieve intimacy, connection, creativity and challenge with every single patient procedure. My passion continues to be dentistry. I am blessed to use my talents through a profession that so powerfully returns to me what I need every day. I channel my need for change into Continuing Education. I have roots with dear old friends, family and many patients who have stayed with me for 15 years.

I am a success personally. I am at peace with myself and with my God. I know I have been given a second chance in my life and I am eternally grateful. I know I must be here for a reason. When I help others professionally, I feel good about myself and feel I am fulfilling my destiny.

I know I am making a difference in the world, if only in small ways. I love changing people's expectations of dentistry. I love making every individual tooth look better than it did. I love helping people get healthier. I love changing people's own self-esteem by giving them a new smile, sense of health and well-being. I love creating gorgeous smiles of which my guests can now be so proud. I love providing dentistry to withstand the test of time. I do believe people with good looking and healthy teeth will smile more in their own life!

www.smilesecrets.com

Henry and Keri.

Love endures all things.

LEADERSHIP BENEFITS

If one is to choose to act like a leader, one needs to see some benefits. Like, WIIFM…What's In It for Me. Why should I take a risk?

The benefits to strong leadership are many:

- Greater emotional rewards
- Excitement and exhilaration of making decisions
- Greater financial return
- Greater control of financial future
- Direction and inspiration for team
- Financial security for team and Doctor
- Now team can be more effective and efficient which equals profitability
- Communication channels are clear
- Expectations for team are clear
- Your guests sense a strong direction and choose to participate
- It's great to be the lead dog

One motivating factor for acting like a leader and stepping up to take the mantle is the financial return. In Michael Gerber's, the *E-Myth Revisited*, we are challenged to look beyond the technician level where many dentists are stuck. The next level is the management level which can earn you another 50% or more above the technician level. This is mainly administrative and clerical but not real leadership.

Which would you rather have? Which one is the better leader?

Produce $1,000,000	Produce $500,000	Produce $1,000,000
OH 75%	OH 50%	OH 50%
Net $250,000	Net $250,000	Net $500,000

Then there is the leadership level which for several more hours of planning and executing a month, you can earn an additional $100K or several hundred thousand in net. This is the bigger picture person who is inspired (or who chooses to act inspired) with positive energy, ideas and plans. A leader inspires greatness and makes others look good. A solid accountable team forms from this inspiration and the leader remains the bright light of positive energy.

LEADERSHIP PITFALLS

Leadership is lonely. You alone make the tough decisions. You reap the rewards or suffer the consequences. Your team will become accountable when you let them be accountable.

Thus, the pitfalls of leadership include:

- Thinking decisions are made by committee
- Procrastinating on decisions until the opportunity fades
- Thinking you need to do everything
- Allowing your team to think you can do everything
- Trying to micro-manage everything which demonstrates your lack of trust in others
- Thinking you can confide in your "best friend" at work
- Playing favorites on your team
- Failing to compliment and give them credit
- Failing to ask for help nicely, please
- Thinking leadership is being their best friend
- Not respecting that line between leadership and team

THE SPEED OF THE LEADER DETERMINES THE RATE OF THE PACK

The team is looking to you for leadership. We are all like a pack of dogs watching to see if there is a crack in the leadership wall. If we suspect a crack, then we subconsciously make it a larger crack just to see what will happen. If the leadership wall is not strong, the workers will find that weakness and exploit it to their advantage. Do you recall having a substitute teacher? Do you recall the group mentality in action?

Everyone admires the bold, courageous and daring; no one honors the fainthearted, shy and timid. Look around at what others have done and what you can also do. Everyone is afraid. The strong act in spite of the fear. The weak cower because of the fear. Timidity breeds doubt and hesitation that not only weakens but can be dangerous. The coward dies a thousand deaths.

The formula for personal development and leadership is the same for everybody.

- You must study
- You must plan
- You must practice
- You must be tested

Some will shrink simply facing the task.

Some will do the minimum and pass.

Some will cut corners and pass.

Some will boldly welcome the challenge of honestly meeting the standards.

Then and only then will you feel the true pride of accomplishment.

Think about this— "Our deepest fear is not that we are inadequate. Our deepest fear is that we are powerful beyond measure. It is our light, not our darkness that most frightens us. We ask ourselves, 'who am I to be brilliant, gorgeous, talented, fabulous? Actually, who are you not to be? You are a child of God. Your playing small does not serve the world. There is nothing enlightened about shrinking so that other people won't feel insecure around you. We are all meant to shine, as children do. We were born to make manifest the glory of God that is within us. It's not just in some of us; it's in everyone. And as we let our own light shine, we unconsciously give other people permission to do the same. As we are liberated from our own fear, our presence automatically liberates others." Marianne Williamson in *Return to Love: Reflections on the Principles of a Course in Miracles*

THE TRANSFORMATION

Dr. Carole Murphy of Hanford, CA

We met Dr. Murphy at the ADA convention in San Francisco. She arrived with the intention to list her private practice for sale as she felt "anything would be better than this."

"I was looking for a way out. I thought of selling the practice and just doing ortho as it seemed like I would have more time to run the business end of things. That scheme just didn't pencil out. I thought maybe of retiring. Things were just out of control. I had purchased my own building and relocated to the larger office. In order to pay for all the debt, my idea was to work harder. I hired more staff and ran from chair to chair. I was making less money, working harder and the staff was driving me crazy. It seemed they needed constant supervision and I could not supervise and do dentistry at the same time."

Dr. Murphy attended Dr. Blatchford's ADA lecture on "Profitability and Numbers," saw some hope and came to our booth. "I was strongly identifying with what Dr. Blatchford was saying and knew this was the avenue for me. He got right to the point, did not sugar coat it and said it like it was."

The biggest impact of the transformation, Dr. Murphy feels is "who we are as a team, selecting the right team members who are willing to change and grow, plus not being afraid to be challenged with new ideas. I actually see them embracing the challenges we have set before us. Everyone, not just me as the doctor, is pulling in the same direction, trying to make our practice better."

"Setting goals openly for ourselves as individuals and for the practice is one of our most important elements which have brought us to today. We all read many books which have helped us gradually become better people and put serving our patients first."

My personal vision has always been to change people's lives. My team has heard me say this enough that they are starting to believe it. I'm thinking of a young girl I just saw for a recall visit several weeks ago. We finished her ortho case several years ago. When her mother first brought her in, she was sullen, withdrawn and not happy with her smile. When she walked into the reception room, I just thought WOW!! She has become a totally different, hardly recognizable metamorphosis of who she once was. She just glows when she smiles. "I'm so lucky to get to do this for people," confesses Carole.

"With my staff problems before Blatchford, I realize now, I was a big part of the problem. I did not know how to get everyone as committed as I was and have us all pulling in the same direction. I started with seven staff and by way of attrition and letting a few go, we now have three full- time and one part time team members. I replaced one with a young man from the real estate lending field. He had no experience in dentistry at all. It was a very scary time for me and I was very uncertain about making this move. When everyone saw how much work he had accomplished and how quickly he grasped the concepts, it just drove us all to do better."

"My team has shifted a complete 180 degrees. The biggest thing is that the team has taken more ownership of the practice that we are all creating for our patients. As the leader, I helped the team clarify our purpose and goals. Then we incrementally built on this with a lot of good coaching and tons of reading."

What I have learned about myself is to be willing to come forward with humility in earnest, admitting my short comings in order to get control of my problem areas first and foremost. Sometimes, I am the one holding the team back. This is a mortifying realization which drives me to be better and better. I can't stand the thought of myself being the weak link.

If one team member refuses to do this then it will hold us ALL back. The cake is only as good as the ingredients that go into it. I want us all to grow as individuals. I can see how much we have grown and accomplished but this is only the beginning.

Setting goals is something I don't have to think about much. They just seem to be inside of me. I just ask myself 'what do you want?' and 'what is it that God may have for me here?' I know for others this is a process that takes some time but for me, it's like asking me what's my favorite color or my favorite jeans in my dresser.

My style of leadership is that I must get the team's input. Otherwise, I feel they may not buy into it. This is probably a big area of growth for me. I try to get them to come up with this stuff on their own with me throwing out suggestions. Many times, they help me see things I would not otherwise have thought of. The basic framework for me is group effort.

Dr. Blatchford is coaching my leadership skills. I found I was mostly focusing on what was wrong and fixing that which is broken rather than holding the bigger picture. Now, we focus on proactive, what we are doing right and how we do more of "right." This has fueled everyone's positive achievement drive. There are still some areas I need to grow.

We have set a monthly production goal of $100K. We have not met it yet but I see this as very doable. I would like us all to experience the excitement of achieving this goal regularly. I would like us to be an office to which other doctors send their implant and sleep apnea patients. We would benefit from more team cohesion and cementing our day to day operations. We also want to work a three day work week.

We needed to implement a better financial policy as our A/R totaled $94K when we started with Blatchford, now down to $55K. It was difficult at first to institute "check, cash, or credit card?" I had to be very firm here and not let it slide when it wasn't comfortable. One thing we did that really helped is we decided to divide the over 90 day accounts between all team members. Everybody had a section of the alphabet and had to call the patients on their lists. They were able to see firsthand how impossible it is to collect past due accounts. They felt our old policy was very inefficient, unproductive and it pretty much sucked! Now, everyone realizes if they leave without paying, it will come back to bite us.

Adding sleep apnea, implants and Invisalign has made it easier to hit our daily goals. New keeps everyone more interested and excited. We are really working on our sales skills by reading and role playing. Our best marketing is internal as the atmosphere and service level in our office has changed dramatically. We need to do more external marketing. Because of adding new services, we have gone into the community for the first time to meet other physicians and dentists. This is not something I would have done otherwise. I think this will have a huge impact as our town is really a regional health center.

The future is unlimited for us and for me. The sky is the limit. I see us doing many more implant cases and hopefully, sleep appliances. I am now single and am excited about the personal goals I have yet to achieve. I see myself very busy and opening a new chapter in my life with community involvement and lots of travel. I see the possibility of dentistry involved in the universal health care cause and wonder how the more volume orientation will play out with more quality orientation. From a positive perspective, services would be expanded to those who are underserved.

www.carolemurphydds.com

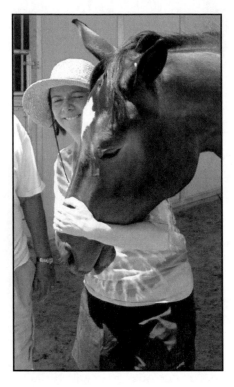

Carole seeking balance in her life.

Skill and concentration outside of dentistry.

THE MICROMANAGER—
HOW TO STRANGLE YOUR BUSINESS

Who is this person who worries about everyone's tasks, thoughts and actions? Who is this person who spends hours after patient care shuffling papers, reviewing completed work, worrying about the schedule and even changing appointments?

Leadership run amok can look and feel like micro-managing. Your staff can tell you when you have crossed the line. Micro-managing is a cousin to the technique of fear; a management approach that keeps a tight rein regarding everything. You are the only one who decides everything.

Micro-managing is a petty approach to managing every detail of your practice. If you are micro-managing, you have a problem. If you feel you must check on every detail, your chosen style is symptomatic of insecurity or paranoia. Your lack of faith and trust in people is repressive.

Your best team members will be discouraged and leave when you focus on problems of details. If you don't trust their judgment or are unwilling to delegate any responsibility, you cheat yourself and them. You cannot build a one person organization that succeeds.

You are acting as a brake to all progress. No one will come up with new ideas or suggestions. You will end up with mindless androids who are only order takers—"this tooth hurts."

How do you break the behavior of a micro-manager? It has to hurt bad enough for you to want to change. You have to see your business is going on a downhill slide or that no one has an independent thought. Once you decide, you will need to evaluate if you have the right staff remaining. You want ambitious, curious people who want to succeed.

Then build your delegation skills at first by giving duties away that are not critical to your business success. Try not to second guess the outcome or feel indispensable. Hopefully, you will realize some of your team members are as smart as you are. Smart staff can give you some smart input.

8

TEAM

MOVING FROM STAFF TO TEAM

The goal is a cohesive supercharged team. We all start with a staff which is a group of individuals who we hope will do the very best they know how from their own individual experiences. They conduct themselves on their own agenda because there is a void in leadership direction, vision and training.

If a group remains at the staff level, the practice moves much more slowly as there are no decision makers unless an individual chooses himself and the remaining staff grant that position. What is the basis of these decisions? What are the guiding principles? Who really cares? The group remains a staff.

Team cannot form without a greater picture from the real leader. People want to do well and make a difference in the world. Without vision, passion and inspiration, people will continue a daily routine which is dull and dreary. Really sharp people will soon recognize the dead end situation and move on. Guess who remains? The staff now consists of average at best as tasks are repeated without direction or enthusiasm.

You can recognize a staff vs. team in any business situation. Initial phone conversations reveal the dull foundation where negativity abounds and the absence of willingness to go beyond the status quo to serve. Staff cannot move beyond "order taking" as that has been their experience. We fill in the blanks and shuffle the papers with no goals in mind.

Oh, for that magic when a group of people come together for a common purpose, moving from individual concerns to the group effort. You can observe trust, great communication skills, purpose, accountability and genuine pleasure working together. It is magic and it can be recreated. It can also disappear very quickly.

A staff is a group of individuals who work hard at their own agenda. Sometimes it feels like a bad hair day when everyone is going in a different direction. There is much wasted energy, inefficiency and the result is the status quo with little movement accomplished.

What are the factors which allow ordinary to become extraordinary? It all starts with the leader. Your job is one of discovery and introspection to find out who you are and why you do what you do. Contemplate the three questions:

- Who Am I?
- What Do I Do?
- For Whom Do I Do it?

As the leader, find that dream. With inspiration and communication, a team can form based on your clarity, direction and depth of sincerity. You must walk your talk and believe in the vision yourself. They must have the opportunity to see something larger than themselves. The leader sets the standards and the climate. Behave like a leader for it is a choice.

Each individual then must choose to be on this bus or choose that this is not the right bus for them at this time. The answer is 'yes' or 'no'. There is no 'maybe.' Your best players want something bigger to happen and if you continue to stall on leadership and staff decisions, your best players will eventually leave or sink to the lowest common denominator.

In this transition from individuals to team, the leader must stand firm and tall. If you continue to rescue with micro-managing or fail to delegate, the team will not form. They know you will continue in your same old way.

Continue to communicate your vision as new solid systems are implemented which will create better service, more efficiency and greater results. We want team to know and own the numbers, be able to make decisions to change trends.

One solid system which must be implemented is a fair and easy bonus plan. If they are truly to be a team and accountable for results, they need to know they will share in the profit from that courage and skill. Develop a solid booking system so a daily goal is reached and exceeded. A reward of efficiency is more time off with pay.

A leader leads with a positive attitude of winning. You need to coach, encourage and compliment. Challenge yourself and continue to create new opportunities for growth with your team. Great people like challenge, changes and becoming better. Write team agreements and live by them. Be the first one to work and do not have a "favorite" on your team. Do not ask your "favorites" what you should do. Your failure to lead is divisive and will turn a team into a staff again.

Be a decision maker. Make your decisions based on your vision. Not everything needs a group vote. You be the leader your team has dreamt of by being decisive, not necessarily popular. Yes, leadership is lonely and good leadership has great rewards.

A leader can still have fun and show your personality. Yet, there are important distinctions. Earn their respect by making your vision clear and demonstrating commitment. Good people disrespect a lack of follow through and will find another place to flourish.

Creating the magic of team from individuals is the leader's job. It is all in your hands. It is a choice and your job is to dream a bigger picture with clarity and communicate it to the team.

GOING FOR THE ONE STOP SHOP

Dr. Philip V. Goduco of Vernon Hills, Illinois (North Chicago suburb)

Now that I am 51 years old, I have reached a major point in my life where I am at the half way mark. Knowing life is short and precious, I want to plan the second half of my life. I want to provide security for my family, so I continue to keep myself open to new opportunities and adapt to change. I want to get great advice from already successful people in my profession so I can take my practice to the next level of success.

I can attribute my vision and drive to the day my family stepped foot on United States soil in 1968 with dreams of higher education and a better quality of life for all six children. Being educators and entrepreneurs in the Philippines, both my mother and father knew that this opportunity along with patience, desire and an excellent work ethic would provide their six children with vast opportunities. My mother worked seven days a week as a pharmacist in two different Chicago hospitals. My father was a timekeeper, accountant, and contractor six days a week. He said, "No one dies from hard work but you will definitely die if you hardly work." All six Goduco's graduated from college and are fully employed with positions they love.

My personal vision involves spiritual growth with God, quality time with my wife and kids, travel with my family, health and prosperity, balance between profession and family, and financial freedom with full retirement plus college funds and to be able to afford the things my wife and I desire. I want to stay positive while maintaining a good personality and sense of humor, my love for my family, my passion for dentistry and the unconditional love I have for God and my wife.

My professional vision is to have a well-organized and established practice with 50% overhead, loyal team members that are well-compensated, net profit of $1.5M, and be well equipped with the latest technologies. I would like to be skilled in all basic treatment modalities and have happy patients referring their family and friends. I want to travel to underprivileged countries to not only teach other dental professionals but to also do charity work.

I visualize being a one stop shop. Upon graduating from Loyola in 1987, I had advanced training from the US Army in all specialties of dentistry. Not only were my clinical and diagnostic skills sharpened, but also my efficiency and speed. Presently, I do all of my own oral and periodontal surgery, endodontic, implant placement and restoration, crown and bridge, veneers and ceramic restorations, removable full and partial dentures, orthodontic , TMD, sleep apnea, laser therapy and oral conscious sedation. I always give all our patients an option to be treated by a given specialist and 95% of the time, our patients choose to be treated in our office. The next skill I will bring to our one stop shop is a certification in IV Sedation.

I have worked successfully with other dental business consultants who really helped to implement office systems, marketing, communications and office protocols. We were doing well prior to Blatchford Coaching. I was looking for a well-respected dental coach who could help me fulfill my dream of running a well organized, lucrative, and profitable dental office. My pressing issues were finding good and loyal team members who were in line with the office vision and goals. Who understood overhead control, debt reduction, office efficiency and had a better balance of time for family and my profession.

After meeting with Dr. Blatchford for the first time, I increased my goals. Now, I want to realize my production goal of $3M within a seven year time frame, become a stronger leader in my community, have a better family/time/practice balance, become more efficient while having fun at work, have more time off with pay, travel with my family and attain financial, physical and mental health.

The first full year with Blatchford Coaching, we produced $1.4M (up $300K from previous year) with 58% overhead, team at 21% and lab of 11%. We worked four patient days, down to three days starting July of this year. We reduced our office debt and funded 401Ks, vacationed four weeks and all three team members continue to earn their bonuses. We have stronger marketing with five websites, magazine and newspaper ads, networking with physicians who are now asking for referrals.

I have also enjoyed extensive training, earning a mastership with Pacific Implant Institute for implant placement and atraumatic surgical extractions, DOCS program for light conscious sedation, laser dentistry, more advanced courses in dental sleep apnea, a Fellowship to the American Dentistry International, and a Diplomate to American Board of Dental Sleep Medicine.

Our aim is to be efficient both for profitability but more importantly for patient care and service. We have the Waterlase MD and Ez-lase, digital x-rays, magnification with loupes with illumination, Diagnodent, oral conscious sedation and the Wand. We focus on Block Booking, scripting, morning and evening huddles, checklists for every procedure and easy financial arrangements. Communication is the key.

The most powerful technique my team and I learned was the ability to use and master the Blatchford Power Questions to enable our office to sell larger cases. We sold an $80K case! A new patient came in from a magazine ad. He was looking for ways to replace his removable upper and lower dentures with something more permanent. He had asked his previous dentist if there was an alternative and the answer was, "No." We did multiple implant placements, bilateral sinus lifts, gum treatment and surgery, neuromuscular therapy with opening a collapsed bite, and total rehabilitation of entire upper and lower teeth with full coverage crowns on implant and natural teeth. I had only dreamed of doing treatment with a case such as this. Now, our goal is to complete one of these cases once a month.

I had always wanted to add two staff members, one in the front and one in the back. My great team of three wanted to keep the number at three. The Blatchford Bonus system is fully understood by the team and they feel they can handle the work load due to increased efficiency and organization as well as solid systems in place so patient care is enhanced and never compromised. The Blatchford Bonus brought team accountability. The three are amiable, enthusiastic and happy. I plan to have my team with me for a long time.

The team is really excited about having conversations with patients and asking the Blatchford Power Questions. Last year the team shared $55K in bonuses. The net in 2008 was $590K and in 2007, the net was $449K. Our office overhead decreased from 65% to 58%. Our goal for this year is move closer to 50% overhead by doing $1.7 million production and collection working 165 days. We are going to a three day work week in July.

The mingling at Blatchford seminars with other doctors and teams who are doing well is a real bonus. The monthly coaching and training from Bill and for our team has been unbelievable. This has enabled me to exert a strong leadership role and my team to be held accountable for our office success. I have learned a great deal just from listening to other doctors share their successes. I enjoy the exchanges of great leadership ideas between doctors and they are well moderated by Dr. Blatchford. I can implement these immediately with my team and ultimately, our patients are the benefactors.

www.goducosmiles.com

*Dr. Goduco
celebrating a large
case acceptance.*

*The Goduco team
from left:
Kate Grainger,
Regina Melman
and Shirley Sujanani.*

*The biggest reason
Dr. Goduco
practices so well.*

TEAM SELECTION

Finding the right group of players is one of the greatest and on-going challenges for a dentist. In America, we have experienced full employment in high economic times which means everyone who wants to work is employed. We have also experienced frightful economic times when people are looking for work. The dental team is always in a state of flux.

I hear dentists say, "she/he was the best who applied and we are just making do." How can you provide excellence for your patients knowing we are working at just below average? Where is the enthusiasm, curiosity and commitment?

"The closest to perfection a person ever becomes is when he fills out a job application form." Dr. Brian Saby of Red Deer, Alberta, shared, "I was going though the process of hiring a dental assistant. One of our applicants had a brilliant interview so we made her part of our team. After starting, it became evident she was not up to the task. When I discussed the problems with her, I simply stated: 'I want the person who showed up at the interview to show up for work.' Her response blew me away. 'It's not going to happen!' was the last comment she made as a member of our team."

Working in our favor is another factor I call the "death of loyalty." Americans shift careers nearly every seven years and companies even faster. Thus, there is hope to find the magic team members who want a new challenge and enjoy people. They are already employed and you must always be looking.

Where do you look and for what are you looking? Furthermore, why would they be looking for you? Finding the right team is a leadership decision and it is a selection process, not a training process. Are you prepared to lead with integrity and a positive attitude? Have you done your homework to discover your own strengths and developed your life mission? Has that been communicated regularly to your team? Is your passion present so your team can catch the inescapable feeling they are truly making a difference? It is up to you.

Work on yourself first as you are interviewing a great candidate, they are evaluating you to see if this is the right place for them. What do you exhibit that makes you different, a place where they can flourish and bloom, too?

What impression does your office make? Is it average and in need of upgrading? Do you have in place the extra touches which attract good patients as well as team? Do you have excellent systems in place which would allow even an average person to show up well? Is everyone cross trained from start to finish in working with a guest? Does your assistant enter treatment, collect funds, issue a statement, schedule and do all the spa amenities plus?

Just when you feel you have the perfect team, a spouse will be transferred, a change takes place and notice is given. April Ziegele, with a tight team of three, produces nearly $2M gross. Her hygienist was moving to California in a month.

After the initial shock, April lined up her ducks by using Craig's List with the ad: We are looking for a dental hygienist for a fun filled progressive cosmetic and implant dental practice in the South Sound. Benefits include working 3 days a week with a competitive salary, 8 weeks of paid time off, holidays, medical and uniforms paid and all continuing education paid in full including all travel expenses. We also offer a 401K, all dental paid and bonuses averaging $5200 for each team member per month! This is a great career opportunity for someone who loves people and to serve others. Sales experience and Blatchford training is a definite plus! See our website for more information. We are looking forward to meeting you and considering you for a part in the South Sound's premier dental team! Please email your resume and cover letter to info@aprilziegele.com.

"We looked at everyone's resume and checked for grammar and spelling. I emailed my vision and asked them if they thought they could align their work goals with mine. If they responded positively, we scheduled a phone interview. I asked them:

- Describe a perfect hygiene job and a perfect week
- Why they are looking for a job, what they loved and hated about their job
- What are your weakest points
- What would your five best friends tell me over dinner
- If willing to travel
- Tell me about your work ethic

I ruled out 2/3 on the phone while listening to "I want to educate about perio." I listened for goals, how much CE they had completed on their own, why they were leaving their job. We then had a working interview with the ones we selected. We wanted to see if they were trainable and eager to learn with us. We interviewed every patient after the working interview appointment. Patients were very willing to help us make the right decision and we knew we could trust them to be honest. Not one of them failed an appointment and they were happy to help. It came down to personality that worked with the team."

Other ads in the area look like this: Full/part time Dental Hygienist needed for hi-tech office, Tues to Sat 8 to 5 PM. Benefits include vacation, health ins., bonus. Fax resume to (253-888-9999).

The right people are looking for a challenge. The average person is looking for an average office where one can escape accountability. The right person wants to grow and learn new skills, like mastering sales skills. The average person would say, "I don't do sales."

One of my mentors has been Les Schwab, the largest independent tire dealer in America with 400 stores in the West and 5,000 team members who literally run to your car to help you. I asked him, "What is your training process to have them respond with such continued enthusiasm?" Les Schwab laughed and said, "You can't train them. You select them. Their training comes from their parents."

According to Jim Rohn of *Leading An Inspired Life,* don't send your ducks to eagle school because it won't work. Good people are found, not changed. They can change themselves but you can't change them. If you want motivated good people, you need to find them.

If you have leadership, passion, systems and accountability in place, the right person will love it. Finding that right person is a constant. Be out there observing people and mixing. You will not find the right person by having a daily lunch in your staff room. Decide what qualities you want exhibited in team members which are generally taught by their parents. If you want your team to be accountable, what does that mean? Will you as the leader still feel you need to micro manage?

Look for people who are comfortable being with others, curious in conversation and have a willingness to be uncomfortable to reach their goals. I want them to be motivated by sharing in the profits and willing to work hard when we work.

It is a selection process rather than a training process. If they have curiosity, passion, integrity and a spirit to make a difference, the training will be easy. Select people for their attitude, the skills will come. You cannot turn a duck into an eagle. They must want it for themselves. Find them.

SAVED FROM *THE* BURNOUT

Dr. Chris Kleber of Coronado Island, CA

When Chris exited the US Navy Dental Corps in San Diego, he started a practice from scratch in a suburb. For 13 years, Dr. Kleber focused on just one practice. Then, he and his family moved 23 miles from the suburb to a coast town of Coronado. An opportunity arose to purchase a Coronado practice as he had dropped being a Delta Dental provider in his primary practice and was now down to three days a week. Chris worked with Bill and enjoyed good results in his growing practice.

Chris operated the two practices for ten years; three days in the suburb, two days at the coast and burned the rubber in between. "I had long time staff in the primary practice and as we marched along, they became more complacent, were paid more and seemed to do less. With several associates, my primary overhead grew from 54% to 73%. I went from "riding the horse" (good profitability) to "carrying the horse" (big overhead to support) and eight staff who were really "on their own bus" but allowed me to believe "they were on my bus."

Some of Dr. Kleber's longest serving team members (15-17 years) started out great but as "I moved toward burnout and lost interest in being a leader, their complacency grew and I 'dragged them along.' They were working less and being paid more. Payroll and benefits swelled to 33%."

The impact was what Chris calls "Killer Sameness"—that is today looks like tomorrow, and tomorrow looks like yesterday." Chris was on a treadmill, heading toward BURNOUT fast and "I could not see it," said Chris. My great partner, my wife, Joy, recognized it, contacted Bill and arranged for us to meet with Carolyn and Bill for a

Summit. We signed up for the full Coaching Program again knowing that we had great results the first time we worked with Bill in 1994. This time required greater determination and resolve and the results yielded my largest yearly net income ($580K) and moving our lives to a better level.

With Bill's encouragement, I closed the primary office and shifted as many patients as possible to Coronado. I kept one part time male employee who was preparing for dental school. Everyone else was either laid off or quit. So I had a 90% turnover.

I have since utilized only pre-dental students from UC San Diego who have graduated college and are applying to dental school to work chairside or reception. They are intelligent, inquisitive, hard-working and willing to work for a "fair" wage without unrealistic expectations. For the rest of my career, I choose to work only with team members who have a college degree.

Chris leads by example. He is the first one to arrive and usually the last to leave. "I make the auxillary's job a great opportunity for someone with curiosity to step up and encourage them to achieve higher aspirations, like hygiene or dental school. This fulfills my desire to mentor future dental professionals."

Chris says "the best thing I ever did was to seek out and marry my wife and business partner, Joy. Her insights into running a business (as her family did) and training as a CPA with an MBA in marketing and finance have proven invaluable in our accumulation of assets, having a good family life and being a best friend and confident. And she is cute, too!"

Dr. Kleber is a numbers guy and with his wife, Joy, who has done the books and paid the bills for 28 years, "we are bottom line planners." We have saved money in pension plans since the start and we now have over $1M saved. We are savers, conservative spenders and believe we can make money work for us and not be a slave to the 'buck.' We take advantage of minimizing taxes through careful planning, budgeting and organization to the fullest extent allowed by law.

Our goals are paying off the mortgage, emancipating our children financially and launching them on a sound financial future, and saving for our retirement effectively. We put 100% effort into this. Even in these challenging economic times, we are in a strong cash position and are using this time to restructure mortgages to lower interest rates while accelerating payments on principle. We are 'empty nesters' and have planned a few fun vacations this year utilizing frequent flyer miles, cost saving vacations coupled with deductible seminars. As an example, we joined the local yacht club and are enjoying the social networking and sailing the club's sailboats for $10 a month."

Dr. Kleber and Joy together have a very clear plan for fiscal responsibility. They live their vision about money and agree how to spend their time having fun. Some people would view them as "too frugal," yet they have a lot more fun and a lot less stress because they, together, know where they are going. They made a brilliant move with their family to Coronado in purchasing a beachfront mansion, so large that it had been divided into three homes prior to the purchase. Their home is desirable for Arizonian desert people to enjoy beach living when it is 115 degrees in AZ. To that end, the Klebers have rented their home each summer to the same family while they have taken their children on 6 week adventures to the national parks of the west. They also took the kids to Europe for 5 weeks (when the euro was 75 cents/ $) using the money earned from the summer rental of their home to pay for the vacations. Brilliant!

Chris feels attitude determines altitude. Successful people clearly see themselves in a future place of accomplishment and reward. They are willing to delay immediate gratification or endure current hardships to get to a better place. "I evaluate this by comparing my daily happiness and assessing our progress toward our economic goals. Correcting my course frequently and minimizing distractions are paramount to attaining true forward movement."

"I am now 55 and still have a few good years left for dentistry. Continuing education keeps me mentally engaged and with 2800 hours of CE, I have attained my Mastership in AGD. I take every seventh week off to unwind from the physical rigors of daily dentistry and a monthly full body massage is a muscular stress reliever that helps to keep me going. Seeing patients three days a week keeps the physical and mental strains balanced for a pace of practice that avoids burnout.

"I plan my work and work my plan. I budget, monitor, use fiscal conservancy and save. My overhead is about 50% with team at 20%, lab at 8%. We save 10% or more personally and pay off debt as fast as possible."

I have worked with Blatchford Coaching in two separate rounds of full consulting services. In 1994, the impact was seeing the 'sweet spot' of profitability at 50%, happiness with seven weeks off and working 180 days with three team members. This is a time proven business model and envied by many.

Eleven years later, it was obvious to others I was losing sight of profitability rules and headed for burnout. With Joy's prompting, I recommitted to the Blatchford model, reorganized our business to serve our life and fund our economic future. It is working well again and I am much happier. I can continue at this pace for a longer time instead of trying to find ways to be distracted and leave dentistry.

I have learned where to concentrate my efforts for the most efficient and effective return. I pay attention to those patients and procedures that put money in my pocket and stay away from things that just feed my ego.

For marketing in this coastal community of 17K, I participate in Rotary, the Island Beer Club (home brewing), and the Coronado Yacht Club. Joy works for the city of Coronado, is in PEO and is joining the garden club. Forty percent of my patient base is from Coronado. I walk the half mile to my office. Can you believe it? YES, YES, YES!!!

I am a reluctant leader. Confrontation had been a shortfall of mine but I am getting much better these days. I can lead when I screw on my hat and get in the game. I lead by setting a desired example of behavior. I have pushed staff members ahead of me and dragged them behind me. Neither works. I show team members I am willing to do whatever it takes and if they cannot take my lead then they are soon gone by their choice or 'I free up their future.' I talk with them frequently during the day individually. I set the direction of the practice. I plan to leave the world and dentistry a better place so Live, Love, Learn, and Laugh because you never know when the clock that ticks inside you will be forever stilled.

www.chriskleberdds.com

Dr. Chris Kleber

Cap'n Kleber

Joy Kleber

WOMEN WORKING WELL

Dr. Carolyn Baldiviez of Santa Maria, CA

Santa Maria on California's central coast is my home and my husband, a lawyer, and I decided we wanted to return to family and give back to the community. We have been blessed with our "nannies," my mom and dad. Our children have such a wonderful relationship with my parents and with two professionals in private practice, it is such a blessing. Vincent and I never have to worry about our children when we are working.

My practice is now in a renovated house and I have started marketing for the first time. I now feel my practice home reflects the quality of my work. I am starting to offer sleep appliances and oral sedation. We are already offering Invisalign.

My experience with Blatchford consulting has been a journey. For the rest of the team, I believe the conferences enabled them to see the overall picture for the goals in our office. The team could also see other Doctors and team doing the same thing and how it works. For the team, I believe there was and is a level of empowerment gained by these seminar experiences. We all learn differently and no matter how hard I tried on my own, I was unable to have some of my team members to see the "big picture." As a team, we have become more committed to the common goals as a result.

I feel when people feel they are truly a valued part of something bigger than themselves, a sense of ownership and pride will follow. This can only bring out the best in people. I happen to be someone who jumps in with all that I have. In realizing we all have different personalities, I was not the best person to show the way initially as sometimes my enthusiasm may be intimidating to a cautious person.

With the information and coaching from Bill, Carolyn & Kaye, the members of my team who are more cautious by nature, were able to feel comfortable with the changes and they also were less intimidated.

With the economic uncertainty, we still finished the year 5% above the previous year. We reached just under $1.1M and did this with only 1000 patients. Our patients are very happy as well with such comprehensive care.

For me, Blatchford reaffirmed it is OK to have the practice which works for me. This is with respect to patient care, number of days worked and the lifestyle I choose for myself. I need a team sharing my vision and goals. Each team member must decide if he/she is onboard and whether they want to make the journey with me. That is their choice and ultimately, my choice.

The Blatchford approach was perfect for me and my team. It is straight forward and it works. I can use the Blatchford principles to guide my way with the practice that works for me. Also, Bill, Carolyn & Kaye Puccetti made me feel that I was more than a client. They truly mean it when they say that they are available for you. They have become part of my team and have shared in my successes and have helped me with my challenges. I have used other practice management companies in the past and I have had other consultants. This experience has been far different than any I had before and Bill has been my coach, well beyond a consultant, as has Kaye.

www.drbaldiviez.com

WHAT MAKES A GREAT TEAM STAY

With vision and strong leadership in place, a team forms. Good people are drawn to others who want to succeed. As the leader, your strong vision shows in words and body language. Your vision shows. People who see the same as you want to help you accomplish your life mission.

Curious and great people want to make a difference in this world. They want to feel needed and valued for their contributions. Good people, when given the opportunity, will rise to the occasion. They want to be accountable, take chances, make changes and move mountains.

Why great people stay is because they feel their skills and contributions are being utilized well and they are fulfilling their mission in life. Yes, compensation is important but it is down the list of more important items. What are they?

- Great people stay when the leadership is strong, clear and consistent. We crave that magic leader who has integrity, humor, and direction and can make decisions while communicating clearly the direction we are headed. Great people do not want a micro-manager who is afraid to let anyone else operate the machinery. We like clearly defined goals on the roadmap to success. We also like it when the leader gives us more than we think we can handle. We like to be trusted by the leader. If there are people on the team who really aren't carrying their weight, we want the leader to make the decisions necessary so we can move forward. When decisions are made not to rid of the deadwood, we will eventually leave and find employment where it is rewarding again.

- Great people enjoy the rewards of being on a moving team. The compensation and health benefits are important but not as important as the rewards received when goals are met. Personal and specific acknowledgement of a job well done is paramount. William James said, "The deepest principle of human nature is the desire to be appreciated." We also find a well-defined bonus system is a constant acknowledgement of skills and tasks accomplished. A solid bonus is based on pro-duction/collection and has an easy formula known and owned by the team. Equally shared, the bonus is calculated on 12 equal fiscal periods so each "month" the team has an opportu-nity to exceed the minimum. A great team member would love it if the bonus actually exceeds our monthly compensa-tion.

- Great people like to be part of a great team. The magic of good people all working together to create something special. It brings power, challenge and joy to our lives. We love the team spirit.

- Great people stay because they like to move forward. They like to meet and exceed goals. Moving forward means holding a larger picture of life in our hearts other than daily routine.

- Great team members stay because we embrace change. We like new ideas that make our tasks easier and more efficient. We do like solid classic systems yet, if there is someone else doing something that allows them to be more effective and efficient, let's give it a try. Together, we read books, cross train, practice sales and role-play. Is it always fun? No, but we know it creates better results so we do it.

- Great people stay because we like a challenge. We are chal-lenged with new technology, new skills, a changing marketplace, marketing, competition and we want to be the best at what we do. Routine and classic systems are always there yet, we stay because we are challenged to be the very best we can.

Dr. April Ziegele's team was featured in our previous book, *Playing Your 'A' Game*. The "guest concierge," Ann Medges adds, "I have been with Dr. Ziegele for 11 years and love my job. I work three days a week or 132 days a year which allows me to be with family, enjoy my home, camping and great vacations. I make a great income to do all the fun things in my life.

Dr. Ziegele continually and specifically praises us with gifts and cards. She allows me to do my job and the freedom to make decisions regarding the practice because she trusts and believes in me.

I stay because I have a vested interest in the practice as a part owner. Blatchford Solutions works. Just do everything they say to do, DO IT ALL. Embrace it, as the leader must lead in order for others to follow. Dr. Z does it all—commitment is huge!"

LESSONS FROM GEESE

Fact 1: As each goose flaps it wings, it creates "uplift" for the birds that follow. By flying in a "V" formation, the whole flock adds 71% greater flying range than if each bird flew alone.

> **Lesson:** People who share a common direction and a sense of community can get where they are going quicker and easier because they are traveling on the thrust of one another.

Fact 2: When a goose falls out of formation, it suddenly feels the drag and resistance of flying alone. It quickly moves back into formation to take advantage of the lifting power of the bird immediately in front of it.

> **Lesson:** If we have as much sense as a goose, we stay in formation with those headed where we want to go. We are willing to accept their help and give our help to others.

Fact 3: When the lead goose tires, it rotates back into the formation and another goose flies to the point position.

> **Lesson:** It pays to take turns doing the hard tasks and sharing leadership. As with geese, people are interdependent on each other's skills, capabilities, and unique arrangements of gifts, talents, and recourses.

Fact 4: The geese flying in formation honk to encourage those up front to keep up their speed.

> **Lesson:** We need to make sure our honking is encouraging. In groups where there is encouragement, the production is much greater. The power of encouragement (to stand by one's heart or core values and encourage the heart and core of others) is the quality of honking we seek.

Fact 5: When a goose gets sick, wounded or shot down, two geese drop out of formation and follow it down to help and protect it. They stay with it until it dies or is able to fly again. Then they launch out with another formation or catch up with the flock.

> **Lesson:** If we have as much sense as geese, we will stand by each other like that.

WHY WE STAY

Treatment Coordinator, Kate Grainger in Dr. Phil Goduco's team of Vernon Hills, Illinois, says she has five reasons to stay:

- I truly love my job
- Dr. Goduco is one of the nicest people ever and an outstanding dentist whose craft far surpasses anyone in the area. He is energetic, personable, and has contagious enthusiasm
- We have a great team. Individually, we are entirely different but collectively, we respect and care about one another. We always have fun
- We have an ideal work environment with a four day week, moving to three in six months. We have generous benefits and some of our compensation is tied to the financial success of the practice
- We are always learning something new. It is never boring and the interaction with our patients is filled with laughter!

Kate adds, "The bonus factor increases our capabilities and productivity by sharing in the profits of the business without losing our goal of placing the health of our patient first. The bonus gives us an emotional attachment to the business with the highest amount being $2300 above our salary. We are fortunate to have patients who have trust and confidence in Dr. Goduco's ability to create their perfect smile.

Kate Grainger

Hygienist Denise Enos on Dr. Dan Vodvarka's team in Eugene, Oregon, obviously, has great passion for her profession. Her bio reads "Denise Enos is a breath of fresh air in dentistry. A Registered Dental Hygienist, she has worked for hundreds of dentists in the last thirty years, focusing her talent and energy as a hygienist for the last twenty of those years and as a dental assistant and in the front office for the first ten years. Her passion is to provide excellent care for patients' overall health. She loves the profession and thrives on elevating their self-esteem, reveling in the WOW moment when she sees it beaming from her patient's newly found smile!

Denise feels she is a part of a bigger, very important puzzle which takes all different shapes and edges to make it complete. "I am accountable to provide on-time patient-centered dental hygiene. My part of the puzzle is to create a healthy foundation for smiles."

She continues, "I feel, in the past, dental offices were separated, both physically and psychologically as there was a 'front' and a 'back.' These days, I cannot imagine working as I have done in the past. Now, we work as a team, and each of us wears many hats, including the doctor. It is so much less stressful when everyone is able to do many different things. For example, it's no big deal to have a hygienist get a PA on a tooth ache, take impressions, assist or make a financial arrangement. And it is not a big deal to have an office administrator seat a patient, take a PA, assist or turn a room around. This includes unloading the sterilizer, developing a pano, taking a patient up front or seating a patient.

Communication is clear and everyone is in alignment. Problems are quickly solved, everyone can "let go" and do what needs to be done rather than the old method of gossiping how this or that happened. Optimally, we all relax, have fun and go down the path together. How great is that?"

Working for Dr. Vodvarka over the last eleven years has been a rewarding experience. I can always count on him to be balanced and consistent. Consequently, we can talk about anything. I have full trust and respect for him and I know I can make a decision and receive support from the Doctor and team. I absolutely believe 100% in the vision he has created. I so enjoy seeing his beautiful dentistry change people's lives. Was he always a good teacher? Yes, however, going through Blatchford's coaching has made him a stronger leader. Having a coachable team is also helpful!

When the goals are not what we expect, we ask the team to think about why this is happening. Is it our verbal skills in how we are enrolling patients? Are we helping to educate our patients on the value of strong, healthier dentistry that lasts a lifetime? Are we consistently marketing? Are we targeting the right group? Do we need more layers? Are we asking for referrals? Do we have an "attitude of gratitude"?

It is an honor and a pleasure to work with a group of happy geese that can all fly in the same direction, straight and focused. I know every day, our team will have fun, laugh and change people's lives.

Team Vodvarka

Tina Burg from Dr. Mark Beckstead's periodontal office in Palo Alto, California, strongly relates, "I have complete faith in Dr. Beckstead as a surgeon as his results are fantastic and effective. This makes it easy to sell services and our philosophy of care. It occurred to me we used to keep a list of satisfied clients we could refer potential patients to converse with if they had any questions or fears. I realize now we have not had to use that list in over two years.

We have a wonderful team I trust to back me up and I work hard to earn their trust. We all hold a vision and a goal to reach and exceed with patient care and treatment, scheduling and of course, bonus. It is good to always be looking forward and up.

I personally have gained so many skills and we all realize the whole office hinges on our job being done well. In our office, we have tons of accountability and responsibility. As we have downsized, each of those areas expands dramatically. We are all much more interested in results and not our reasons. This is a refreshing focus.

I value the culture we have created around the clarity and vision of our leader. I appreciate the humor when one of us is not at our best, we can crack jokes and lift the mood. I love that everyone on the team is looking for ways to make systems better, stronger, faster. It is a dynamic environment and there is always more to learn and do.

I have great confidence in Mark's surgical skills, his fiscal sensibility and generosity towards us (pension plans, health care, bonus and vacation time!!). The truth is we work because we need to so he makes it a great place to be. I feel he invests much in each of us and stands back once we are on our feet. He will listen, be reasonable and upbeat about any suggestion made to benefit the whole.

I have worked for people who are not good teachers or coaches. They are disappointed when results don't occur. It feels like a setup for failure if you do not know what is expected of you. One day about four years ago, I was struggling personally and apparently it showed even though I tried to suppress it. One day, Dr. B asked me to meet with him. He asked what he could do to help me like my job more. It was such a kind way to approach something that wasn't job related but it did serve as a catalyst to make some changes that benefited more than just me.

Kim Stephens from Dr. Ron Zokol in Vancouver BC:

"I know this sounds corny and will swell Dr. Ron's head, but I have my dream position. My good days do out number the bad and I am the only one who limits my success. I love who I work with and everyday there is laughter and mutual respect. I have a place where my boss encourages me to grow, learn and be an active part of society. He allows me the time needed to support my family. And, oh, yeah, even though the base salary is not bad, the bonuses are better!

When I was hired, I worked under someone who did not believe in the "Blatchford Way." Her main daily task was to protect **her** job. The first six months were tough. I had very little influence until I learned to go around the staff member. At the Blatchford DYNAMO, I learned we could not succeed unless all the staff members were on the same page. We had one person who was keeping us from moving forward. I went to Dr. Zokol with the need to renew his team. He trusted us and removed that person's influence. I promised him we could work together and reach our goals.

The new team had great ideas, worked hard and we wanted to learn new things. We believed we could achieve all our goals. Now, Dr. Zokol allows us the freedom to run with ideas because he knows we want to succeed as a team. I stay because of respect given, the great team, the challenge, the freedom and the patients.

Kim Stephens

PARTNERSHIPS THAT WORK

Dr. Ira Shapira and Dr. Mark Amidei of Gurnee, IL

Twenty year partners in Delany Dental Care LTD just northwest of Chicago, Drs. Shapria and Amidei had a very successful income but not a quality of life. They had three offices, 31 staff and several associate Doctors. "Managing the group and putting out fires occupied much of our time and we had a lot of after hour responsibilities," recalls Ira.

Now, they have one office with seven full time team members and one part time. "There is much less aggravation, stress and our net income has stayed the same. We have paid down debt. The REAL CHANGE is we have a great increase in personal time," Ira shares. They now alternate four day weekends with half the team and one Doctor free every other weekend. Dr. Amidei adds, "My life has found time. Time was never so precious to me until I really found some. Bill was always about quality of life and not dreaming of it for a later date like retirement. Our profession allows us to dictate our life. We just didn't know it. Again, QUALITY OF LIFE IS WHAT'S MOST IMPACTING."

At first glance and even delving deeper, the partners are quite different. There is about a 15 years age difference. The temperaments and skills differ. Ira analyzes Mark—"my partner is very detailed and sets specific goals for me to meet on a regular basis while I tend to focus on the bigger picture and the future. Mark is the CFO and I am the CEO. We have checks and balances to tone down my unbridled enthusiasm with workable operating strategies. The two of us together are stronger than either of us alone. Our partnership is like a marriage with give and take. The sum is greater than the parts."

Mark adds, "Being in a partnership, our personal goals are a bit skewed timewise but we have very similar values or we wouldn't have made it this far…20 years and stronger than ever. I have five children under 12 and Ira's family is all grown and out of the house. Fortunately, we are always able to discuss our needs and wants and with Bill's common sense approach of mediating our ideas, we always come out on top. Ira and I have become even better at understanding one another. Bill has provided us help with the simplicity of what we think is complicated. Obviously, Ira and I have infinite respect for one another and that's the glue that keeps it together."

On attitude, Mark shares "As Bill always reminds us, attitude is a choice. You can wake up in the morning and choose to be a grump or a star. It is your choice…I choose to win. I tell my kids about choice anytime they are down or in a rut. 'Why have you chosen this today?' People learn to recognize it on their own, especially children. There are times when I'm a grump. My assistant, Stacie, is very good at saying 'Why are you giving me the "elevens"?' The "elevens" are the wrinkles in my forehead that started after about forty. I thank her and shape up quickly. The moral here is Stacie can comfortably share when I need to make a different choice. I know how to receive it. We all created team covenants about conduct, communication and service. It works!"

Dr. Shapira feels attitude is crucial to his success. In looking at a glass as half empty or half full, "I grew up with a mother who said, 'if you add a little, it is overflowing,' and that is how I tend to look at the practice. I am always excited with the wealth of possibilities that exist."

"Mark is a problem solver. It is the blending of our disparate personalities that makes us strong. We share strong respect and affection that lets us work through our disparities. Like a good marriage, there is give and take. We value our difference as much as our agreements," indicates Ira.

There are motivating factors for both Drs. Amidei and Shapira. Mark has five children under 12 and is part of a large Italian family. His mothers' family immigrated to Chicago-land in 1950 with six siblings. His father was courageous enough to leave on his own and immigrated to Toronto in 1950. When he arrived, he contacted a woman by mail as he knew she had immigrated from a neighboring Italian town. She later became his wife. "I am as fluent in Italian as English. Four years of high school Italian and a minor in Italian literature at Loyola University allow a strong and continual bond of my heritage." Births, baptisms, birthdays, graduations, holidays, anniversaries, cousins, illnesses and tragedies all play an important part in Mark's life. Taking care of family is the key motivating factor and having more time from work is most important.

Dr. Shapira's wife has had breast cancer and a double mastectomy in 1991. "That year, we decided not to worry about future retirement but to start taking it now. We spent ten years enjoying life and then, Elise was diagnosed with ovarian cancer. As I write this, we just returned from two weeks in Aruba. We live our lives to the fullest, enjoying our retirement as we go. Elise is currently in remission and has been through seven bouts of chemo and I have had surgical treatment of prostate cancer. We have spread our retirement over 18 years now and would love to for another twenty years. There is not one trip or adventure we regret. Bill calls it "Retire As You Go" and my partnership with Mark makes this easier from a practice standpoint," Dr. Shapira said.

Dr. Amidei says, "Our debt reduction has decreased our pocket change. Reducing the debt by $200K a year, we'll be debt free in three years. Prior to Bill's coaching, we always carried debt of $800K. We now minimize expenditures and buy what we can afford. We don't need every gadget that is sold in dentistry to make ourselves work best. Our overhead is just over 55% but that's OK as it used to be 80%. The team knows what 20% is and they surprise us every month with their bonus. Last year, we had our best year of production yet, up $150K from the prior year. Although the economic feel is down right now, we are earmarking next year to be up another $300K. We'll all work hard at it.

"We are not close to retirement but always planning to retire within the practice, said Dr. Amidei. "If my health is good, why not continue to practice a few days a week? Planning the Blatchford way will allow for a comfortable retirement with plenty of time for leisure and occupation. I know it will work."

When the partners showed leadership by shifting their practice, Ira found he had so much free time he started two new businesses. One is Chicagoland Dental Sleep Medicine Associates and the company and website of I HATE C-PAP both of which greatly expends the practices of Doctors treating sleep apnea. He also is using his 25 years of experience in sleep medicine to create a course for dentists wanting in depth knowledge of sleep apnea. The classes are limited to six Doctors with emphasis on follow-up of an hour of monthly consulting as part of the program.

Ira simply says "The bonus system has instilled ownership in the team. What could possibly be more empowering and productive? I have trust in my team and respect their efforts. They are partners in our practice and treat it as their own." Mark adds, "Team….Wow what a word… You know when I first began using the term it always felt weird. It almost sounded fake. Now, I'm constantly complimenting the team in front of patients just because I really appreciate how very hard they work for us and themselves. They constantly are trying to improve the moment."

"There is not a better motivator than positive influence, a concept I wish I had used years ago. We'd be so much further along on our journey. As long as the journey is enjoyable, sometimes you don't necessarily have to have a destination. It can change from day to day, always in a better movement forward. I want the team to continue to create this journey with us, each adding to it in their own special way. Like, caring for the patients and listening to their stories. The time availability now exists to listen and really spend quality time connecting."

"Has the team shifted? Oh yeah," says Mark. "We look back four years ago and what we now do automatically was so foreign. How were we going to do this? Well, I'll tell you, this Blatchford program, when practiced and constantly reinforced, trains the mind to be confident and caring. We are open about what we have to offer and, best of all, the openness either is well received, the patient leaves with a good feeling, comes back, completes his treatment, fully understanding what is involved and happy to pay in advance OR the patient leaves happy with a referral to a place that will best fit at this point in the journey. No hard feelings…. just a feeling that if they could, they would be a part of our place and maybe, just maybe, in the future they will. They leave saying 'What a great place …I just can't afford it now but I sure want to.'"

Dr. Shapira feels there is integration of all aspects of treatment. "Mark follows block booking very strictly as he does primarily restorative. In my schedule, it is less followed but we do respect the time of large cases. Sleep apnea is a big ticket item. The one hour consult is inviolate with over 95% of patients starting treatment and many sleep patients converting into full restorative and reconstructive patients. We talk about TMJ and neuromuscular to sleep patients and about sleep to TMJ and pain patients. We discuss occlusion with CEREC patients. I will often see my schedule very busy with sleep patients. When this occurs, we will, with the patient's approval, move restorative dentistry into Dr. Amidei's schedule. Our large cases often come from sleep patients and Mark will produce much more income on my sleep patients then I will." Now, that is a real partnership!

Mark adds, "Ira and I have been CEREC docs for almost 20 years starting with CEREC One, which we produced more than $6M in production. We now have CEREC 3D. I couldn't live with out it. It is so satisfying and efficient to complete treatment on the same day. We also use a rubber dam on absolutely all operative procedure, even extractions. The rubber dam is key for me. I've received great influence from good clinical programs to improve our skills but mainly, the

Blatchford program has given us the confidence in motivating a patient to follow through with the more complex cases. I still have a ways to go and know the journey will never end. There is confidence gained through Bill's guidance."

Dr. Shapira feels "marketing is a joy. I have learned the art of press releases rather than advertisements. For sleep apnea and TMJ patients, marketing is the major source of new patients. Restorative patients and cosmetics are usually patient referrals so we do intensive internal marketing."

Dr. Amidei adds, "We have tested the waters by spending up to 16% o f our collections on external marketing. Bill coached us to 8%. We have found external marketing is not effective for general and cosmetic dentistry but it is fabulous for sleep and chronic pain dentistry—wants vs. needs. We know this as we kept excellent records of patient's entry. The results of our two year marketing survey was very revealing for our mix of treatment vs. money spent. Caution: This is true for us right now and may not be the answer for you."

Internally, they use Smile Reminders to confirm and contact patients with bulletins on whitening specials or treatment for the first caller to fill a space in the short call schedule. "I call all my patients on their birthday which takes about ten minutes during the day. This is a huge deal to the patients. Some patients find out my birth date and call to wish me the same in return, which is a very neat little perk," Mark shares. "Our hygienists also collect for treatment in the hygiene room and if there is any subsequent treatment, our assistant schedules which frees the coordinators in front to take new patient calls with a sense of caring and no interruptions. This is an integral part of our new patient experience."

In the community, Mark lives just ten minutes away and finds he is involved in areas which are important to him like the local church and school, Rotary, health club, Toastmasters, Ski club and he is active with his son's hockey team.

Both Doctors agree their morning huddles are key. "It took us a while to make them productive. They note creating value in hygiene for uncompleted treatment with photography and power point of the patient's photographs.

We think the future of dentistry will be fantastic. "I'm already trying to impress the profession to my children as it is a profession of rewards and satisfaction. Dentistry and our partnership have enabled me to live a very fulfilling and prideful life. We are well rounded in all aspects, the profession, the business, and most importantly our personal lives have been regained.

I attribute the success of our practice to the continuous drive my partner and I have always had toward education and its impact. We have learned to treat one another as very close brothers who are fond of each other.. I have a great deal of respect for Ira as my mentor and partner. He has a great respect for my appreciation of him and my willingness to have taken his knowledge and experience and developed my own stride.

Our practice is like a baby...... it must be constantly nurtured, fed and stimulated so that it will give fabulous rewards. The key is in our own motivation and desire to have an excellent attitude every day and to be thankful for what we have accomplished in our journey.

Thank you for the opportunity to participate in this book. It is a nice way to thank you both in return for what you have done for us in the last five years. It has been challenging but what would a journey be like if it were always predictable?

www.delanydental.com

Dr. Ira and Dr. Mark.

Partners and respectful friends.

WORKING SMART

It's no secret. We have the best profession in America. Dental school applications are higher than ever. For the first time, GPAs of entering dental students exceeds those applying to medical school. We surpassed physicians' income several years ago. The average dentist makes a very good living. Is there more?

It's about lifestyle and balance. Americans are workaholics. Present dentists are sons and daughters of working class people who learned hard work equates with good. Dr. L.D. Pankey spoke to dentists about balancing work and play, love, and worship. Where are you in your balance today?

It is a challenge for dental entrepreneurs in setting parameters to avoid having dentistry be their whole life. Life is precious. Slow down enough to question yourself. What do I want? What can I give? What do I want to be remembered for? What do I need to change to be on that memorable path? Who can help me?

During your 35 years of practice life, you could have 70 months of vacation time while producing a very good income and providing excellence for your patients. The keys are passionate leadership, solid systems, updated clinical skills, sales skills, and current marketing. These keys can gather a team of people who see what you have to offer and want that, too. That vacation time equates to nearly six years so you really only work 29 years! All these rewards come from focused leadership and a team serving your guests well.

Too often we meet dentists who can't remember when or where their last vacation was. They work evenings and miss their children's T-Ball games. They work 4.5 days a week (really five) and go to the office on the weekends under the guise of "I love dentistry." They take a week off a year and some long weekends yet, not enough to really sharpen the saw and refresh. We are a nation of tired and frustrated dentists. They continue to work with staff members who drain energy from them and to schedule patients who cancel and don't pay their bills.

Working longer hours at the office or bringing charts home to workup treatment plans on patients who have not even indicated they would be interested in your ideas of treatment for them does not create more income for you or help you serve your patients better.

Many dental offices are inefficient because they do not work as a team. There is a division of labor and "there are certain things I do not do." Cross-training and accountability is a must and it includes the Doctor.

Demographically, dentistry is a desired and needed service. There are one-third more dentists of retirement age than graduates each year. For this reason alone, we must become more efficient for the hours in our office. The answer does not lie in hiring more help. It requires engaged and passionate leadership. The bigger plan must come from the top and be a consistent message.

Leadership determines the commitment to block scheduling for efficiency. Once a guest says "yes," to the plan, treatment should be completed in blocks of time rather than seeing them four to five times for a crown and root canal. We are a busy society and your reputation can be enhanced by excellent planning. Examine your schedules for the last 90 days to see where you could have been much more efficient, effective and profitable. How many more hours were available? A day? A whole week? Most dentists are taking their vacation time at the office due to poor scheduling.

In observing dental office sales skills, most staff and Doctor fold at the patient's question of "what do I really NEED?" and take advantage of the insurance trap or use the predetermination close. Lacking direction, staff defers sales to the dentist who wants to please. Diagnosis remains small so the patient will say "yes." We are a sophisticated society and modern sales skills are right brained, the opposite of the scientific sales approach. It takes real leadership and dedication to learn and master what is currently needed to sell dentistry in a general practice.

We must serve people well yet we dislike it when our charity work was not our choice. Create a day each quarter when your team and possibly other dental offices volunteer to treat patients who do not have access to care. You serve your profession, your community and it can be a spiritual experience.

You can design a balanced practice life fulfilling every dream. The practice should support your every dream, not merely leave you with the leftovers. It is a challenge to do this on your own. Every great athlete has a coach. How will you work smarter?

MOVING UPTOWN

Dr. Bernee Dunson of Atlanta, GA

"We as a team and a practice have grown, defined who we are and who we serve. Our practice is best classified as a general dental practice with a focus on sedation dentistry and implant reconstruction. We are better than good, in my opinion and working towards being great." Well said, Dr. Dunson!

Before joining Blatchford Coaching, Dr. Dunson had been considering the possibilities of a move "but it just never came together. It seemed like there were unanswered questions and some fear. There were good reasons to move. Fifty percent of my patients did not even live in Stone Mountain and my family didn't even live in the area where I practiced. But I avoided pressing the button."

In meeting with Bill and Carolyn, we discussed my goals and vision of an ideal practice. We further discussed facing one's fears and not letting anything prevent you from achieving your dreams. The conversation with Bill served as a catalyst to allow me to isolate my fears, confront them with rational efforts and 'go for it.'

In 2005, several office projects weren't quite right or fell through. During this time, my team was participating in the Blatchford Coaching process and we received a collective boost of energy, efficiency and productivity. This was my most productive year to date. We realized over $100K increase in collections. I started with seven staff and ended with four.

The next year, I was the regional president of American Academy of Implant Dentistry as I was moving my practice 15 miles to Midtown Atlanta. It became a full time commitment to plan and run a dental meeting in Charleston, SC and my team really supported me.

We had a very successful and informative meeting. It was "First Class" and a lot of fun. In addition, we doubled the treasury money for our district.

The timing of this event diverted my attention away from the big move. We have been in our office for two years, are proud and happy with our move. My vision of what and how I wanted to practice has served me well.

As an undergraduate, I had the privilege of serving as an assistant with a general dentist who was doing dental implants. This exposure sparked my interest in implants. At USC Dental School, I received a tremendously strong education in occlusion and aesthetics dentistry while choosing electives courses in implant dentistry. Near the completion of my dental training, I decided to balance my functional aesthetic training in a GPR that was strong in surgical concepts to increase my surgical acumen. My choice was Columbia University at Harlem hospital GPR where I trained with eight oral surgeons, two prosthodontists, two periodontists, two endodontists, an orthodontist as well as some very talented attendees and residents.

Now, my goals were to participate in a graduate periodontic program followed by a graduate prosthodontic program. I was accepted at USC Periodontal Program. Yet, in a thorough review of the curriculum and program, I determined only about four months of the 24 month program focused on my interest of implant dentistry and perioplastic surgery. One of my classmates at Columbia knew of my spoken interest and was aware of the hospital-based Implant program at Loma Linda. After much research, I decided on this program, (three years in length) the only one of its kind dedicated to implant surgery and implant prosthodontics. WOW! I was so excited as I felt this was the program for me. It was a great opportunity to have exceptional "interest-focused" training. I decided to defer my acceptance into grad perio at USC and apply to the Implant program at Loma Linda University. I was accepted and started winter of 1994.

As a resident of Loma Linda, I was based in Atlanta with two implant directors where I served as resident and associate. I did rotations in oral surgery, anesthesiology, ear nose & throat, and orthopedics at Emory Adventist Hospital, an affiliate of Loma Linda University. One week each month my first year, and two weeks every other month in my second and third years, I spent training at Loma Linda in California.

The program was quite a sacrifice but extremely rewarding for me with such "focus-training." My training was in implant soft and hard tissue surgery and implant prosthodontics. I also received I.V. and oral conscious sedation training which has proven to be a great asset to my private practice.

My practice today is best described as a comprehensive general restorative practice with a focus on cosmetic implant reconstruction and I.V. sedation. I have been able to serve as a referral source to several general dentists and two prosthodontist in the metro Atlanta area. If given the choice of doing this again, I would not change my course of training. I consider myself fortunate to have the vision and the guidance to pursue my goals.

I use I.V. Sedation in my practice every week sometimes several times per week. I could not see practicing my craft without this very valuable, very safe tool in my skill set.

I give honor to my mother and father, Dr. Charles and Mrs. Bette Dunson who served as education pillars in the Albany, Georgia community where I was raised. The four siblings were encouraged by our parents that you 'Educate for Life.' I adopted this philosophy and it has fueled my intense drive, ambition and perseverance. The older sister is a massage therapist, one brother is a chemical engineer and the youngest sister is a chiropractor.

In his quest for the ideal team, he feels communication is of paramount importance on the journey to greatness. For Dr. Dunson, finding the perfect team comes from the 3 P's—Patience, Persistence and Prayer. They are working on being proactive, diligent and consistent to the purpose.

With their move so new, they have jumped into marketing to become known. They have partnered with a lot of non-profits and serve as sponsors. "We use a regional metro publication to advertise our services. We are launching an educational radio address and we also provide auction items for independent schools.

The majority of our new patients are referrals from existing patients. We emphasize our internal marketing, constantly communicating with our current patients and providing five star service. We do receive new patients from our marketing and advertise directly to the general Atlanta population. We are using Rocket Dog Dental and have two ads running right now. We are targeting baby boomers and corporate people (Atlanta is becoming the NYC of the south with many corporate headquarters like Coca-Cola, UPS, CNN, Turner Broadcasting and Home Depot). We have advertised in many magazines targeted towards various audiences, such as lifestyle, corporate women, legal as well as community magazines of the Atlanta Metro area. We sponsor local events, participate in fundraisers and run promotions several times a year. Our overall goal is to let Atlanta know we are a five star practice that provides leading edge services and treatment.

Dr. Dunson will be the only dentist on a weekly radio show discussing various health topics. He will appear at least once a quarter. Because the show is sponsored, there is no fee from Dr. Dunson to appear. Additionally, he will be giving daily dental notes on a morning spiritual program, one of the largest in the Atlanta area. The message will play during the morning drive for a monthly fee.

New skills added are CEREC 3D and Biolase MD. We find these new technologies coupled with our unique training has been quite rewarding. The laser facilitates many of the procedures we perform surgically and most importantly, it expedites healing, minimizes trauma and provides a better, less painful experience for our patients. The laser is truly a winning investment in our practice. CEREC has the obvious benefit of convenience and minimizing crown delivery appointments. CAD/CAM technology dramatically improves our diagnostic capabilities for implant and restorative dentistry.

In the summer of 2009 I will be launching an educational center, the Atlanta Academy of Reconstructive Dentistry. The goal of the academy will be to share my passion and knowledge with other dentists interested in implant and reconstructive dentistry.

www.dunsondental.com

Dr. Bernee Dunson

DON'T SETTLE FOR LESS

In my twenty years of coaching Doctors on business, I observe there are certain doctors who always have great teams, even with turn-over. You will observe certain college and professional football coaches have a consistent record as well. There are certain behaviors of leaders which create team excellence on a consistent basis.

Doctors who have remarkable teams are very clear on their **vision**. They have done their homework on themselves and have defined who they are, their aspirations and inspirations and speak that consistent message in their words and body language. They have been able to move those lofty words to a street level of inspiration so everyone knows and can take action as if that vision is their own. They can **communicate** with consistency on their standards of service and clinical excellence.

Systems are in place to support that vision so no one needs to use the "hold button" to ask a repetitive or redundant question of the leader. Systems to support your vision are so critical. Without strong systems which support the level of service, efficiency and clinical skills of the team, you are in "free fall." When a new person comes, you have little structure for them to enter and the end result is system changes every time there are new personnel. My college roommate was an A-7 pilot flying off of aircraft carriers during Viet Nam. I asked him if it wasn't unnerving to have a new crew rotation when he landed at night in a storm. He said, " The systems are so strong, the whole crew could change and we would be fine."

Because of this clarity of vision, **hire to match the vision**. Keep looking until you find the right person to possibly even inspire a higher level for the team. Where dentists fall short is settling for "the best one who applied." A winning college football coach holds the standard of vision. His players must meet that standard and play his game. Your team will not form with strength if the leader allows a lower standard in attitude and skill. Keep looking.

In possible candidates, look for a positive **attitude** over clinical skill. You can teach skill but you cannot change a poor attitude. Many dentists hire and then cling to their new employee "hoping her attitude will change because she is the best assistant ever."

Give up on the **concept that you can change** someone and remake them into someone who will perform exceptionally. You cannot change a duck into an eagle. Strong leaders recognize this and keep looking for the right attitude which matches the vision.

After you hope you have found the right person to join your team, you must spend the **time and money to train** them. Who will train them? You must have systems in place which support your vision of service and excellence. Spend the time in numerous weekly trainings and monthly verbal skill training sessions so the "newbie" can be incorporated into your team as soon as possible. A review is good for the whole team. Work together on the books you want read, the scripts, sales skills and patient protocols which brand your practice as excellent. Because you are always working on cross training, existing team members can be an important part of her training. When there is a fair and consistent bonus system, your team will want to have the new person succeed as soon as possible.

We have all heard that team turnover is expensive so avoid it. What is expensive is not having a strong vision or the willingness to communicate it and not having strong systems in place to support that vision and willingness to settle for less.

As you are training a person whose vision and attitude match, you will find the consistency of a training program to be appreciated. Do not give up here. This concept will help integrate the new person into the team and become a valuable team member who contributes to all their bonuses. The right person will want to be **accountable** for numbers, service levels and even bring new and better ideas to your team if they feel you are putting effort, time and money into their training.

Hold yourself and your team to a higher standard. Don't settle for less as mediocrity will creep in, your best team members will become discouraged and possibly leave. It takes strength and courage. Keep looking to find the right person.

WORK SIMPLIFICATION

How much thought, time and training have you invested in making your business department more efficient and effective? We devote most of our attention to efficiency with our technical skills. Yet, what is noticed by patients is your value of their time, especially in the business area of your practice. A side benefit is the saving of your time thus creating a lower overhead and greater net return.

Time or the illusion of time and efficiency is a highly prized item. Anything you can do to create the result of more time is highly valued by your team, yourself and especially your clients. If you could do the same work in less time, wouldn't that be a goal? How about working three days instead of four? What kinds of systems would that take?

The business of dentistry can become a big dinosaur for many reasons—a revolving staff, no real direction, favorite duties as well as non favorite tasks, layers of management, not knowing the numbers and more. One of the methods of becoming more efficient is to do what we call a Task Analysis which is an Excel spreadsheet which everyone on the team completes, including the Doctor and spouse, if at all involved (think errand person, parties, gifts, books). We want to see what everyone feels are their tasks, how much time they spend, what is being done, who else could do it and who could be hired to do it.

When everyone has completed their task writing, we come to the analysis part where each task is discussed, defended with questions of "how does that fit our vision of service?" What is being omitted, what is being duplicated, why, why, why?

A Doctor was spending half a day a week on lab work, pouring models, etc, because he had always done it, felt he should and he kind of liked it. His staff challenged him to send it to the lab and he now has more time and is not so grumpy.

Having a website is critical to serving patients well. When there is a question, people immediately think of the Internet for the answer. Make your website very user friendly with health forms and new guest entry forms which they can complete on their own time. You and your team need to speak frequently of your website and refer people there for easy directions, contact numbers and links to your specialists.

Becoming paperless this year is a step towards efficiency. Many dentists are still hanging on to charts and papers while trying to go paperless. Doing two systems takes even more time, energy and creates inefficiency. By being paperless, each team member becomes accountable for entering their data. With monitors in each area, assistants and hygienist can enter treatment, schedule appointments, create the insurance routing (either electronically/digitally or handing the papers to the patient) and collect the money.

This system allows the receptionist to become a relationship expert both on the phone, answering your web inquiries ASAP and encouraging your new guests as they enter your practice.

Ultimately, the Doctor is responsible for treatment entries. With time, training and encouragement, assistants and hygienists can enter the treatment at the time of service and the Doctor can review and initial. How about creating an opportunity for the assistants and hygienists to write the referral for the specialists? Learning to cut and paste can provide a very efficient system for time.

Eliminating accounts receivables is efficient. Collect their portion or full amount at the time of service and have insurance reimburse patients, utilize outside funding to the fullest and eliminate statements, by refusing to be THE BANK and cross-train so everyone can collect money at the time of service.

Think of all areas to become more efficient. If the task is worth doing, do it once and complete the work. Cross-training is a must. A great team of three (plus Doctor) can handle a practice producing $2M with a major emphasis on doing it once, eliminating repeats, cross training and being paperless. With the Task Analysis, work can become more streamlined and efficient. A goal is more productive time and less time in the office doing unnecessary tasks which someone else can do more effectively.

TEAM RULES

- Coach calls the game
- Be on time. Lombardi's time is 15 minutes ahead of regular time
- Wear your uniform. Be proud, look your best and make your team look good
- Prepare yourself mentally to play the game
- Wear your game face proudly
- Play full out as you never know which play will make the difference
- Start your day with an effective morning huddle 15 minutes before your first play
- Be accountable for your actions. If the ball comes to you and you miss it, create a plan for that not to occur again. Accept responsibility and move on
- Do not hog the limelight. There are no stars on a winning team
- Make your teammates look good. Give them credit all the time
- Do not start derogatory or gossipy conversations about your coach, your team or the fans and do not listen to any team member who is the gossip. Instead, take them by the arm to share their "story" with the person who is the subject of their wrath. Bottom line, no trash-talking on the winning team.
- Treat other team members how you want to be treated
- Do not make anyone smaller than you
- If there is a problem, go to the source
- No whining. Instead, contribute positively and constructively. If you do not agree with something, think of a different plan and present it. Whining is a losing skill.
- Never admit to anyone you are tired, angry or bored
- Never carry a grudge. It is a waste of everyone's time
- Include everyone on your team in communication and training
- Holding "secrets" will destroy a team

- Learn something new everyday. Read a sales or marketing book and apply it to your game.
- As a team, donate skills and time once a month to community service—walking dogs at the animal shelter, serving homeless meals, adopting a single-parent family, etc
- Do volunteer dentistry in your community once a quarter. The whole team participates.
- Either you have your reasons or your results
- Be a team player 100%. During the game, you are focused. Home or relationship concerns are not part of your work conversations.
- Do not consume food in the work areas
- The winning players are those who think and know they can win
- Learn the most important skill in sales—listening.

TEAM PITFALLS

- Having the wrong team and not recognizing it
- Having a micro-manager as the leader belittles team and no one wants or needs to step up
- Failing to communicate the vision or hold it as your own
- Sub-grouping or gossiping about other team members, Doctor or patients
- Failure to form a real team
- Becoming stuck in tasks by loosing sight of the bigger picture
- Allowing an attitude of mediocrity prevail rather than one of winning
- Forgetting who we are serving
- Not having an effective bonus system
- Failure to learn and apply new technical, sales and marketing skills
- Not having regular morning meetings or weekly staff meetings
- Working overtime and blaming it on someone else
- Continually running late in hygiene and in the Doctor schedule will decrease new patient flow
- Allowing personal issues to pervade the practice
- Allowing non-professional behavior to be the practice norm
- Super-stars are generally not great team players

BLATCHFORD GUIDING PRINCIPLES
OF <u>TEAMWORK</u>

- Don't fiddle with the bonus system
- All team, including the receptionist, needs to be current on emergency procedures
- Give your new team member a chance to succeed with excellent training, uniforms and bonus plan from the start. How committed is "conditional"?
- Position yourself on the high end of team salaries in your area
- Team salaries are ideal. On hourly, how do they earn more money?
- Do not hire anyone whose first question is "what are the benefits?"
- Plan your calendar 12 months in advance. Vacations are scheduled at the same time.
- In figuring bonus, count 12 "fiscal" periods of 15 work days each so team always has an equal chance at bonus. Or determine how many days you will be working for the year and divide by 12 to come up with days in the cycle.
- BAM is the basic level of financial solvency when bills are paid. It stands for Bare And Minimum. Team overhead should be at 20%
- As a team, donate your time once a month to community service—walking dogs at the shelter, serving homeless meals, adopting a single-parent family, volunteer dentistry day for those less fortunate.
- Watch your conversations in treatment rooms. Others can hear you. Is it the right thing to say or do?
- Don't gossip about anyone
- Don't carry a grudge.
- If you feel a team member is not measuring up, communicate directly and immediately what you need, set guidelines for improvement and monitor the progress.
- Complete your team's dental work at "team day" every quarter when we all volunteer.
- Avoid sarcastic remarks

- Listen to your team
- Dress for success. Review quarterly your wardrobe/image. New uniforms every quarter
- Rid of scrubs, for sure
- Let your team overhear you showering specific praise on their skills and attitude in front of patients and dental colleagues. If not, why do you keep them?
- Remember, no one makes it alone. Have a grateful heart and be quick to acknowledge those who help you.
- Encourage your team to display one or two family or interest pictures
- Hire people smarter than you
- Hire curious people
- Demand excellence and be willing to pay for it.
- Often, tell your team how terrific they are and that you trust them
- Allow your team to grab responsibility. Get out of their way
- When you run habitually late in the evening, you will have high staff turnover
- Be the first person to arrive in the morning.
- Remember team birthdays. You plan something special
- With your present team, write an office purpose and read aloud to start your weekly team meeting
- With your team, write agreements and commit yourself to following them
- Do not call your team, "my girls." Avoid labeling them "front-end girl" and "back-end girl."
- Hire team who are people oriented. You can always teach the technical skills
- Insist team members leave the office during lunch hour, even for a walk around the block. They need "cob-web clearing" time.
- All team wear nametags, including the Doctor.
- In hiring a new team member, check out their car for cleanliness and order
- Showing favoritism will help destroy teamwork
- Meet quarterly with each team member to evaluate progress, expectations and goals for the next quarter, year and five years
- When a new team member is hired, share your expectations for continuing education opportunities and requirements. How

many days are expected, who pays and what is the expected result.

- Encourage your team to make mistakes. Have them evaluate situations and make decisions. Praise. Discuss other choices later.
- Never decrease salaries. Eliminate a position, if you must decrease overhead
- A bonus is a bonus is a bonus. Encourage team to avoid adding another payment based on bonus
- Be a team player
- Unless the spouse is THE registered hygienist, THE full time receptionist or THE full-time assistant, there is not an actual position in the office for him/her.
- Celebrate successes, no matter how big, or how small.
- Celebrate holidays, birthdays and special occasions.
- Remember when conversing with others "be interested, not interesting"
- Celebrate accomplishments no matter how small
- If you bring up an issue, always bring a solution
- Remember the "give, get, give" philosophy
- At your PM huddle, always acknowledge your team for their efforts during the day

9

OVERHEAD

OVERHEAD

This is the biggest factor in figuring your net return. It is really very simple. There is gross income before any expenses are paid. When you pay all your expenses, including rent, laboratory, team and their taxes, dental supplies and more, this is your overhead expenses and the remainder is your net.

The big problem with overhead is we allow it to be whatever it is and we take home what is left over, whatever that is. This is backwards because we allow our expenses to run our business.

Since you are in business to make a living, a profit, how about starting from that position? Decide what percentage of net you want to support your lifestyle, pay down debt, save for retirement and fund emergency savings. It is possible to have 55% overhead which means you take home 45%.

What is sad to see is a highly skilled dentist producing $1M and allowing the overhead to be 80% so for all that effort, the net is $200K which must include debt reduction, taxes, retirement and savings plus living expenses. No wonder they are frustrated.

Be tough. Be smart. State your net first and make your overhead work for you, not wag your tail.

BLATCHFORD FORMULA FOR DETERMINING OVERHEAD PER HOUR

This computation allows you to see how much you make per hour.

1. In determining what it costs to operate your office, remove from consideration: Capital expenditures (anything over $2000 per month), continuing education courses and travel for those courses, doctor benefits which are legal but do not influence the cost of producing a unit of dentistry in your office (ex; auto, AACD convention in Hawaii, etc.).

2. Total overhead per month and subtract the lab bill. This lab bill should reflect number of units this month multiplied by your lab fee per unit. If you use a Cad/Cam, assign an amount.

3. Divide overhead by total hours seeing patients equals cost per hour without lab.

4. Divide the number of providers; for example one doctor and one hygienist equal two providers.

5. This equals the cost per hour per provider.

6. Time procedures, including diagnostic time, prep time, seat time and add in the lab bill for laboratory procedures.

7. As you can see, once the lab bill is removed, the cost per hour for hygienist is same as for the doctor.

Blatchford Solutions
www.blatchford.com
(888) 977-4600
Copyright email: info@blatchford.com

PERCENTAGE OF OVERHEAD IS A CHOICE

Too often dentists place much emphasis on gross production rather than net return. What you bring home is your choice by being very aware of expenses, having the intention and action to earn and keep 45%. Currently, dental overhead in the US is approaching 78% which means net return is a low 22%. How is it that some dentists are able to operate at 55% or under?

When economics have been in a good place, dentistry is on people's priority list and being successful is easier. Yet, most dentists, even in good times, find the money rolls through and there never is enough. What continually causes the squeeze and a feeling there never is enough?

Blatchford Doctors are big believers in budgets. Too often, the connotation of budgets is appalling as it feels like a diet. We avoid budgets because we feel we would be restricted or denied the fun stuff, the choices. A solid budget allows necessary purchases plus equipment, improvements, continuing education and the fun stuff, too. A budget is based on percentages which allow you to monitor on a monthly and quarterly basis. What is currently happening? What choices do I need to make to keep within budget to take 45% home?

A dental budget has rent at 5%, equipment at 5%, marketing needs 3-10%, lab expenses should be over 10%, dental supplies at 5%, and total team expenses at 20%. **This item is one which you can control**. It is the largest item in your budget and most offices are staffed at closer to 30%. If you are producing $100K a month and are not watching your numbers, your lack of leadership in this area is costing an extra $10K in net for you.

It is easy to abdicate leadership and choice regarding team when you focus on the technical dentistry. A team member says, "I need more help in the front." Without looking at your budget, your numbers and failing to questioning the "why," or you have failed to implement a fair and very motivating bonus, you say, "OK, take care of it." You have just committed yourself to an annual $30K plus and allowed your team to dictate overhead.

Your team should be privy to your budget, percentages, targets and goals. When they know the numbers and that a fair bonus system is a part of your practice, team becomes accountable for those numbers and for making the practice work. Good team members make it their own practice.

What does it take to have team at 20%? Leadership, a road map of the future, strong systems like block booking, complete cross-training, coaching to goal at morning huddle, weekly staff meetings about numbers, monthly training sessions, computers in every room so hygiene and assisting can enter treatment, schedule, produce insurance form/ charge slip and collect the money, increasing collections at time of service, applying the 80/20 rule to your practice so marketing money is effective, being positive, energized and the most important, everyone is mastering sales conversations with guests by reading books, role playing and encouragement. It also takes a doctor willing to diagnose long term treatment plans rather than single tooth dentistry as the blocks need to be filled to goal.

Besides looking at the numbers of staff at 20% of production/ collection, other indicators of overstaffing could be:

- More people working in the front than those producing the dentistry
- Layers of supervisors and managers
- Having staff members who have little or no patient contact

When a dentist feels overhead is just one thing that happens and he/she is not in charge of net income, it hurts your family, your team and your patients. When finances have control of you, do you make decisions about patient care in a different way, like choosing a less competent lab, diagnosing only what you feel they will surely accept rather than discussing with them long term dreams and treatment plans?

Does your financial pinch force you to offer less than ideal? Do you offer less so the patient will at least accept something?

Choose your 55% overhead by creating budgets and living within the numbers, especially for team, the one area you can change. Make the bold decisions to take home 45%. It can be yours because of your leadership.

Bill Blatchford DDS

A MAN FOR ALL SEASONS

Dr. David Ward of Woonsocket, RI

Dr. David Ward is a general dentist in the blue collar town of Woonsocket, RI. His father was a dentist and David is the 9th of 10 children, all who worked their way through college. Before meeting Bill, he had converted an old Victorian house into his dream office with eight treatment rooms, 14 full time and part time staff and an associate. Working 5.5 days a week, his overhead was 80%.

His dream practice was turning into a nightmare. Staff issues consumed him and debt began to pile up. "I had always thought the only way to make more money was to work more hours. My wife was discouraged because she thought I loved the office more than family time or special time alone with her."

Now, he has three full-time employees with two hygienists sharing one position. By implementing block booking, he is able to work four days a week and takes seven weeks of time off with pay, produces $1.5 M in a small mill town. He is producing more now in four days a week than the former 5.5 days.

Dr. Ward feels the biggest gift is his happiness. Longing to retire before, he now wants to be involved in dentistry as long as he can. Bill has helped him expand his leadership skills in all areas of his life. His family is very grateful for the new Dr. Ward.

"My personal vision seems to be a work in progress. I tend, like so many dentists, to over think many of my decisions. Where do I want to take my practice and who do I want to ride the bus with me? My vision centers on my ability to treat most of my patient's desires right in my own office. With Bill's encouragement, I have expanded my capabilities. When my patients ask about cosmetic procedures, I can share I was trained at the Rosenthal Institute and can meet their high expectations. When they ask about implants, I can place and restore my own implants. My vision is to give my patients the best and most comprehensive care without their having to leave our practice."

Dr. Ward shares his staff evolution. Before Bill, (BB) David felt it was just normal to have constant staff problems. "I really couldn't call my co-workers a TEAM." Now, he understands if you don't have a solid team all pulling together for a common goal, you are lost. He feels attitude is the common denominator. "You can teach skills but you cannot teach attitude," David concludes. In choosing a team member, Dr. Ward wants to find out, 'is the glass half empty or half full?' David has also learned people are motivated by different things. "Money and bonuses are important but the most motivating and important is being shown sincere appreciation. They want to know that without them, the office would not be quite as efficient, pleasant or inviting," Dr. Ward has wisely learned.

"The team also needs a coach or leader. In fact, they need a great leader. I tend to avoid rocking the boat. Bill has been instrumental in helping me realize I can improve and my team actually needs good leadership to thrive and excel. I realize I was not born with terrific leadership skills, but I am convinced working with Bill has helped me to see that inside of me of me there is a great leader who continues to grow daily."

"We set goals as a team because what we decide has a direct impact on their lives. This year, the goals focused around productivity and patient retention. We are going to increase our efforts to make guests' visits as pleasant and surprise-free as possible by knowing everything from what treatment they are expecting, follow up phone calls for clarity, to financial obligations. We want to maintain a great relationship with our existing patients, knowing who are our top 20% of patients and who could potentially be in that top category."

Dr. Ward finds the numbers game in dentistry very challenging. He admits he did not even know there were certain parameters to meet financially in order to be successful. Dr. Blatchford pointed out his staff overhead was nearly 40% even producing $900K and his overhead was over 70%. Now, his team costs are at 23% including bonuses and overhead is at 60%.

"When my vision is clear, team members can grasp and run with the concept. Their bonus is directly related to attitude and job performance. Then, systems begin to matter and follow through is critical. My team loves it when they get a bonus, but understand it is not a right or a guarantee. I am amazed when we do miss a bonus, everyone pulls together to work harder. It is very rewarding to realize you have the team support."

Dr. Ward and team focus on efficiency by instituting Block Booking. They are now much more productive with a consistent stream of income. We have become much more comprehensive. "Before, we worked tooth to tooth, now we share what would help to improve the smile and dental health." Treatment rooms have computers and appointments are made chair side. They use Smile Reminders with fantastic results. "Now, we send email and text to confirm appointments as well as communicate with newsletters and seasonal greetings. Our patients love how we are in contact with them on a regular basis."

"We used to carry $100K in receivables and sent hundreds of monthly statements because that is how my father (dentist for 37 years) used to do it. The effect of instituting "check, cash or credit card" is amazing and we daily use Care Credit as well as arranging for fee paid up front. We send a handful of statements and our receivables are negligible."

www.beautifulsmilesrhodeisland.com

Dr. David Ward.

SIZE MATTERS

Within the artistry of dentistry, attention to details and numbers affect the end result. The same applies to the business of dentistry. Size matters. Numbers make a difference and it is not all about being big. The Doctor with the largest gross is not the winner if the net return is 20%. Why do you choose to work so hard for so little return?

Dentistry is a lot like fishing stories. We remember the largest number we ever produced and round it off to the nearest hundred in speaking with other dentists. Do we ever mention net or numbers that count? I remember as a rookie dentist, hearing those boasting conversations and being frustrated because I thought they were true and I also thought gross mattered. No one ever mentioned net.

Paying attention to practice numbers ensures an excellent outcome, just as in your technical work. Ignoring numbers is a choice which can result in numbers moving in the opposite directions rather than having a good result. Slipping, sliding and guessing are not so good when size does matter.

A million dollar practice should net $400,000. Why would you work hard to produce a large gross and take home less? Which would you rather have—a practice gross of $800K and a net of $350K or a practice gross of $1M and take home of $200K? These are choices we make about size.

Let's examine more "sizes." Not only is there a choice about gross and net, there is also a choice about numbers of new patients and case acceptance. Some dentists are crying for more new patients yet lack the skills of relationship and discovering dreams and wants. New patients are wasted in this environment. With current sales training, you can do well with one quality new patient a day.

Instead of large new patient numbers, it takes focused sales skills where conversations are not about NEED and pressure to purchase.

Relax. Find out who they are, what they want and how you can help them. Every team member needs to be on board with good personal skills.

Another place where size does matter is the percentage spent on staff salaries. A general practice should goal at 20% of production spent on team salaries, taxes and benefits. We have seen practices as high as 39% spent on team. Now, that is a big number, not one of which to be proud. A dentist would be working hard to support the team. How does it get so big? Many reasons but it basically occurs because of an absence of real leadership and planning. A better question is "how can I get my staff costs in line?" Even a million dollar practice can operate with three team members plus the Doctor. Yes, they need to be the right team members. Keep looking until you find the right ones instead of hiring three to do the job one could do. Work shouldn't be noisy.

Now, size matters regarding the Doctor, too. If you are a seasoned veteran and taking over 60 minutes to routinely prepare a crown, you have a case of the "slows." Combine that with a staff of six and you are working hard, very hard. Take more classes and create efficiency skills in the treatment room. Work from a laminated checklist and avoid being a "diddler."

Size matters in scheduling treatment. If you do not know your overhead per hour, how can you cover it each hour? A big overhead and little income is not a pretty thing. Combine an 80% overhead with a team of 6-8 all involved in the Crown of the Year Club and dentistry is not so fun. An average overhead is about $250-$300 an hour. Do you have a goal of covering your overhead per hour? Consider, too, just reaching your overhead per hour is a tie game.

Size matters in the relationship of your lab bill to production. It is very difficult to make a good living in the Crown of the Year Club. You lab percentage should be in the 9-11% range for a general practice which means you are diagnosing beyond the magic insurance maximums. Congratulations! You are the right size.

Size matters. You want a higher lab bill, a lower team percentage, a bigger net vs. gross, and a higher case acceptance from fewer quality patients. Go for the right numbers; some to be large, some to be small. Size does matter.

Bill Blatchford DDS

FEAR IN THE AIR? MAKE A PLAN

Whether economic changes are real or not, the media and politicians are feeding a frenzy of worry, concern and even fear. Your patients are starting to pull in, your team is watching cautiously and even dentists are looking concerned.

We have had at least ten years of economic growth and being a dentist has been anything but difficult. We have exceeded physicians for net return and enjoy much time off. Any dentist can make a decent living in a growth economy. You may have become complacent about systems and allowed your overhead to creep up, knowing you can always produce more.

In good times, a $1M practice ($83K a month) could have a 75% overhead (the national average) with six team members and the dentist wants it better but the urgency is lacking and the dentist is not motivated to make any changes because life continues well. Without any changes, this exceptional practice with a high overhead would be challenged to weather three months of $60K production as the overhead would then be 100% and the net to the Doctor would drop to zero. Imagine the impact!

During changing times, dentistry moves down the list of priorities. Without sales skills and solid systems in place, patients will easily revert to "just fix the worst one" and your practice becomes a member of the Crown of the Year Club. Your team starts to believe this is the standard. But you failed to be a real leader and keep your overhead low, especially during changing times.

Being a leader requires having a strong vision of where you are headed. This vision needs to be clearly communicated and owned by the team. A real leader continues to make the bold decisions necessary to keep the practice healthy and viable. Your team looks to you for enthusiasm and confidence. How is that working for you?

At Blatchford coaching, we work with our Doctors and teams to know and own their numbers so their overhead is 50-60%, not the out of control 75 or 80%. To keep the fears at bay, you must have confidence that you are in control and you are following a plan. You always make your retirement contributions even in changing times. You always pay your bills on time and you operate your home and office on a budget which is not a diet but a road map for wise choices. Your team knows the numbers and they are accountable to have meaningful conversations with your guests about their dreams and wishes for continued healthy smiles.

If you are teetering on the edge of high overhead and the wind starts to blow, you have no wiggle room. It is easy to have a whole team in a depressed state, creating a spiraling vortex. *The Secret* shares the laws of attraction. If you are in a funk because you failed to prepare, you will share that depressed conversation and bring others into it. Why would you ever mention the stock market or failed mortgage situation with patients or your team? These are inappropriate conversations and they are like a flashing neon sign of how you are feeling.

Examine your financial plan regarding your reputation in the community. If during easy times, you became tightly niched in a modality which is optional you may want to shift that reputation by widening your base. You don't want to be so exclusive that you are no longer viable. Being obstinate will make you unemployed.

You may not be able to afford your team of six during tough times. We have found in the Blatchford Coaching, with technology in place, you can operate a large practice with three to four solid team players. Your total team expenses should be at 20% or below.

If you have been an insurance provider, this is not the time to change that relationship. Continue to accept their insurance and shift the responsibility for collecting to the patient by collecting up front (offering outside funding) and giving the completed insurance forms to the patient to send to their carrier.

Why not be prepared? If you reduced your overhead to 60% and the economy recovered, who wins here? You win and your team. Best of all, your patients who want you to be successful, win, too. If you need some direction and confidence to make the right choices, help is available now.

RAISING FEES

"Value has been defined as the ability to command the price."

Dentists' overhead has increased from 45% thirty years ago to the average of 75% today. Your net return is squeezed to 25% or less. Dentists' net income has been cut in half as a percentage of doing business. What are some viable solutions?

Dentists bought into the insurance programs in the early 1970's as we agreed to accept their fees. Thus, our fees have been eroded as other expenses continued to rise with inflation. There is something wrong in a practice when you continue to treat patients from certain insurance plans, all the while worrying about the cost of the laboratory procedures and materials for this patient. If we have to compromise our standards to treat a patient for low fees, why do we continue on this path?

To encourage you in making a fee increase decision, you need to know the numbers of your practice. Many dentists do not know their overhead per hour. What does it really cost you to diagnose, prepare and deliver a single crown in your office? In your overhead expenses, do not include extraneous items allowed by the IRS but have no bearing on cost analysis of your treatment. An example would be a car, continuing education in Hawaii or if you were able to pay $90K cash for an equipment item this year. To properly figure overhead per hour, you need to amortize that item over its life and use that monthly figure. When you have that figure which could be in the $250 an hour range, share it with your team. Compare your overhead to produce that crown to your collection amount for that patient. Will you be surprised? If you already know it isn't that great, why do you continue?

Another spreadsheet which is extremely useful is the 80/20 Pareto principle of determining who is purchasing the most and the least. Knowing who is on which list during the last 12 months of practice helps you make marketing decisions as well as financial decisions such as raising your fees, laboratories to use and continuing educations classes to improve your skills. Even if your computer software will not do this automatically, the 80/20 spreadsheet is so valuable you can afford to do it by hand.

As you list your patients who had treatment in your office, also list their insurance company or plan. The group of patients creating 80% of your income should reach about 20% of your patients. Study the top 20% and try to replicate these. Now study the bottom 20% as you actually lose about 10% on this segment. Who are they? What treatments do they accept? How much time and energy is spent on keeping them in your recare program? Looking at your overhead per hour in producing treatment, are you really making any money on these patients?

Of course, the leader's vision comes into play here and if you are fully knowledgeable of your numbers and feel you are making a conscious choice to continue to serve this patient on this plan and not compromise with a less expensive lab or cut corners, then proceed with our admiration. If you feel you are a victim, do something about it now.

There are Doctors charging far below the norm for their treatment. We have seen denture fees trying to compete with denturists for $1000 a unit. If your stated fee for a unit of dentistry is $750 and you are accepting $500 from a plan and it took you two hours and 15 minutes, you have exceeded your overhead per hour of $250, this is not good.

I find it fascinating that many Doctors charge the same fee for a veneer as their accepted unit fee by insurance. Veneers are not even covered by insurance. If you are skilled with artistry and use an excellent lab, you must charge in the $1200 range for your veneers. Why would I think your veneers had value if you charge $980 and someone else charges $1350? Which dentist would produce a better result? If you are the best in your area, your fees should reflect it.

Bottom line, raise your fees frequently and justly on the items which make a difference like crown and bridge, dentures and veneers. Quit doing treatment on patients where you feel you need to send the work to a less expensive lab and compromise on materials to make it work. Do your best and be compensated justly. The right patients will see value in your work.

BLATCHFORD GUIDING PRINCIPLES ON NUMBERS

- Choose to lead your practice at 55% overhead
- The Doctor and team members need to know the numbers—how many new patients does it take to reach goal, what is break even point, how do we figure bonus?
- Pay your withholding tax on time
- Don't be embarrassed for your team to know how much you net. Usually, they are shocked at how little.
- Make a budget for dental supplies which is 5-6% of collections
- Increase your lab bill to 15-20% of collections. The average dentist spends 8% on lab
- Your staff and lab together should equal 35%
- Doctor's daily diagnosis needs to be three times the daily production goal. Some people will say, "no, not yet."
- Learn to read a profit and loss statement or work with your accountant to make the numbers meaningful to you.
- The leader needs to make the necessary changes when numbers do not show up well for a quarter
- When purchasing another practice to add on, look for net income and quality of patients
- Make your practice better, not bigger. If you're not making it financially now, do not add more.
- In sharing the practice budget with team, take out the deductible expenses which are legitimate but have nothing to do with producing a unit of dentistry
- Do not plan to retire on the proceeds from your practice sale.
- Staff for the low month's production, not for the highest production ever

BLATCHFORD GUIDING PRINCIPLES
ON OVERHEAD

- Do not hire an associate unless you intend to sell your practice
- Before hiring an associate, are you turning patients away because you are too busy?
- Share your overhead figures with your team. It makes production and collection goals more meaningful
- When your overhead is 80%, it is hard to feel the joys of dentistry

10

SALES

SALES CONVERSATIONS

It was less than 15 years ago when dentistry formally recognized the process of having a patient say "yes" was called sales and not hidden by Case Presentation.

The skill to master is called sales and the more you study, the more you learn it is simply a conversation. Yes, it is a guided conversation but just a conversation with a friend.

We still hear from some staff, "Oh, I don't sell. I want nothing to do with putting pressure on my patients. That is just wrong and I won't do it." They are right. The old method of sales was to move people into a corner and squeeze them by putting pressure until they purchased or left upset. As Brian Tracy says, "pressure sales are Neanderthal sales."

Even in dentistry, teams and Doctors are slowly moving from NEEDS based to WANTS based questions. The paradigm shift is "no one needs what we have to offer." If they don't NEED it, then our conversations are about what they WANT.

How can you be putting pressure on people when you are talking with them about their favorite subject—themselves, asking what they think about their smile and teeth?

Conversations can only be about them. We use the 80/20 rule here, too. Your guest gets to talk 80% of the time and you only have 20% of the time to ask questions. If you flip this equation, you may be violating the "no-pressure" rule.

With "no-pressure" sales, it is OK for your guests to say 'no, I don't think so now.' They will be back because they still have a nice relationship with you.

It sounds easy and it is. The important point to remember is sales is a life-long learning process. Blatchford Doctors read, read, read and apply. They write scripts, they role-play and practice, practice, practice. When you think you know it, but really don't, you will "wing it" and the conversation will not move to the result you desire. It will just be an interesting conversation.

In Blatchford Coaching, we spend half the time on sales and half the time on leadership with the other half on systems. So 150% effort is needed. Are you up for it?

THE NICHED PRACTICE

The Smile Stylists
Drs. Jason and Colleen Olitsky of Ponte Vedra, FL

We opened our start up practice less than three years ago. Bill has guided us from the beginning and encouraged us to furnish just two of the five treatment rooms. We see one patient at a time with 90% cosmetics. We do our own 15 hygiene patients a month. We work three days a week with just one team member besides Jason and me.

We decided we could practice anyway we wanted. We now look back at our initial business plans which we took to banks with the model we knew; six chairs, working 4-5 days a week, having 5-6 staff and seeing lots of patients. That was what we knew from working at a managed care office for 3-4 years.

We feel our vision and attitude is a huge factor in our success. We have written goals in a number of areas in our lives—family, personal, business, health and finance. We try to review these everyday to keep focused and motivated, knowing that if we keep pushing in the same direction, our goals will eventually come to reality.

Michael Gerber's *E-Myth Revisited* was one of the first books Bill recommended and in the book, Gerber mentions you need to envision what your business will look like 10 years from now and start acting like that from the start. Family is most important to us and therefore, we work three patient days a week. We had our first baby boy, Chase, and he will grow up knowing family is most important to us. We travel a lot to visit our families in Ft. Meyers and Philadelphia. Jason is a Hornbrook instructor as well. Chase has been on 32 flights and he's only eight months old. We really work on balance in our lives.

We also have several other businesses we have started. Wall Smiles sells stock photos to dentists for office display and also provides a place for dentists who don't want stock photos to learn portrait photography via a DVD and course. Our other business is Smile Stylist Inc. which is a license for dentists we feel share the same level of education and passion we do for smile makeovers.

We want to make Smile Stylist a household brand name to help the consumer with their research since the term cosmetic dentist means nothing and is therefore misleading. Our goal is to increase the awareness of the need for patients to do their research and decrease the number of unhappy patients with complacent cosmetics. We have also worked out the logistics of opening a satellite office in New York and hope to see patients this spring.

A positive mental attitude is huge! Dr. Blatchford stimulated us to read books and in three years, I have read over 230 books on personal growth, marketing, networking, sales and biographies. You never know when a concept is going to hit you and say 'aha, I get it now.' Having a positive attitude is something we work on every day. It is hard work, but we know how important it is. We keep each other up.

We started with Dr. Blatchford before we even opened our practice. We had an exceptionally great first year and this has continued. We do struggle with overhead, our loans (new office and equipment) are $14K a month, we spend on average $10K on marketing a month and our lab bills are huge, about $25K a month. So, already we are at $52K a month with nothing else added, like rent, team pay, dental and office supplies, CE and travel and insurance. We are looking forward a few years to when our loans are paid.

We are applying the 80/20 Pareto study to our practice and fortunately, it is easy to see where we made the most money and how it coincides with what we love to do. Our 90% comes from cosmetics, smile designs, full mouth rehabs and bonding/contouring. We decided not to concentrate on our hygiene program. We have also learned we don't want to treat every patient. Money is not the most important thing; happiness is. If we get the "weird" vibe, we typically raise our fees by about 50% and hope they do not proceed.

We follow Block Booking very strictly. Our financial policy of 'check, cash or credit card' was the way Dr. Blatchford had us begin. We never knew any differently. We have no A/R and the majority of our cosmetics patients pay up front.

We are very involved in marketing and networking. We market heavily to become known as the place to go for cosmetics. We network and become involved in fashion shows, model agencies and photographers. We become useful to them and make connections so it is not about us but about how we can help them. We've learned to say yes to opportunities, you never know what door they may open. A good example is an extremely successful patient invited us to brunch (it was my birthday and I almost declined). We ended up spending the whole day with him and really hit it off. It turned out he was interested in our business ideas and could be a source of funding. He is a very generous person and someone we can look up to. He has referred us $140K worth of smile makeovers this year alone. We couldn't imagine not having him as a part of our life and how we may not have become friends if we had said 'no' to his invitation.

We are super-niched and we really don't want to add much new. We recently added no/minimal prep veneers as we see many young patients. We now look at our cases differently and most are a combo of no and minimal prep. We went through the Misch Institute and found we weren't passionate about implants and it really didn't fit our vision of who we were so we do very few implants and we are fine sending them to specialists. We realize by mainly doing cosmetics, we will have ups and downs as far as production/collection but we are OK with having some really big, as well as really low months, we've learned to look at the big picture and have a long term view of our lives.

www.olitskysmiles.com
www.smilestylist.com

Drs. Colleen and Jason Olitsky.

Baby Chase hits Jacksonville Beach.

Marathon finishers.

Voracious reading on sales, business and marketing.

Marketing beautiful smiles at Runway Shows.

BURNING LEADS

Burning leads is the dreaded result in businesses in which the marketed and the sales force is either untrained, not motivated or the internal systems are not in place to handle the new client. The net effect is a real loss as the new client from marketing is turned off and responds with a 'no."

Dentistry is new to marketing. Our product is one of emotion and desire. We are uncertain how to approach attracting the outside world and there are no certainties in marketing, no guarantees that one approach will be the magic bullet. We are all hoping what we do will bring in new patients.

Yet, in many cases of dental marketing, we have not evaluated our internal structure and sales skills to make certain we can handle with care the new clients inquiring about our services. In many practices, there is a real disconnect between the "marketing" department and the "sales" department.

We believe every new call should be handled the same as how it has always been done. We are learning a client responding to your message from print ad, radio, direct mail or website is different than an internally generated referral who has endorsed you. A marketed client has no relationship with you and is still in the "looking stage." They are evaluating your connectivity of relationship on the phone as well as doing their listening and watching during your initial conversations.

What is a marketed client looking for? There are all levels of inquiry yet, basically, they want to know:

- Can I trust them?
- Do they care about me as a person or just a tooth?
- Do they see me as an important individual or is it about them?

Make certain there is great communication within your team about what marketing offers or materials you have contracted. This is who, what, when, where and why. Share the marketing pieces, when they will be offered. Who are you appealing to and what results are you seeking? Write possible scripts for phone inquiries, emphasizing emotion and right-brained thinking. Change from your former "order-taking" mentality ("just the facts, Ma'am") to asking questions, making them feel heard and making it easy for them to enter your care.

Talk as a group about some of the barriers you might have to entry. One might be "It is our policy for new patients to have the best thorough exam with our wonderful Doctor first. Then, on the second appointment, you can have your teeth cleaned." Instead, ask, "What would you like us to do?"

Your potential clients are viewing websites 24/7. We are finding people are calling with, "I want eight veneers and a lower bridge with no gold showing." It is appropriate when specific dental treatment is requested, to ask, "Where are you in your research?" Some marketed patients have researched what they want to have done and now are interviewing potential dentists to find one they trust to do the work."

You are on the list for potential dentists. Make the grade by asking, "What qualities are you looking for in a dentist?" "How can we make sure we satisfy your needs?" This will open a whole box of emotions, history and important information.

In addition to mastering no-pressure sales skills, examine your internal structure for appealing to marketed clients. Greet them by name, find out their favorite beverage, providing it and more each time. Be on time and avoid long forms to complete while they sit alone. Shorten your forms and answer the questions with them on the first visit. Ask them questions that share their thoughts and feelings. Make certain you listen well; responding with more questions.

Build trust by asking questions. Do not talk about yourself. Your office can speak your brand with nicely framed after pictures, elegance, discussions in quiet spaces, guest comforts during treatments, complete bathroom amenities and an upscale yet small reception area. Practice as a team before launching your marketing. Be ready to meet their needs.

You have committed money and time to marketing. It will make your phone ring. Your job now is to connect quickly and listen well. Make your internal skills match your marketing and master sales skills to help them uncover their dreams. Avoid the dreaded burned leads.

Bill Blatchford DDS

ORDER TAKING VS. SELLING

We are always thinking of different ways to present, motivate and "educate" on dental sales. It is a challenging topic as most Dentists and dental staffs believe they are complete and service patients well. "We keep our Doctor's book full." Let's look at it a different way.

Yes and this is the real question, "With what quality is his/her book full? I see an important part of the Five Star Service is complete discovery through focused questions, real listening, understanding their dreams and delivering.

Contrary to that, in most dental offices, we find order takers. In the big sales world, there is a distinct difference between an order taker and a master seller. An order taker in a dental office is comfortable only looking for the superficial reason your guest enters your office. When the questions start with "What is your major concern today", the answer will be something immediate and small. This is how a practice ends up as President of the Crown of the Year Club. Ask small questions only and you will receive small answers only.

This will keep your schedule full and the staff feels fulfilled. Your schedule becomes a log jam (an Oregon term) of running, fixing and patching. This is the point where it seems overwhelming for a Doctor to see the bigger picture and how would they ever be able to do a larger case so "I will just 'watch' it or hope we can discuss it at the next recare visit because I have no where to treat anything larger."

If your staff and the Doctor are order takers, your practice will reach a plateau and remain unfulfilling for years. It takes boldness to break out of this routine of order taking to find the time and master the skills of real sales.

Real sales begin with absolutely no agenda on your part. The Boat Salesman of the Year said, "I never begin with a boat in mind." A focused team player begins a conversation with a clear mind and no smile planned for the guest. This is a real challenge because you and the Doctor are so trained to discover pathology, to fix and mend.

Move from order taking to real sales by thinking of the bigger picture. Your mind set needs to be, "I am here to help my new friend discover why he is here and how we can help him." "I am the conduit to help him uncover the bigger picture."

Begin with "how can I help you today?"

"I am here because my wife made the appointment."

"Why do you think your wife sent you to us?"

"She thinks I have neglected my teeth and my teeth could use some care."

"What do you think about that?"

"Well, she's probably right. I just haven't taken the time and felt they were not worth it."

"Are they worth it to you?"

"Not in the shape they are in."

"When did you and she first notice this?"

"She has been talking about it for ten years."

"She must really love you. What have you tried to make them look better?"

"She bought me some white strips"

"How did that work?"

"Some of my teeth got white and it made the others look worse."

"What else have you tried?"

"I just try not to smile real big."

"You said you are a teacher. How does that work for you?"

"I have heard I am known as 'Mr. Grumpy.'"

"How do you feel about that?"

"Not so good."

"So your students and your wife would like to see a big smile from you? Here are some pictures of smiles. Here is a gentleman who didn't care for his smile and look what we were able to do for him. What do you think?"

"Looks good but I will bet that is very expensive. I am a teacher, remember?"

"It might be a considerable amount of money. You could make convenient monthly payments. Would that work for you?"

Talk with your team about the difference between order taking and master sales. Be in the big picture crowd by working as a team on scripts, role playing scenarios, reviewing the progression of larger cases and why they were accepted, reviewing the cases which are in limbo and what could have been different. Celebrate your listening victories and the times you were so engrossed, the conversation just flowed.

Bill Blatchford DDS

GENIUS ATTACKS KILL THE SALE

In most dental sales conversations, there comes a time sooner or later, when we believe we have the exact solution to the patient's "problem." This genius attack kills the sale. Why? Because we have not thoroughly developed the patient's wants and desires and helped them uncover their own value systems before we blurted out a solution or an answer to a question or problem they really do not yet own.

Whether you share your genius solution with words or there is a show of great knowledge, it is definite your "genius attack" has halted all thought processes and sharing from the patient.

Most of the times, we are so excited to share with the patient the whole process. We start talking with unbelievable speed because we are sure we know enough of what they want and besides, this is THE answer, in your esteemed opinion. We share models, pictures and explain the techniques which we will use to accomplish this bit of genius. We pack our lecture with features like, "you can take the bleach trays home and use on your own time" or "oh, veneers are thin and small, like fingernails."

You will note the patient's body language and glazed eyes. Their reaction at the reception area is "what did he say?" "Why do I NEED this?" If a bolt of lightening strikes, they may say "Go ahead." Most likely it is "I need to think this one over" or "I need to talk to my spouse" which is the universal excuse of "I just don't want that now."

Asking questions instead of acting on your genius attack is demonstrated in the Socratic Method. Socrates knew when we stopped asking questions, we stopped learning. Without asking questions, we assume we know the answer which is really just based on our own perceptions. Others also learn more about themselves when we ask them questions instead of lecture or "educate."

Dr. Glenn Spencer of Bloomfield Hills, MI shared his "genius attack." The Spencer team had developed a mutual admiration with a lovely patient for twenty years. As her dentition failed over the years, Glenn assumed he was in control and knew what was right for her. He added more implants to her locator partial. When the treatment was complete, Fran said, "Glenn, when will I get my permanent teeth and not have to take this out all the time?"

Needless to say, Dr. Spencer learned a costly lesson as Fran now has six healing implants and ten units of crown and bridge.

Dr. Spencer feels this is one of the hardest lessons in his 32 year career. Thinking he knew the answer for Fran, "I let down a wonderful patient and friend."

To be successful in sales, you need to hold your tongue. Take a deep breath. Look your guest in the eyes and smile. Do not act on your impulse to solve their right- brained question with your left-brained solution. Hold that thought. Ask another question, even a relationship question. How about, "Could you clarify?" "What exactly do you mean?" Is there another question you want to ask me?" "I am confused, can you help me?"

Your job is to get back in the game by involving your patient. Allow your genius attack to fade away. Sergeant Schultz was much smarter than he appeared when he habitually said, "I know nothing."

Video tape yourself in a live patient conversation. In replay, you can easily spot your genius attack where you start lecturing, thinking you are educating or selling. Real selling is finding out what they want, not what you want. Learn from your mistakes.

You will always have those genius attacks. 'A' gamers simply do not act on them. Ask more questions and deeper questions. Listen intently. Find out what they want and why they want it or your genius attack will kill the sale for sure.

Bill Blatchford DDS

DOING WELL IN MICHIGAN

Dr. Urszula Firlik of Grand Rapids, Michigan

My practice grew 50% after working with Dr. Blatchford, both in production and collection. My team has enjoyed big bonuses as well as small bonuses. Bonuses were a great motivator initially, but I found that giving my team members more time to be with their families also has a positive impact.

There is more organization and direction, as opposed to chaos and unpredictability, in my practice. Having a daily goal; morning huddles; and setting clear expectations for my team, like scheduling and block booking: all these things make my day smoother, less stressful and more pleasant. Dentistry is more fun.

Bill always stresses that we should look at the positive things - in the practice, in my team members, and in patients. I like to think I've become a more positive person. It is so easy to focus on the things that aren't going right or on mistakes, but we try not to do so. My team and I try to be positive, enthusiastic and always have a great day, even if things don't always work out for the best. Starting our day with a positive quote puts everyone in a good mood and sets a great atmosphere for the day.

Getting out of my comfort zone hasn't been easy but it has brought wonderful results and after a while, it's a good feeling of accomplishment. Things that I've done that were uncomfortable at first were:

- Spending time with patients, asking them questions about their dental goals
- Learning new clinical skills, such as sleep apnea and Biobloc/ orthotropics
- Meeting with ENT specialists, sleep medicine physicians, and others to discuss the treatment modalities that I offer

The best thing that happened to me to help me grow, in addition to Dr. Blatchford's coaching, was to take his advice to read books on leadership, sales and marketing. Those topics were most helpful for the business side of dentistry, especially "customer service": giving patients what they want and not what I think they need.

My team stays motivated, I believe, with open communications. We've learned to listen to each other, and any problems are brought into the open at the huddle or meetings. There is mutual respect. We all have unique talents, and we try to emphasize that a lot. We believe in compliments, talking about problems openly, and not finger point-ing. I've set clear expectations for my team members, and that has been a tremendous help. Every year, my team learns new skills. My employees attend the same seminars and lectures as me, and learn as much as they can about new treatments. They are able to talk to patients with confidence about their care.

In our hygiene department, my hygienist learned about laser therapy and is incorporating it into our practice. This has been a very positive change which is well accepted by our patients. Adding sleep apnea treatment and dental facial orthopedics (Biobloc treatment) has cre-ated great results. Now I can treat patients needing these services, which in the past I referred to specialists. I can treat them here and my patients like that. The benefits of dental facial orthopedics over tradi-tional orthodontics are so great that increasingly more patients accept this treatment for their children.

I want to continue to build my relationship with medical special-ists to create sources of referrals. I also want to continue to be involved in community activities where I can educate the public about develop-ments in new fields of dentistry.

I think the future of dentistry is very bright.

www.drfirlik.com

A POSITIVE ATTITUDE

Dr. Josh Hong of Goodyear, AZ

The grand plan for Dr. Hong was to continue to heavily grow his insurance based dental office to its greatest capacity and efficiency as he created, constructed, and marketed a dream office to be the best of the best in restorative and cosmetic dentistry and delivery of customer care. Dr. Hong and his wife and business partner, Karen, have positioned themselves well in developing skills and business mentors to have this fee-for-service start up become reality.

Josh and Karen are POSITIVE and see the light. They understand the Law of Attraction, relationship and inspiring leadership. They both give great compliments to the clinical skills and study in which Josh has participated at the FACE, Foundation for Advanced Continuing Education with Dr. Tom Basta and Dr. Jeff Brucia. They also give much credit for their business direction to coaching with Blatchford.

Dr. Hong's first office was very busy with a dental associate and a staff of two in the front and two clinical staff producing $800K and net of $300K. The Peoria office was about 20 miles from property he had purchased in Goodyear. Should he continue to operate two offices totally different in appeal? The Peoria practice was profitable yet, was the antithesis of what Dr. Hong envisioned in his dream. "Dr. Blatchford encouraged me to apply strong business principles to the insurance practice, increasing the value and net to eventually help finance my dream practice."

"It was very clear from early in my career to invest in continuing education. Drs. Basta and Brucia forever changed me as a dental clinician to achieve the highest level of restorative and adhesive dentistry. I started to realize my first office did not fit my goal as I matured as a dentist. In the search to build my ideal office, I looked for a coach. I had learned a lot from the Pride Institute, Dr. Michael Schuster and Dr. Dick Barnes. I felt Dr. Blatchford's Program fit me as I am a dentist first and a business person second. During this whole transition, I feel my wife and I have gone through a transformation, too. We have matured as business owners, as leaders in our community and as people."

"I realized to achieve my goals I needed to be a student of business as well as clinical dentistry. I now understand the responsibility of being a leader so I am studying and training to be that leader in my office and in my community. We set very high standards for ourselves which push us to be our best, push us to be smart and push us to be profitable."

Karen adds, "We have been in business eight months and finally broke even. This may seem like a long time but we have a solid clear vision and we have not deviated or compromised. We work in a results based economy which is different than an hourly mentality and we have set some really big, hairy and audacious goals which we have met."

"Through Blatchford Solutions, I met dentists and dental offices whose visions were very similar to mine. When I discovered these offices produced two to three times more with far fewer team members, I learned what my ideal team member would be like, someone who is a leader in the profession and in the community. We look for someone who has invested in education and life. I now work with two exceptional ladies who understand and share my vision.

One is my wife, Karen, whom I met while in UOP Dental School. Besides giving me two beautiful children, Keilani and Kaileia, she has seen my transformation as a clinician and as a business partner since my career started. She understands FACE culture and she fully participated in the Blatchford Program. Karen has a shrewd business mind with exceptional skill in marketing and networking.

Our only other team member is the right person in personality, curiosity and skill. She is completely cross-trained and works in networking. The Blatchford Bonus clearly plants seeds of ownership. It is a win-win. Since we are just a team of three, we are extremely efficient. We all schedule, collect, have phone skills, treatment plan and assist each other. Their job descriptions are to make me profitable, shares Josh.

I am a student of the law of attraction—you attract into your life what you think about the most. Energy flows where your attention goes. We started a fee for service practice from scratch during the most economically challenging times of this century. I cannot control that but I can be selective on who we hang out with, what we watch and hear. We do not have much room for negativity. It is easy to have negative thoughts and experiences. It is also easy to have positive thoughts and experiences. I choose positive because the more positive I live my life, the more positive people I will meet.

Attitude plays a huge role. I monitor attitude as a family man, as a clinician and as a business person. It is important that I feel good spiritually, physically and mentally. I have a meeting with myself once a week, once a month and once a year to evaluate progress in different areas. I have a monthly call with Dr. Blatchford and bi-monthly with Jeff and Tom. Results are a good indicator of my attitude.

My three dental teachers have changed and shaped my dental career: Dr. Basta, Dr. Brucia and Dr. Blatchford. I see and experience their professional status and accomplishments. Yet, these people work harder than anyone I know. Their dedication, commitment, stamina and quest for excellence are life-changing experiences for those around them. I understand to have a meaningful life, I need to find meaning in the responsibility of different titles I have in life.

I set goals in these different titles I have, like dentist, father, husband, son, community member, etc. I have twenty year goals broken down into ten year, five year, yearly and monthly goals. And I review these goals with my teachers.

We have three team members in our office and we are all leaders. However, there is only one boss and that is me. I have to have a clear vision of what we, the team, can accomplish. My wife, Karen, is also a team member and we work quite well together. It took several years to set a few rules we follow. We treat each other with respect and integrity both at home and the office. Karen understands at the practice, I am her boss which means she supports me in being the office leader. Karen explains the rules: Many gray areas exist when you are a husband/ wife team. Differentiating work from family can be challenging at times. We don't hold grudges. If there is a conflict, we talk about it. We always look for win-win situations. It's not fun for one to win and the other to lose. We don't have to agree on everything. But it is important for us to support each other if one were to make a decision and the other one follows. We also know our limits, and respect when the other doesn't want to talk about the office. Karen adds, "As a leader, I have had to accept Josh is the boss. He sees the big picture and I am better at implementing the big picture. I motivate my team by empowering them to make decisions on how to implement the bigger picture. I do instill guidance when needed and set clear expectations."

We, as dentists, are gods at our office. Both FACE and Blatchford create a humbling experience to help you open your eyes to your current situation. This has helped me grow. I am the dad to two young kids. No one taught me how to be a dad. I just learned to act like a dad. At work and in the community, I act like a leader. I continue to act like a leader by continually surrounding myself with people who are smarter than me, by reading and learning. Karen says, "Some new skills I have been developing this past year are verbal skills for an insurance independent office, case presentation for large treatment plans and the verbal skills and networking skills with a desire to be a better leader."

Six months into our new start up office, our goal is $600K. We are working 183 days, taking two weeks vacation time and taking more than 200 hours of continuing education. We have a nanny who watches our children full time but when we take continuing education, we like to travel with them.

We have really emphasized community involvement by working with local businesses, being a dental consultant for the local hospital, active member of Rotary and Toastmasters. We are Ambassadors for AZ Dental Assoc. and members of the Art Council. We want to be the official dentist for several pro sport teams. Our goal is to attract clients who are leaders in the community like dignitaries, government officials, business CEOs and important decision makers. We want to do eight full mouth cases and eight smile enhancement cases this year.

We are holding a Town Meeting in our studio. We are involved with the local Biggest Loser of West Valley, working on our Mayor's reelection campaign and sponsoring different music/art events. We always brand our name: Joshua Hong DDS. Karen says, "We are trying to think outside the box by hosting events that create foot traffic and exposure."

Karen adds, "In January, the Cancer Treatment Center of America here in Goodyear sent us their first patient fighting for his life with oral cancer. Dr. Hong is the first dental consultant at any Cancer Treatment Center (there are four in US). Any client who needs any dentistry within two years of starting any chemo or radiation from the shoulders and above must have the dentistry completed before they can start treatment. Not only are we changing the world one smile at a time, we are also saving lives. It is an exciting time!"

We feel we are walking billboards and internal marketing is very important to us. We understand that people do business with people they like. We have check lists for everything. Our systems are written and get modified. If we have a problem, we talk about it and move on to the next project. Karen adds, "to contribute to our efficiency, we have incorporated digital, paperless, Smile Reminder, all cross-trained,

Care Credit, online forms and some other fun toys Dr. Hong utilizes like Diagnodent, Velscope, Basta Gnathograph, fully adjustable articulator.

"At first when Josh told me about Blatchford Solutions, my initial reaction was that we can't afford that right now. However, a little voice said, 'listen to my husband and trust in his instinct because we would find a way to make it happen. It turned out to be one of the best decisions we made. If it feels right, it probably is," Karen says.

Josh adds, "Currently, I do my own hygiene because I like to spend time and make them feel comfortable. The relationship time is essential to build. These are challenging times and I feel we need to be even more proactive to attract patients and make them comfortable enough with us to go ahead with treatment. We need to be even more visible in the community."

I live my life like I have lived my life before and I have a second chance at life. Life brings me much joy and challenges. There is no limit to our achievement. Because I realize I have unlimited potential, I will keep doing things that challenge me. I want to remain in constant contact with FACE and Blatchford.

Karen adds, "Thank you for being our inspiration to follow our dreams. I am fortunate to have such amazing mentors. I feel confident if I don't know the answer, I know where I can find it. We truly appreciate our relationship with Blatchford Team and feel very honored to be in "THE book." Thank you.

Josh concludes, "I have an attitude of gratitude. I have built my dream office on a solid foundation. I have a healthy body and mind I am married to a wonderful wife and have two beautiful children. All this is great fuel for success. My plan is to keep learning and be grateful for what I have. I need to be focused and disciplined on achieving my goals and dream big."

www.joshuahongdds.com

Dr. Josh Hong completes FACE Institute.
Dr. Gerald Preiner, Dr. Josh Hong, Dr. Tom Basta.

THE MYSTERY OF PATIENT DECISION MAKING

We are constantly amazed by how we are all so different. From the initial phone conversation to a possible stalled relationship at "let me think about it," we are trying to figure out others, what's wrong with them, what is wrong with us and why they are not like us. We are perplexed when a decision is made so quickly and are frustrated when there is a non-decision. How can we all be so different?

Psychologists present theories on personality development and argue their cases. Human behavior is a complex and changing dynamic. There are few solid classic answers.

Many decisions today about dentistry are now optional. Because what we have to offer is no longer a needed service (like emergency room medicine), we now must become mini-psychologists and make some inroads in understanding human behavior.

What we do know is everyone comes pre-loaded from the factory. We are born with certain distinguishing styles, pace, personalities and because of this, develop definite skills in making life work and dealing with others, including how we make decisions.

The first key is to know and understand ourselves. This is huge and will never be fully accomplished. Are you not still learning life lessons? Can we change? What effect is our environment, our birth order, our friends, our home situation and past life choices? Does our past dictate our decision making style?

Because two people interact in a sales conversation and one of them is almost a total unknown (your new patient), it would be a real asset to assess yourself or have a counselor do a third party assessment of you. One of the pitfalls in sales is to think everyone makes decisions and has the same values as you. Teeth, their pathology and how they look are exceedingly important to you yet will be much lower on the priority list for others.

Before cosmetics entered dentistry, diagnosis was based on pathology, not desire. Once our guests became aware of appearance choices which were not necessary, sales skills became mandatory. With the explosion of web traffic and inquiries, we must learn to work quickly with people making inquiries who are sometimes just a few degrees above the dreaded cold calls to someone seeking action now. We must become so aware of others personalities and how they make decisions about their appearance.

We cannot use our predetermined personality traits as an excuse for behavior or conversation if we are to be successful in business and sales. Know yourself and meet them more than half way.

Awareness of how we attract or offend others is so important. Yet, even more than awareness about ourselves are the absolutes of taking action in learning skills to put ourselves in a more neutral zone when dealing with others. Listen on the phone for clues about their pace and drive through their questions, demands or hesitations. Your job is to match their pace, be focused and patient. Put them in the driver's seat.

Ultimately, it is the guest's decision, not ours. We cannot put pressure on our guests. Particular personality types are more quiet, need information, confirmation and time. The decision making process can take two years. Your personality may perceive the case is lost. Here are some ways to keep the relationship going without pressure while the decision making process is occurring:

- If you have uncovered in the initial relationship building, an interest in something outside the office as animals, wine, sports or food, good for you. This then is an opening to share a new restaurant for lunch, a wine tasting, dog show, etc. A phone call or card about that subject could continue every couple months. This does not need to be a mutual subject but one you have recognized as important to them. You might learn something, too.

- If a case could be perceived by the guest as "complex," arrange for non-pressured, non-clinical setting to have you, the guest and a specialist to lunch and become acquainted as people. You would need to work with your specialist and let them know the purpose and goal.
- If you have been a good listener from the start, usually you can recognize the signs of a more cautious decision maker. Assure them in the consult process, with "you are in charge. You can do the work a little at a time or all at once. You can choose to have me do the work or someone else. We want to support you in making your decision but the time frame is definitely up to you." And then, be comfortable with it.

How people make decisions is a life-long learning process and we, in dentistry, are just starting the race. It's not over till it's over.

Bill Blatchford DDS

These "**Blatchford Power Questions**" were developed by Dr. Bill Blatchford and are intended to guide the doctor through the initial new patient consultation.

How can I help you?
Tell me more about that…
Have you considered what this treatment/result might mean to you?
How long has this been a problem?
Have you considered how this affects your life?
Where are you in your research?
Have you considered a budget for this?
What do you mean by "that's a lot of money"?
What would work for you? (what monthly payment works?)
Do you have a time frame?
What would you like to do next?

DO YOU WANT FRIES WITH YOUR BURGER?

McDonald's has made money with the easy question always asked, "Do you want fries with your burger?" What do you suppose the answer is the majority of time? Are you offended when you are asked? Of course not. It is simply a choice.

In sales, this is called "taking the order." It is so easy and profitable to apply to dentistry. As the worst single tooth scenario is usually diagnosed on a recare patient, ask if they want fries with their burger by saying, "The one next to it is very much the same. Would you like to do that at the same time?" Will you cry if the answer is no or will the patient be upset you asked?

Even when a guest is in the chair for a unit of dentistry, it is acceptable for the assistant to ask, "Would you like fries with your burger?" Referring to the tooth next or opposing, any team member needs to ask for the order. How much more time does it take to prepare and seat two teeth? Time is about the same as one and here is the business reason—your net nearly triples when you do two units at a time.

Every guest is well aware of their time, busyness and the need for efficiency. You know your patient's mouths and habits well enough that you are really offering them more time in their busy lives and serving them well by making the offer.

Make "Fries with Your Burger" a team slogan. It is fine for patients to say no but you always offer. Dental labs indicate 95% of their work is single tooth dentistry. We even have team members asking, "Would you like fries with that burger?" The patient laughs and says, "What do you mean?" Make it fun and create an opportunity for your guests to say "yes" to fries.

Bill Blatchford DDS

BLATCHFORD GUIDING PRINCIPLES FOR SALES

- Buy a three minute egg timer for the dentist to turn over upon entering hygiene recare exam. When the sand finishes, so does the dentist
- Our goal in sales is not for the dentist and team to EDUCATE the patient to do the treatment themselves
- Give your guests the opportunity to talk 80% of the time and you are allotted only 20% of the time
- Don't speak "dental-ese" to patients. They don't know what you are talking about
- Do not send new patient forms in the mail. It's busy work, they forget and then you have made them wrong. This is not a good beginning
- Every patient is an "A" patient until they prove themselves otherwise
- Ask team and guests about their favorite subject—themselves
- Place your demo skull in the oak case, put it in the trunk of your car and throw away the key
- Greet guests by name when they enter your office
- New patient screening exam by the Doctor lasts three minutes
- Give "A" patients a second chance, but not a third.
- Develop a team library of books, CD's, videos of motivating, positive material on leadership, sales, marketing, and attitude adjustments
- Have your own mouth restored to ideal by paying full fee to another dentist
- Never criticize another dentist's work. Say, "It looks like dentistry has been an important priority for you. Good for you."
- Avoid educating with x-rays. Your guests do not see the different little gray lines. They trust you to make the call.
- Do not draw tooth pictures on the bracket covers for patients to understand.
- At the sound of the first technical term, you lose your guest even though they may nod their head in understanding.

- Present life time treatment plans to your guests. Do not become known as "Dr. Patch."
- Practice new sales scripts with video at team meetings until you feel comfortable
- Sales are mastered by everyone on the team, not just the Doctor
- In sales, know your fees. You lose cases by having them ask someone else
- Watch great interviewers on television to see how they create relationships and gain people's trust by asking questions.
- Closing a case is not, "do you understand?" or "do you have any questions?"
- Don't prejudge your patients. They will continually surprise you.
- Do not diagnose your patient's pocketbooks
- In successful sales, one real key is to ask questions.
- Thank every patient for caring about their teeth, no matter the condition of their mouth
- Diagnose life-time dentistry. It may be completed a quadrant at a time, however, you and your patient know where you are headed.
- Decide what you want your reputation to be in 20 years. Diagnose that kind of dentistry and treat guests who see value in what you have to offer.
- When a new patient arrives, greet them by name. Shake their hand and look them right in the eyes
- Encourage your team to be genuinely interested in people by asking questions
- Let your team enroll the dentistry.
- Shift your sales paradigm to "No one needs dentistry."
- All people want to look good, feel good and last a long time. Have your guest thinking on these lines.
- Everyone who shows up in a dental office is seeking help
- Ask future focused questions like "What do you want your smile to be like in 20 years?"
- Patients want the benefits of treatment—not the process
- Ask questions like, "How would a nice looking smile affect your job?"
- The dentist is only needed for technical advice after the guest has said "yes."

- No patient ever comes in with a problem. You cannot solve their problem before they own it. You will turn them off completely.
- If a new person calls to have their teeth cleaned, clean their teeth.
- Become skilled at conversation so patient talk centers around "smile talk."
- Decide what is your standard of care for which you want to be remembered and diagnose to that level on every guest.
- A closing question is "Can we go ahead and schedule an appointment for you?"
- Never send a guest to your receptionist for financial arrangements until you have closed the case and the guest has said, "YES, I want to go ahead."
- The first 12 words out of your mouth need to be a compliment.
- Patient's concerns about treatment are usually time, money and pain
- During the three minute hygiene screening exam, the Doctor is asking four questions: Do they have teeth? Are there holes in the teeth? Is there infection? Is there potential for treatment?
- For sales, digital pictures are unbeatable. It is instant and patient's awareness is keen.
- When the new guest says "yes" to records, they include: digital pictures, FMX, digital pan, bite-wings and study models.
- Do not try to compete on the basis of price. There will always be someone who will do it for less.
- Watch the Doctor start buying back the case as tooth pictures are being drawn and explanations of how to do a root canal is shared. See the guests eyes glaze over.
- Avoid diagnosing guests according to how they look, speak, what you think about their insurance or what their house payment might be
- Help people have the dentistry they deserve by mastering your sales skills
- Learn to be comfortable with silence. Ask a question and let them answer
- Don't put words in people's mouths and ASSume you know. Listen up.

- Let the guest view their pictures and ask, "What do you like best about your smile?' Is there anything you would like to be different?"
- Dentistry is an option, not a right.
- Sales is never mastered as the marketplace is constantly changing
- You feel phony when learning new skills like sales. Stick with it and you will feel uncomfortable then comfortable and finally integrated. Most people drop out of any new skill at phony.
- Create a small consult room for three equal size chairs and no table
- If you feel the need to demonstrate fixed treatment, do not remove the teeth. All they see is pegs. It is FIXED so glue them on the preps.
- Do not present Plan A, B and C. Present only the best and phase the treatment if needed.
- Never present treatment before the patient is ready
- If money is never mentioned as a concern, changes are good they are really not interested.
- Welcome your guest's questions. You know they are interested.
- The Doctor tells the guest the fees.
- The Doctor does not make the financial arrangements.
- Dealing with "objections"
- Your competition practices sales skills daily.
- Be a Nordstrom—always compliment your guests on their choices
- When a guest says "no," it simply means, "no, not now." Move on and don't try to talk them into it.
- When a new guest arrives, greet them and take them immediately to the consult room for your conversation in private
- Have your medical history forms and entry papers on your website.
- In a sales conversation when the guest asks about time, you ask "what is it about time that concerns you? The length of the appointment or how soon can we complete?" Do not ASSume you know what they are asking.

11

COMMUNICATION

COMMUNICATION

Morning huddle is a coaching time, **looking four days out**. Find ten minutes a day to do this with your team. It is critical that everyone is on time for this meeting. The receptionist needs to communicate at the morning huddle to Dr. and staff what is needed to make goal every day. Start with an inspirational message from the Doctor with enthusiasm. Doctor always coaches to goal four days out. Coaching four days out is critical, if you are to reach your long terms goals.

An evening meeting held for five minutes at the end of the day forms completion. What is important is the exchange of compliments, what worked well and if it did not work well, what they will do about it to make it different tomorrow. A copy of tomorrow's schedule is distributed.

Communicate with weekly staff meeting and the BMW 4x4 where skills are built. BMW 4 x 4 is Blatchford Motivational Workshop held for four hours every four weeks and focuses on skill building (role-playing, video-taping, scripting, erasing cancellations, marketing brainstorming).

USING THE RESOLUTION CYCLE

Learning to communicate about upsetting situations and unfulfilled expectations takes focus and an intention to recommit to the team. We all hear things at work that jar our senses. Sometimes, we may feel left out. We can feel picked on or feel we just don't fit in. Sometimes we are bold and sometimes we are very shy. Sometimes, we feel isolated and alone. How we communicate our feelings and reactions makes a real difference in the continuity of a team.

One of the first premises about feelings and communicating them is "choice." We are always at choice in how we choose to conduct ourselves, react to others, or present ourselves to others. You can say, "He really made me angry." The truth is I chose to become angry over what he said. This is probably the most adult form of conduct and responsibility we know. It is a difficult lesson to learn, yet once learned, there is real power in knowing you do have more control over your emotions than you realized.

We see team being formed because of a leader's sharing of his/her **Vision**. At the top of the cycle, the leader's passionate vision is what has inspired us to want to help the cause or be part of a greater effort than ourselves. We all want to make a difference in this life. Most of us are searching for that cause or leader where we can share our talents and find that end result so rewarding.

The leader of a church, school, community, nation, dental practice, or business has a vision or direction to which we find commonality and chose to aspire. The words of that vision inspire us to join that team. You see, without vision, we are just existing, coming to work and just going through the motions until 5 PM. We have no vested interest and really don't care about the results. It is just a job. Therefore, without vision, a real team of people moving together will not form.

Team is the group that joins together in a community of results. We want something to happen differently. The team is working together for a common good and they keep the bigger picture in their minds which is the Vision.

In any marriage, group of friends, dental office or political party, something can occur which causes **Conflict**. In a team, where there is conflict, we no longer see the Vision as clearly. It is becoming clouded with words, actions or innuendoes. At this point, we are not moving forward. We are dead in the water. We may even be moving backwards until this is resolved.

Sub groups of workers, church members, nations, legislators or dental staff may form. The bigger vision is not there and smaller groups opposing each other may form. It may be groups or it could be just two people who feel misunderstood but do not have the resolve or skill to communicate well. The greatest causes in all mankind can be lost here, right here, right in front of our eyes and we can't see it or we are stuck in one of the opposing groups.

In conflict, some people chose to quit and go away. Some may quit but continue to look like they are part of the team but they are dead weight. They are obstacles in our way.

Our primary goal should be to get back to Vision as that is the only avenue by which we can continue to move forward. Have you ever wondered why soap operas are fascinating to people? If things are too good, a conflict or surprise is written into the script to keep turmoil going. How boring if everything turned out well!

It may take some outside coaching or help to recognize the 'ugly pink elephant in the room' and create some action. What needs to happen is the Conflict between the groups, troops, individuals or partners need to be **Confronted.** An adult confrontation is a win-win and does not start out "YOU did…." The greater good is at stake here and unless the conflict is confronted, we cannot return to vision. We will stay in the muddle, good people will leave and our dreamed of results will not occur.

An adult confrontation starts out "Here is what I see. This occurred and I felt...." What did you see? Is there anyway we can resolve this?"

Then the valuable **negotiation** can occur. Can each party see how the other viewed the occurrence? Can we find common ground to move forward? Can each give a little and make a **resolution** to move forward with new agreements for conduct?

Once the resolution occurs, the conflict is resolved and we move again to Vision and the glorious time of real TEAM.

Every Doctor or team member can recall or cite right now events that have occurred in their life where conflicts became the norm and ruined any chance of great results. Conflicts are normal occurrences. It is what you, and your team, choose to do about the conflict. The choice is to head toward resolve to get back to team or to wallow in the mud of conflict for the rest of your journey.

Happy Travels!

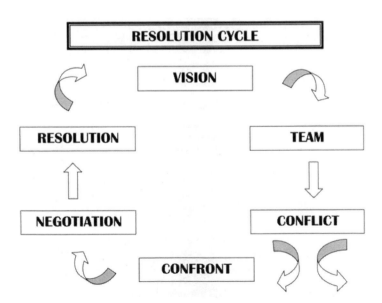

TEAM BUILDING

Group Problem Solving

- All ideas are good ideas
- Listen to the whole idea—don't interrupt
- No attacking ideas or solutions
- Build on each suggestion or idea
- No defending any ideas
- Be unattached to your ideas as being the right ones
- Allow the group to formulate the solution—synergistically
- Be open to solutions you never thought of
- Believe there is a solution—to every problem
- Be willing for the right solution to surface

To instill the kind of vitality needed to fuel the vision, we need:

- A mutual feeling of caring about each other, a feeling that our colleagues and team members are WALKING BUNDLES OF UNIQUENESS
- The freedom to be emotionally vulnerable, open and receptive to the wants, needs, problems and possibilities of others
- A reduced amount of "telling"—that is, abrasiveness, knee-jerk machismo, directness, pushing and crowding. Let team members feel involved

BLATCHFORD GUIDING PRINCIPLES IN COMMUNICATING

- The agenda for team meetings comes from a week's worth of thinking by team and Doctor. Stick to agenda only, no new "urgent" items
- Doctor does not lead the team meeting
- Team meetings are focused on "forwarding the action." Look for bottom-line action, a source person to be responsible and a completion date
- Write a "no whining" agreement. When a staff member or Doctor sees a problem, instead of grumping about it, your conversation must be focused on a solution
- Stamp out immediately any friction between team or Doctor
- Learn to make specific requests of team with deadlines to move the action forward. Team then can negotiate
- Learn to communicate with your team. Silence can be misinterpreted as anger, upset, shyness or snobbery

12

SCHEDULING

BLOCKS

One of the top systems Blatchford advocates creates efficiency, promotes larger conversations with patients about treatment, encourages team work, promotes a team goal, promotes organization and leads to a happy Doctor. What more could you want?

Block Booking is not difficult. Everyone understands the concept. What block booking takes is total commitment to make it happen. We are all looking for cracks in the wall of leadership. If you as leader allow scheduling to falter when you had committed to block booking, NO KIDDING, your team sees this and will follow accordingly.

It is very clear when Bill is coaching his Doctors, if block booking and daily goals are being followed by looking at the numbers. That is the value of coaching by an outsider. Yes, Bill is on your team but he will not allow your excuses.

BLATCHFORD GUIDING PRINCIPLES FOR BLOCKS

- Block booking from 1:30 PM to 3:00 is the "aerobic phase of dentistry" These are single fillings, checks, adjustments, etc.
- When you start diagnosing life time dentistry, the number of emergency patient decreases
- Productivity only occurs when the burr is turning
- Presenting lifetime dentistry which is more permanent is a way to fill the morning blocks
- Have your young child write a sign: "We want our mommy/daddy home in the evening and Saturdays." Post in the window with your new hours.
- Reserve each day from 3 PM to 4:30 for seating crown and bridge. It is rewarding, easy and guests love it. Your receptionist now leaves on time too.
- Work a four (three) day week starting on Monday
- Working evenings and Saturdays will produce a real following of "C" patients
- No patient leaves without another appointment
- New guests usually call to have their teeth cleaned. Agree and then ask "would you like for the Doctor to check them, too?" 99% will agree.
- Confirm your hygiene patients by email
- Buy enough tray setups to be prepared for the day
- When a dentist has outside business interests, make it clear to callers and the dentist, Job 1 is first class dentistry. The Doctor can return calls only at lunch and after work.
- The hygienist calls perio and injected patients in the evening
- If you are using a dragnet to canvas the city to fill hygiene, you are encouraging your practice to be filled with "C" patients
- If the hygienist has a new patient scheduled in the morning for a cleaning, be totally prepared for the possibility of full records
- Work a four hour morning and take a full hour for lunch
- Eighty percent of Doctor goal should be met in the four hour morning
- Schedule your consult appointment with new guests for right after lunch

- Block booking means you see only one patient at a time
- Put a seat belt on your Doctor chair to encourage Doctor to stay seated until scheduled treatment is complete
- Does your day start with four people in chairs at 8 AM? Why?
- New guests are scheduled to have their teeth cleaned in the morning when the office is not so busy
- Emergencies are scheduled in the afternoon only, unless it is a real emergency on one of your own patients. Reserve 1:30 to 2:30 only
- Hang your doctor's roller skates in the closet and throw away the key
- Start, Finish, Stop. Do not go on to the next patient until all scheduled treatment is finished
- Schedule no more than three patients for the Doctor each morning
- One receptionist can handle everything in the front if block scheduling is strict and the team is mastering sales skills.
- If a guest is late, do not try to complete all scheduled treatment and make the next guest late. Release them on time
- Create a new reputation of timeliness by seeing your guests on time and finishing on time
- Have a three day turn around agreement with your lab to seat permanent work
- Don't mix charity patients on your productive days. Quarterly, schedule a volunteer day when all team serves the needy
- Don't take charts or x-rays home at night. This includes doing computer work at home
- Schedule to a production goal every day
- If the Doctor chooses to treat family and friends at no or reduced fee during productive hours, the full fee is counted (production/collection) for bonus calculations
- Keep your watch five minutes fast
- Do not allow an emergency patient to disrupt a previously scheduled "A" guest
- Plan your office calendar 12 months in advance
- Doctor never makes appointments for guests. "I want to see you in a week" is taken literally by patients.
- Schedule one hour team meetings once a week whether you need them or not

- Schedule team meetings during productive time, not during your team's lunch hour
- The purpose of the morning huddle is to connect as a team and to coach to results
- If hygiene is part time, schedule your team meeting so all are present. Take a vacation every six weeks to sharpen the saw. You can stay home but cannot visit the office
- All team take vacations at the same time. If you are gone and we did well, we might not need you
- Schedule your last hygiene patient 45 minutes before the end of the day so all can leave on time.

ANTICIPATING A
FATHER-DAUGHTER PRACTICE

Dr. Les Miller of Lawrence, Kansas

I have always loved clinical dentistry. I have had a CEREC since 2003 but have struggled with the leadership and the business of dentistry. In 2006, I was producing $55K a month and had $120K debt on the practice. I was 60 and retiring was a financial impossibility. My daughter Kelly was a second year student at UMKC School of Dentistry.

I hired Bill because of his ability to customize to fit my specific needs and his straight coaching. I truly wanted to get from where I was to where I needed to be. After about six months, I had increased my collections to $56K. In hindsight, I thought that I could get results by putting Bill's systems in place and expect the team to take it from there. That is like preparing for an exam by placing the test book under your head while you sleep and expecting osmosis to do the job for you.

I needed my team to be with me to make this happen. I asked them for their opinion as to why we weren't getting the big results. The team felt they were doing all the things that the more successful teams were doing. Well then, why weren't we getting those results? I took my team to the next seminar with instructions to mix and ask questions with the other 25 offices. What were they doing that we were missing? All we needed to do was duplicate what those successful practices were doing.

Part of the problem we discovered was we had a staff, not a team. The other part of the problem was me and my leadership. I had to get out of my comfort zone and be a better leader. If I were a better leader, a team would form because they would have a common purpose and vision. I promised myself to be accountable for the leadership of the practice. I have demanded accountability from each member of my team and I have expected them to hold me accountable.

We set our collection goal at $90K which is a daily goal of $6K. We have reached $87K, our highest ever and are pleased. The big deal is what happened to our profitability. In one year, my net income more than doubled, while my overhead dropped from 65% to 52%. My practice debt will be paid off over a year ahead of schedule this summer. Now I am really looking forward to my daughter joining me when she graduates. Our goal is to increase the number of new patients entering our practice (not my forte), as my daughter Kelly is graduating in May. Initially, she can be my assistant to gain some knowledge and she will do dentistry two days a week and I will work three. My goal is to help her increase her speed, have her gain a bigger picture of all the treatment possibilities in dentistry and share my passion.

By the end of the year I plan to have increased my production by 5% ($2500/mo) and have Kelly producing $30,000/mo. Our new patient flow will need to be around 25 per month. The office will move from 3.5 days per week seeing patients to 5 full days, possibly 6. We have three team members at present plus me. Our BAM is $66,000. When Kelly starts, she probably won't have her dental license yet and will basically be there to support the team as an assistant. She will also learn the systems we have in place, learn the scripting, cross train, and hopefully learn some from me. I do not plan to have her salary as part of the BAM. Hopefully she will soon be adding production after getting her license by doing dentistry. An additional support team member will be added when the demand is there. As this will increase the BAM, the team will be involved with that decision.

All of this will require a team effort. Kelly and I and the rest of the team will need to become more involved in the community. We will also be expanding our services through dental appliances to treat OSA, esthetic dentures, and Dr. Kim Kutsch's Carifree science. My team and I are extremely excited to have Kelly join the practice. I know that I will have so much fun in the process. At the same time, I know that

I will be challenged by these changes in our practice and the condition of today's economy.

All of us will have to grow personally to achieve these goals. Whether Kelly stays here in Lawrence for the long haul or ends up practicing dentistry in Ireland in a few years (there is a long term boy-friend involved here), I know that this opportunity to practice dentistry with Kelly is here only once. I can hardly wait!

Bill and Carolyn have made a big difference in my life. They came up with a Custom Plan for my practice. They and their team were there for support. Bill challenged me when I needed it. I know that Kelly and my team and I will continue to grow professionally and personally with Bill's coaching.

Dr. Les Miller's model train hobby.

THE BLOCK PARTY

Scheduling in blocks of time is not just an academic exercise. Almost every dentist knows of this path to profitability and ease of practice. Fewer dentists actually adhere to it. Why doesn't everyone use it since it is so simple? The answer is: a matter of the leader's commitment, drawing your line in the sand.

Your gross and net are largely determined by what you choose to do in the first two hours of practice. If the leader sets the stage with coaching to treat one guest only with four units of crown and bridge, three hours of veneer preps or a cosmetic denture, your day will be wonderful and goals are met.

If, on the other hand, your leadership or lack thereof, did not draw a line in the sand and you are scheduled for two hygiene checks before beginning a single filling and a "look-see," your whole day is not much fun. The real question is, how committed are you to a perfect schedule?

The Doctor determines a total daily goal by digging deep within to examine life style, financial goals and his/her own willingness to move forward into uncharted territory. Looking five or ten years ahead, what would you like your net to be? What is it now? Create a plan (scheduling, skill building, marketing, conversations, etc) to reach that five year goal for net.

From the five year goal for net, what do you want to net in the next 12 months? Divide that number into 12 equal periods to set your daily goal. Many Doctors feel BAM determines the daily goal. We coach you to push yourself beyond this with thinking into what will make my life work well and reach my goals? I guarantee your team will cheer you on if your goal is higher than BAM.

Your commitment is demonstrated by establishing a daily office goal which is comprised of individual hygiene (should be $800-$1000) and a total Doctor goal. In your morning blocks, 80% of the Doctor goal should be accomplished in a four hour morning.

Work with your team on skill building and conversations with guests to make your morning blocks sacred. What is the production amount you need to have in the morning blocks before a guest's name goes on the books? Could everyone on your team explain the philosophy of blocks and what is your block minimum? Does your team know the figure of 80% of Doctor goal? Does everyone on your team think blocks, anticipate conversations and execute well? They will if there is a fair bonus attached to their accountability. Your team will make a consistent difference and contribution if they feel there will be rewards.

Your commitment is shown by your leadership in a meaningful ten minute morning meeting where blocks are supported and schedules discussed. Are you coaching four days out? Does your walk follow your talk? If the morning blocks are not happening, how do you change thinking, desire and action? Write on your hand, "If it is going to be, it is up to me."

Block booking makes your office experience different. Catch the enthusiasm and pass it on to your guests. One benefit of the block scheduling is total service to your guest. Once one decides to improve their health and smile, they want it now and expect focus and experience. You can present block booking to your guests by saying, "we do this so you have 100% of our Doctor's time." The team then needs to ensure the Doctor stays with the patient and completes the treatment by having a perio patient scheduled in hygiene and no other patient (not even a "quick, look-see") is allowed opposite your sacred block. Here again, you walk your talk. You promised your patient they would be THE ONLY ONE. Do it!

Leadership is called forth to help alleviate the team's fear of a blocked patient being a "no show." If you collect in advance for the treatment, your guest is as committed as you. If your team has created a brand of "on time" behavior, like patients are attracted to that commitment and will respect your time. If you have built skills in sincerely allowing your guest to feel their decision to proceed is theirs and not being motivated by your goal or your agenda, you will have a solid patient experience.

A short but important evening meeting, post production, filled with sincere specific compliments for team and looking at the week's schedule will reinforce the commitment to blocks.

Another important part of block booking skills is to "know when to hold them, know when to fold them." Hold the morning block until the afternoon of the day before. The whole team knows the amount of treatment acceptable to have a guest have the block. If by the afternoon, it is not happening; your team can create a meaningful morning with several patients from your short call list who are waiting for treatment. Rejoice and make them feel as special as your larger treatment.

Real block booking allows you to have time this week for a guest who accepts a larger case. If you are booked with blocks three weeks out, you have probably set a low daily goal or your team is not privy to the goal. Real block booking happens every day because of a committed leader who walks the talk. Email us some of your schedules. Show us your blocks. Make it happen. Give it your best!

13

LEADERSHIP REVISITED

LEADERSHIP REVISITED–
KICKING IT UP A NOTCH

The dentist's ability to lead is the most critical piece for practice success. Earlier, we shared the basic essentials of building a strong leadership position with vision, communication and decision making. A number of just graduating dentists are seeking our business coaching advice even before finding a place to practice. These are leaders in the making.

Now, we want to share the next level in leadership which must inspire. It is principle centered and strong. In framing a strong leader, the strength is in the vision and passion for life. The strength is not in being dogmatic, 'my way or the highway' and walking over people. We need strong leaders in dentistry who are willing to stand for what is right for them. We need passion in the profession.

If you are not the leader you would like to be and the leader of whom your team dreams, coaching can help you create a stronger stand. The result would be a team who is accountable and excited to march forth with you to get the job done.

HOPE IS NOT A BUSINESS STRATEGY

During challenging and changing economics, a dentist needs a plan to provide emotional stability in projecting optimism for yourself, your team and most important, for your patients. A plan keeps your fears at bay like the confidence of a road map. You anticipate making the tough decisions because you are the owner and leader.

As the media continues to whip us into a frenzy, patients start to pull in. As your staff perceives patients pulling in, your team starts questioning and verbalizing their own fears and now, the dentist is feeling concerned. A real plan of action is needed as to how and when decisions must be made by the leader. Hoping things will get better on their own is not a good small business strategy.

Create a plan of action which will serve you during tight times and when you are "in the money." Every practice is unique yet, there are commonalities which must be addressed. Your largest expense in a general practice is staff. This is also one of the few pieces of overhead which you can control. The national average now is over 30% spent on team. The number should be 20%. Blatchford offices really work at being 20% including bonus and benefits to team. If you were producing $100K a month with staff costing 30% and now production/collection drop 20% to $80K monthly average, you staff is now costing 37.5% or $10,000 over 20% which could be used for education, marketing or debt reduction.

Too often, dentists staff for the month of their highest production ever or the number they have heard their neighbor dentist has produced, rationalizing, "we have one extra in case someone is sick." Good people like to be busy and challenged. This is not the time for "extra staff."

At this juncture, Doctors decide to "outrun their overhead" by producing more. What treatment have you turned away? What patients could you not see? How will you produce more? Hope will not work here.

The better plan is to create solid systems and work efficiently so that three well-qualified team can do the work of five or six. These are the toughest decisions a Doctor has to make for staff becomes like family and are good friends. No one said it would be easy to be the leader in tight times. These decisions come back to the leader's vision, the importance of which cannot be overlooked. If your vision is to be a protectorate no matter what the cost to you, then keep your large staff. That is a decision, too. If this is truly your choice, to spend the money on team, even if you do not have a fully scheduled day, then DO NOT COMPLAIN TO THEM THAT YOU HAVE NO MONEY.

With technology today, becoming paperless and using a communication tool like Smile Reminder, one person in the front can well handle a $1M practice. Even health history and entry forms can be accomplished easily on-line. A great website with map, easy directions, team introductions, and, patient testimonials can speak well to an inquiring patient.

Block booking is essential for a happy team of three. Know your daily goal and what dollar amount of treatment must be in the morning blocks. Everyone plays the game full out.

Another great system is to have the hygienist and assistant complete the check out with each guest by doing the scheduling, entering treatment, producing an insurance form and collecting the money. Thus, your receptionist can concentrate on phone conversations of a selling nature and be able to service well those patients present in your practice.

This is not the time to drop insurance. Stay the course and communicate with patients about their options. This is the time to add sales skills and learn to converse with patients about their hopes and dreams. Forget the old pressure techniques of "you NEED to have this done NOW" or trying to educate patients. They will respond to easy open-ended questions about their smile and dreams. You can reach beyond "just fix the worst one now."

With a team of three, you will be in a position to bonus, even in tight times. Team becomes very motivated with a bonus system which is paid monthly. Who wouldn't want to lead a motivated team? Your leadership decisions will create a happy place, even in tight times.

Bill Blatchford DDS

MAKING BOLD MOVES
OR RETREAT TO SAFETY?

I have been asked why some Doctors can really pull it together while many perceive they are happy where they are while others struggle making decisions and taking action. There are lots of answers and reasons why we are all different yet, there are certain characteristics of very successful doctors I have observed. It is about behavior and behavior always is a choice, unless someone has a gun to your head. In all situations, there is behavior that works and behavior that doesn't work.

Our growing tendency in America is to blame someone else for our behavior that doesn't produce the results we want. Or, we don't know what we really want but feel that whatever we are doing today isn't it. Dentists are small fish in a big puddle yet, most of us spend time comparing, idolizing, wishing and hoping. But, when it comes time to make the big decisions, the actions are one of retreating back to their comfort zone.

Successful dentists exhibit behavior which is bold. They have taken the time to see clearly who they are and where they want to position themselves. Their vision is in place and they believe it will happen. They surround themselves with a team who see the same and support that vision. They act like that leader. They start exhibiting behavior that will have them reach that path and they start acting as if they have reached that position. Asking Tom Watson, the founder of IBM how they became so successful, he said, "We figured out what we wanted IBM to look like in ten years, and then we started behaving like that from the start."

Most people will tell you they will do most anything to change things in their life. Is that true? Generally, people will do and behave in a manner that is comfortable for them. They will do anything that doesn't require them to step outside their comfort zone. But the moment they reach the terror zone, that point where we all have to take the proverbial leap of faith, most people will rather step backward into safety than step forward into growth.

People (and dentists are especially good at this) base their goals on what they have accomplished before. If they have always increased by 5%, that is then the goal. Base your goals on what you really want and make the bold decisions to make that dream goal a reality.

What does it take to move you out of your comfort zone? The pain of the present must be so clear and hurt bad enough that you can taste, know and feel the new and better results will be worth going through the unknown for you. What would it take to support a new bold goal, be it moving, adding another practice or changing the direction of your practice and treatments?

Changing the behavior of the Doctor comes first and the right team members will see it and want to be a part of your growth and change. The right people will support your decisions. Behave as if you are on the path now.

We need strong systems to support a change. Do you have business systems in place which create respect from your patients, your team and yourself? Time is a big indicator of respect. Do you have a systematic daily booking which allows your guests to feel served well in a timely manner or are you still double booking and a single crown prep appointment has the patient holding on for two hours?

Making the bold decisions creates a team with systems of accountability and rewards. They behave differently because they are needed and wanted. They hunger for regular and clear vehicles for communication. Do you value your team enough to train together on a monthly basis so everyone is speaking as one? Or do you have layers of paperwork and managers of managers with more people doing the paperwork than the actual dentistry?

Do you have hygienists and assistants scheduling, entering treatment, producing insurance forms and collecting money? How would this change the sense of service in your practice?

Furthermore, do you feel the pain enough to see how hard you are working to produce $1M and take home only $200,000 and that includes debt reduction? Behavior that works is being bold enough to do something about your pain. Are you ready to change your behavior? Do you deserve to win bigger?

Bill Blatchford DDS

TRANSITION MADE PERFECT

Dr. Tom DeLopez of Tallahassee, Florida

Already successful, why would you add a larger practice to your existing practice?

- I wanted to do more of the high end challenging dentistry and I wanted to create my ideal practice
- The team had more ambitious goals than mine and they were on fire to double the practice, work the same number of hours and take six weeks off a year. The only way to meet their goals was to do more crown and bridge. I love designing smiles, crown and bridge.
- Bill said 'go for it, pay him what he wants and do it.' His nudge pushed me off the fence. I would not have done it without Bill's encouragement and advice. We were only three months into the coaching program but all of Bill's coaching was helping us go gang-busters, so he had established a trust with me.

The terms that made it work were:

- The seller's office was very close to my office.
- The seller did solid dentistry, so I was not buying trouble. As he did large amalgams there were a lot of patients who could benefit from crown and bridge. Many patients will step up and do the work and many will choose to do just one filling at a time and leave.
- I was his personal dentist and we stressed that in the retirement letter
- The fee was half of one year's gross
- The seller and I both sent out welcoming letters
- The seller had chipped front teeth, so I did three ceramic crowns and put his picture in my Smile Gallery on display in the welcome room.

- All the 'new to us' patients were treated like existing patients in that there were no initial exam fees.
- I had initially built my office for two dentists so the facility was ready to handle the increased patient flow.

Melding the two teams:

- I took two of his team but they did not work out. In retrospect, I kept them too long. I was faster to evaluate replacements and a few did not make it.

We made the schedule work by:

- Rigid block booking
- Collecting at time of service, so no billings or receivables to collect
- Small fillings were scheduled at the next recall
- Crowns were done as soon as we could schedule

I never had any doubts. I bought another practice in 1983 and paid for it the first year. I wish I had done Blatchford earlier as I would have purchased another friend's practice when it became available in 1990.

Was this the right move for you?

- Are you kidding? It was more than paid for in two years.
- With people controlling expenses right now, the more patients we have, the better, even if you don't see them for a year or two, they still think you are their dentists and when they break a tooth, they come in for a crown.
- You will lose a lot of these new patients, no matter how well you treat them. They might just not want or value the kind of treatment you provide.

www.tallahasseesmiles.com

*A jubilant Dr. Tom Delopez winning five awards (most ever)
for photography at Florida AGD.*

TIME AND EFFORT VS. RESULTS

We were born into a time and results based world. We think if we work harder and longer, we will achieve our dreams. Our fathers and families are part of this culture and it is so ingrained, we do not see another avenue. We work long hours, more days than necessary, Saturdays and evenings. Some Doctors do not take lunch, thinking they will produce more. It requires a paradigm shift to move from a time and effort thinking to a results based thinking.

The results based thinking is being paid for creativity and you are more creative when you take time away from work and are refreshed. Instead of thinking vacation is a reward for working long hours, think of vacation as a requirement for creativity. How do we create the opportunity for six to eight weeks of vacation?

Our most productive offices are working the least amount of time. Working three days a week, they are discovering taking every sixth week off will increase creativity. It doesn't matter if you leave town or stay and enjoy activities with friends. When Doctors are working six days a week, they fearfully drop one day and production increases. They drop to four days a week and production increases. Why?

You need time away to refresh and be the most effective when you work. What happens in a five day a week practice, Doctor and staff is tired and they take "vacation" at work. They are inefficient and ineffective. They are in a low productivity mode. Team is probably being paid by the hour so why not continue to work and even have some overtime? Work can never be completely finished in a dental office.

Have you noticed some very creative moments come when you are running and exercising? Your mind needs time away to dream and develop solutions and plans. We need to create a new cycle of rejuvenation and a higher level of creativity.

The mechanical stage of time and effort thinking creates burnout. Then, we feel we need a vacation. As a profession, we need to take more time off and think bigger. Our teams are currently on time and effort based economy as this is the thinking of their environment. Moving them to a results-based economy demands an effective bonus system which creates accountability for results. For the paradigm shift to be effective, a team will form when they are paid for their professionalism by being on a salary. The outcome is accountability for results rather than working more hours and making a greater effort.

Ask any team member working a five day week, "If we paid you the same as you are earning now, do you feel you could produce the same or better in four days or even three days?" What do you think the answer will be?

Dr. April Ziegele works three and one half days a week and in the book, *Playing Your 'A' Game,* she relates the average bonus is currently $3100 each above their salaries. The goal is to double that which means two more smiles per bonus time and equals to talking with about ten guests of their dream smile. Team is actively looking for the opportunity. "There is no more complaining, gossiping or whining because we don't have time anymore. We have a credit balance because the team recognizes that is their money. They have bought into the "ownership" of the practice due to bonuses and "it makes my job so much easier," says April.

Dr. Curtis Chan of San Diego makes a point of vacationing every six to eight weeks. He and his wife Mae are madly in love with their four children and take every opportunity to grow and create with them. The team takes turns manning the office and answering the phone but all take vacations at the same time.

If real results are your goal, the profession of dentistry offers you the opportunity to shift from time and effort economy to results based thinking. Take time to regenerate, rejuvenate and recreate. Shift your thinking from working hard and squeezing in a vacation to using time off to reinvigorate your practice.

Bill Blatchford DDS

HAVE YOU REACHED <u>CAPACITY</u>?

We all operate to the level of systems, knowledge and philosophy of which we are familiar. And generally, we operate at our full capacity. We feel busy, possibly overworked and the classic of being under rewarded for our great efforts. Doctors producing $350K annually feel stressed and at capacity while another Doctor grosses $1.5M and feels he couldn't produce anymore.

They are both right. It is your habits, relationships and your structure which keep you where you presently are and keep you at a plateau. Because we feel busy at the level we are, we tend to view others who are producing more as, "they must be cutting corners somewhere and doing something illegal or immoral."

If dentists could visit other practices and see their books, they would be amazed to see the differences in gross and net return. As you move to the larger numbers, it is a given—you must be working the same or fewer regular hour days, not more to produce more. If you are at capacity, how could you fathom someone else doing more dentistry in fewer hours with a small skilled team?

In talking with Doctors, I find there is frustration at the level they are yet they have reached their ceiling of complexity. To gross and net more, changes would need to occur and when you are at capacity, it is difficult to see the changes needed to move to the next level without outside help. Dentists tend to dwell on the HOW rather than the WHAT of an idea.

The bigger picture will be realized by the WHAT. In order for change to occur your WHAT or vision needs to be crystal clear. You need to be able to communicate what you envision with passion and energy to your team so they are moving at the same speed, preferably just ahead of you. The bigger picture of where you are going will motivate people, especially if there is a declared bonus system for team efforts in reaching numbers.

What new numbers? What new treatments will you be learning and adding? What will have you excited enough about the future to make the necessary changes in your systems and thinking to break through your present ceiling?

You must change your own thinking on capacity. Our daughter is in dental school where prepping a crown with waxing, casting takes a full term. Remember feeling at full capacity? Most practicing dentists could now complete their two year clinic requirements in two days. You have grown and react differently.

In rising to the capacity of our systems, we need to change our thinking. As a new pilot, I felt the Cessna 150 landing at 70 miles an hour was at my capacity. The Comanche 260 lands at 90 miles an hour, the Cessna 340 at 130 miles an hour and the F-18 pilot lands at 200 mph on an aircraft carrier. We are held hostage by our habits, thinking and systems.

In creating new systems and thinking for the next level practice, don't worry about the how. Concentrate on the WHAT for you. Consider and get excited about these possibilities:

- Can I reinvent myself and move in a slightly different direction to renew energy and passion?
- What skills would I need to add or eliminate?
- Is my present team the right team to help me move to the next level?
- What could allow me to be the leader my team is longing for?
- What would my workdays look like for maximum efficiency?
- What could be added or subtracted from my leadership position as well as team duties?
- What systems could be instituted to make it easier for our guests and for our team?
- Could we collect differently? Treatment plan differently? Schedule differently?
- What communication systems do we need in order to train, motivate and keep us in the game?

- What kinds of marketing do we need and does it match our office and sales skills once the guest arrives to meet us?
- What kind of help is there available to make this happen?

In looking at all these questions, your tendency will be to stop and get stuck in the "how will I do that? Where will the money come from? I don't have the knowledge." Keep focusing on WHAT do I want by seeing each of these possibilities clearly. If you worry about the HOW, you will never reach the WHAT. If you can clearly see the WHAT, the how will appear. It sounds like magic and it can be.

Bill Blatchford DDS

WHERE IS YOUR DESERVE LEVEL?

A deserve level is an interesting psychological barrier that is so real, yet invisible. This deserve level influences your life, your decisions and your life choices. There is an invisible floor and a ceiling which you have created for yourself. Whether you realize it or not, you have a floor under which you will not operate. We are as uncomfortable breaking through our ceiling—like having more fun than we deserve, having others recognize us for being special, having more money than we had planned. We have individual and unique standards for everything in our lives—not just money but happiness, stress, work, play, friends, relationships, physical fitness, family conversations, professional achievement and so much more.

Our deserve levels are invisible and only show themselves when we are nearing our floor or ceiling which is the comfort level we have set. We will do anything we can to stay within that comfort zone. Most people have little problem with the floor but struggle with the ceiling. Bigger or better really holds people down, thinking "I do not deserve to have things this good." The problem with individual deserve levels is we do not allow ourselves to think and dream beyond our own experience level. If you have not seen it or felt it, you are likely to refuse to look at the possibilities for fear of failure or what others would think.

Some examples: a dentist most likely would never sleep on a park bench and be homeless. Yet, the divorce rate is significant when building a new home which may go beyond the comfort level of one of the partners.

A dentist might have a deserve level for work which indicates to him that being busy, no matter how productive is more worthwhile or worthy than doing nothing. Work plus the amount of busyness equals a noble activity. Thus, the dentist would rather be busy in the practice than work on systems allowing him to be more productive and profitable. His measure of self-worth is more tied to being busy than being productive and more profitable. Hard work can be a virtue which indicates a low deserve level in the value of time. Do you recognize yourself here?

This deserve level can relate to the time and effort economy (each hour equates to a pay level) verses the results economy which is really where dentist's thinking should be. Working hard is the time and effort economy. Working smart with systems in place allows us to think and act in the results economy. Where are you in your deserve level?

The ceiling struggle for dentists can be about net return. Why do some people earn a net of $500K and some struggle to earn $200K? Perhaps they do not believe they deserve to break through their ceiling to $500K for whatever reason.

How much money are you comfortable having in the bank for savings? This is demonstrating your deserve level. Look at the behavior of many lottery winners which many aspire to be. When it happens, many times the big money becomes a burden and they spend it as fast as they can to come back to their deserve level of struggle. "This is where I deserve to be."

Having deserve levels helps us make decisions, avoid situations which are uncomfortable and make us stay within those boundaries for security. That is the positive. The downfall of ceilings in your deserve level is it keeps you in the arena you have experienced. If you have never heard of any dentist with $1M net, it is out of your realm of comfort. Without counseling and coaching, you cannot break out of your ceiling. Your present deserve level wants you to be comfortable and will do anything to keep you in the zone.

If a coach could start with a clean slate, it would be much easier. We all come with baggage, including our own deserve levels. With counseling and coaching, you can raise your deserve level.

If you had no fear, what new ceilings could you create? Check out your happiness quotient, your physical fitness, your weight, your net, the amount of stress you allow in your life, your willingness to be fully present in conversations and relationships. Where are your ceilings and how is it keeping you at a plateau? What do you need to do about it?

Bill Blatchford DDS

WHAT IS YOUR PURPLE COW?

Seth Godin's book, *Purple Cow* shares how a cup of coffee became Starbucks, ice cream became Hagan Daz, a secretarial chair became the Aeron chair. The *Purple Cow* is turning the ordinary into the extraordinary. Selecting a different path in branding and marketing can help you be known as something special. How can you apply this to your dental practice?

Cosmetic skills were so new and different 15 and 20 years ago. Now it looks like cosmetics are done by everyone and it is nearly a commodity. This means some dentists now feel the competition is based on price. To continue to stand out in dentistry, make yourself different by applying the Purple Cow principles and seek a new treatment modality to add to your repertoire. How can you turn the ordinary into the extraordinary?

In some areas, dentists are pining for new patients. What are you doing now or could do to be different and turn that ordinary experience into something memorable and creative? Find a new skill to add which will bring different clients to your practice.

To make this successful, revisit your vision of excellence, caring for others and making a difference. What could you do that would be consistent with your own vision? What you add must be consistent with who you are to be successful.

At our Purple Cow seminar in Chicago, five general dentists shared five new skills they have added with great success. Interest, curiosity and an investigation of need in their area combined to create excitement in the community. A professional DVD of these five dentists is available on www.blatchford.com. In this short article, we will share just two of the five Purple Cow ideas presented.

How about adding cosmetic dentures? What? You hate dentures? For many dentists, the lowly denture hasn't been broached since dental school. Think of this. What do you charge for a full mouth reconstruction? People who lost their teeth early would give much to have a full set of beautiful teeth and gums which fit well, occlude properly and possibly even be implant supported. This is a whole segment of population, many with means, who may have had very ill-fitting and embarrassing dentures for years. What they really dream of are beautiful smiles and teeth on which they can count. They want teeth like everyone else.

What would it take for you to turn a disliked treatment of dentures into something rewarding? Reconsider current classics from Dr. Carlson, Massaud, Turbyfill, Barotz and many talented others. Occlusion, proportion, gums, shading are all important considerations.

To be successful in offering cosmetic dentures, you and your team need to shift your paradigm about denture wearers and make a turnaround of need to desire. There is a very strong desire to have what they perceive others have and the sales process is based on desire, not technique. Make them feel special.

Within this shift, from denture commodity to desire, you will want to be treating your guest with as much service, fuss and artistic endeavor as a cosmetic case. Consider fee plus lab and make them a spare set. You will be relieving one of their greatest fears.

Another Purple Cow could be sleep apnea for it is an area of great medical concern with sleep clinics in every city. Few simple solutions exist, yet people with sleep apnea have a shortened life, lessening brain activity, increased heart problems and sleep apnea can occur even in our youth. Consider investigating the skills needed to successfully treat sleep apnea with a dental appliance where compliance of the patient is much more successful than other modalities.

Contact the Academy of Dental Sleep Medicine (ADSM) for courses on sleep apnea to become qualified. Check their website www.dentalsleepmedicine.org. It is so important to develop the skills and knowledge as this is from a medical field and medical insurance is billed. Aside from skill, you must follow the protocol of testing prior to your appliance and testing after. In trying to predict the future, it would appear as the boomers mature, other dental and medical specialties will claim sole ownership of sleep apnea relief. If you are interested, qualify early. Some of these patients could develop into larger dental cases.

Marketing for sleep apnea? Start with asking your patients, "Does your mate snore?"

Bill Blatchford DDS

BIG WORLD, SMALL TOWN

Dr. David Painter of Auburn, Indiana

It's a big world out there. A question often asked is 'Can the Blatchford Blueprints work in a small town?' Dr. David Painter has been a Blatchford client for five years and he practices in Auburn, Indiana (pop. 12,000) with his wife, Julie, and sons Cowboy Dan and Lil' Joe. Dave and Julie keep active with their children's activities and sports. Dave is also an Auburn City Councilman and an active Kiwanian.

From Dr. Painter— Our rural Indiana patient base is more blue collar with ties to manufacturing (auto and steel). Our service mix shows our patients are more focused on function and less on cosmetics. We do bread and butter restorative dentistry. Even in this small town, we have an ample supply of dentists. Auburn has ten dentists. The drawing area has 40,000 and 16 dentists. I chuckle when I hear others say there is a shortage of dentists.

When I started dentistry, I felt underappreciated. I realize now, I was demonstrating myself just like any other dentist...'caring environment with highest quality.' We worked 210 days a year in the Crown of the Year Club insurance driven practice. Honestly, after ten years in practice, life was frustrating. I wanted and needed a change...and in the mail came the 80/20 Blatchford CD. From then on, my practice has changed for the better.

My practice has changed to a slower more purpose driven practice. We now have a sharper vision and focus on our services. We see fewer patients, work less hours and are better rewarded for our efforts. We are attracting more patients who appreciate what we do and are willing to pay for it. We now offer patients unique treatment modalities and amenities.

To become unique, Bill encouraged me to obtain new clinical skills as well as sales skills. Dr. Blatchford coached us as a team to focus more on listening rather than recommending treatment. He said, "When the patient is ready, the Doctor will appear." With role playing and reading, Blatchford Coaching has helped the whole team communicate better with patients.

Bill asks you to challenge yourself. He coached me to expand my knowledge base and offer a broader range of services and this requires more CE. So, I did:

- Misch International Implant Institute to learn bone grafting, implant placement and restoration. Dr. Carl Misch is a national treasure
- Miami Valley Hospital to become IV Sedation certified. Dr. Dan Becker is very thorough and you learn it the 'old school way'
- Hornbrook Institute for live patient hands-on smile makeovers
- Invisalign I and II
- Somnomed for sleep apnea care

The addition of IV Sedation has had the most dramatic effect on my practice. IV Sedation allows you to handle larger cases with more ease. It makes implant placement appointments smoother. It is quicker and more reliable than oral sedation and more importantly—patients love it. Over the last three years, IV Sedation has grown to about 25% of our practice. IV sedation has helped differentiate my practice as I am the only general dentist with an Indiana Sedation Permit in northeastern Indiana.

To have our patients say 'yes' to these new skills, Bill has coached me to be a better listener. I have learned to ask questions and shut up so the patient has a chance to tell me what they are thinking. Bill has coached me and my team to accept the fact that teeth are optional and people can live without them. We do not have pressure conversations in our office. We don't beat ourselves up when patients decline care. Life goes on—live it.

Bill has really worked with me on leadership and developing a great TEAM who shares my vision. The team makes or breaks a practice. When we started with Blatchford, we were overstaffed and under paid. My inexperience as a manager/owner showed us we were not 'together' and frustrations would occur.

I find the leadership/decision maker role much more comfortable now. If a concern arises, it is addressed and not let to simmer and boil over later. We now have three very well compensated team members; we are more productive and happier. Monthly Blatchford calls help keep me focused and sharp. I also like to read, read, and read.

I feel the most important attributes a team member can bring to the table are attitude, personality and being a team player. The four of us really pull together to accomplish a lot. Our patients notice and do appreciate the extra effort.

We continue to be coached on systems and patient interactions. We work together on role-playing client interactions with a video. It is interesting how you *think* you look and sound and now can see how you *really* look and sound. We discussed how other businesses role-play and learn sales. They decided to make the most of it. We script out our usual patient interactions so we can focus on really listening to our patients.

As a team, we want to be efficient for our patient's comfort and for us, too. We want to get the job done so we can lead our other lives, too. To that end, we have:

- A large wall calendar to set up the next year's office calendar in October/November. We look at team's vacations, CE desires. We plan 170 days. Everyone has input.
- Blatchford Block Booking—every AM is saved for longer procedures. Hold those blocks open!
- Thursdays are sedation/large case day. On Thursdays, there is no hygiene and we are done when we are done. It is our most productive day and we usually complete by 1 PM. Three and one half days a week works for me!

- New patient conversation—we want to know how we can best serve them. Everyone participates. *Blatchford's Power Questions* make the conversation easy for everyone.
- Cross training really pulls the team together and I have even learned I can work without an assistant sometimes
- Computerization—we fully utilize our computer network and software. We are fully networked—eight computers throughout our small office, digital x-ray, digital photography, e-claims, and email. We continually learn how to better use technology to improve our practice.

The Blatchford Bonus system unites the TEAM. All the practice numbers are open and it helps the team understand the business side of dentistry. The bonus unites our team to make every patient experience the best it can be. It encourages cross-training so we serve people well. We all can answer the phone, interview a new patient, make money arrangements, assist the Doctor and so on. We respect each others positions and can easily cover when needed.

Energy was created in a goal setting session when one team member openly said, "I'd like us to get $$$$ bonus every month." Everyone on the team concurred and *they* began to figure out what it would take to reach it for the year. When the TEAM buys in, it creates success.

Our monthly BMW (Blatchford Motivational Workshop) or 4x4 (four hours every four weeks) is our most important meeting of the month. We role play, discuss our successes and where we need improvement and implement changes. It is the quickest four hours of the month and most valuable.

Dr. David Painter.

Cowboy Dan, Lightning Lil' Jo, Dr. David Painter.

OPPORTUNITIES

Knocking on your door right now are opportunities. One is the possibility of an associate with no obligations or buy-in promises. You say, "But Blatchford has always advised us against moving towards associates." You are correct.

There are several reasons I have advised against associates in the past:

- Usually, the solution of an associate is the result of small diagnosis and being so busy, you are unable to see anything but needing more help. An associate is not the answer for this. Better leadership and team learning skills will help solve this.
- Usually, there really is not the income to warrant an associate so the net is divided. Not a good answer.
- Usually, there is a tired dentist who infers to the young associate, there is a future buy-in, "maybe." The tired dentist has not thought through the economic and emotional ramifications either short-term or long-term. The tired dentist feels he will become the eventual partner of privilege and "cherry-pick two or three large cosmetic cases a week and work as long as I can." This dentist is a real dreamer.

However, there is an opportunity developing because of changing dental demographics which could be of help and interest for some. About one-third of the dental graduates presently are female. They are graduating as professionals during their prime child-bearing years. Many are not purchasing practices and yet, want an opportunity to continue their skills with no obligation of purchase or responsibility at this time.

Right now, in your area, there are graduates who are choosing not to work full time but have good skills. If you are moving towards specialized skills and can see the opportunity for someone to work several mornings a week doing routine dentistry, give this some thought. Never before has there been this demographic opportunity.

We have an "internship contract" which allows a 12 month position with no obligation for continuation or purchase. It allows you to specify duties, hours, types of treatments which keep you in control. If the first 12 months are a success, you can renew for another year, again with no promises.

Be in contact with me if you feel your numbers and time would warrant an associate ship of this kind. We want this to be a win-win situation.

TUNNELS WITH CHEESE

Life comes at you fast in today's world. Why waste time trying to reinvent the wheel? Why run through tunnels where it would be a miracle to find cheese? Use your head and the knowledge of a trusted few to find those tunnels with cheese. Here are some examples:

Transitions: Keep your eyes open if you are either the buyer or the seller. In the real world, realtors cannot represent both the buyer and the seller but somehow, in dentistry, that important ethical and legal fact is overlooked. The young dentist believes he has impartial counsel saying "he was so nice to me." Investigate if one is representing both buyer and seller. Who has your best interest at heart?

There is cheese at the end of the tunnel when the senior Doctor can continue to increase his net instead of sharing it. There is very little cheese when he sells half to someone who has no patients to bring to the table. Do the math. Does one plus one equal three? The cheese at the end of the retirement tunnel for most dentists is to stay in control, keep practicing in some fashion and do the "retire as you go" program. Solo practicing dentists are virtually unemployable. Will you find cheese at the end of the tunnel if you think you are now employable and can take directions from others?

Hygiene: Most practices spend too much staff effort to keep hygiene full. Hygiene is always in a state of flux and an important part of dental practice success. We are finding most dentists are "over hygiened" when examining capacity vs. demand for services. The cheese for hygiene is when you are bursting at the seams, have reserved daily time for new patients and sift through those patients who have accepted your work or who are not ever going to accept it from you. Most production comes from new patients. Cheese in hygiene is a tight schedule with demand larger than capacity.

Office building: The cheese for your practice, in most situations is a five year lease with renewables and the option of moving to a better part of town. Many dentists dream of owning their own building, which usually ends up being too large and pretentious. It becomes dated in design and after twenty years, the dentist says, "I'd really like to be five miles south." Rent is only 5% of your overhead. The cheese is in being flexible.

Marketing: The cheese for marketing is to do your own due diligence. Study your demographics and avoid copying others from dental forums whose criteria, area or skill does not even match yours. There is cheese when you do select some methods of marketing and work with your team on discovering the source of new patients. Another marketing tunnel with cheese is adding skills that make you unique and more easily distinguishable. Absolute cheese is acquiring an additional practice and merging. With scripting, you can make the selling dentist a hero in the eyes of patients who loved him and acquire some nice cases. While 6500 boomer dentists retire, new graduates total 4,000. One third of the classes are now women and only half the women are purchasing practices. Thus, it is a buyer's market. This is guaranteed marketing to add to your other marketing efforts.

Budgets: Au contraire, this is not a dirty word. A budget is not a diet but rather a solid plan of money action. Cheese is when you create a plan for home and for practice and stick to it. Your team should be aware of your budget and be accountable for their part of the budget. Overspending is a disease; no cheese.

Staff: A great team is small and skilled. This is where the big cheese is for those who are great, with rewards of a strong bonus plan. Your team budget should be at 20% of your gross collections. A dental team is for the fabulous few who see the opportunity, are curious in learning and growing and want to be responsible and accountable.

Work with people who can help you find cheese. Find a coach with integrity who holds your dreams and his own. Work with team members who also see the possibilities of tunnels with cheese and are willing to take a risk with you. The cheese is worth it.

Bill Blatchford DDS

NORTH TO ALASKA

Dr. David Nelson now of Homer, Alaska

When we met with David and Luanne Nelson, their plight seemed dismal. Happy people by nature, it appeared their present practice situation was like a train wreck. A great dentist with many skills and a talented supportive new wife, they were practicing in an area of Milwaukee, WI which was rapidly deteriorating. Of the seven dentists in the building, only two remained. The other was a pediatric dentist who was there on a very limited basis. The barbershop, at this location since 1980, refused to renew their lease for safety purposes. There were several break-ins to the building and a patient was robbed at gunpoint in the parking lot. The police were called several times and they considered putting bullet proof glass in the front office. The new owners of the building had armed guards patrolling the parking lot and building since so much was vacant.

Therefore, when they joined Blatchford Coaching, we asked them at their first meeting in Chicago, "if you could be anywhere in the world doing whatever you wanted to do, where would you be and what would you be doing?" Both Nelsons answered, "Homer, Alaska, doing dentistry, hunting, and fishing." Dr. Blatchford asked, "Why aren't you there doing that?" and this is their story.

David and Luanne call this their "Miracles"

David says, "I have always been positive and worked hard. I was an Eagle Scout, won a Senatorial appointment to the Air Force Academy, first candidate accepted at Marquette Dental following my undergraduate junior year and Marquette offered me a teaching position upon graduation from dental school. My father always encouraged me to put forth my very best effort.

In Milwaukee, I was firmly entrenched in dental insurance since I started in 1980. Participating in network provided a great way to attract patients and establish my office. Problem was, I never stopped participating and continued signing up with enthusiasm and optimism, harboring the belief that the more patients I had, the more successful I would be; the longer hours I worked, the more profitable I would become. I could not understand how I could work the hours I was working, increasing production, yet becoming less and less profitable.

I was too tired at the end of the day to even try to figure it all out. Besides, it was more fun to fly off somewhere on weekends to tack on more hours of continuing ed (I do have thousands of hours over 30 years) with the belief the broader based and better my skills became, the more I could help my patients, the more they would appreciate my skills and the more I would be paid. Just one problem—this is not a part of the insured's mentality, saying, "will my insurance cover this?"

Annually, I made my trek to Alaska. My office was decorated with Alaskan photos, mounted antlers and snow shoes. My Dad was a Navy weatherman stationed on Tanaga Island in the Aleutians and I loved to imagine what an adventure Alaskan life would be like. I actually obtained an Alaska dental license with the thought of going up and working the summers or working for Indian Health Service. Just in case, of course.

I pray a lot and am grateful for each of the days given to me and everything in it. I admit I was getting to the point of praying to get through each day. I loved my work, it just wasn't any fun. I was working about 60 hours a week and my income was steadily decreasing.

My wife of 23 years filed for divorce. My patients were very kind, offering books, marriage counselors, words of inspiration. One eventually called me to have coffee. Luanne and I were married a year later and she continued working at a title company.

My "dream team", (hygienist of 22 years and her sister-in-law receptionist) quit, claiming loyalty to my first wife. The real reason, I found out later, was they appeared to be taking home more than just their paychecks. I hadn't been paying close attention nor did I have systems set up to prevent this. I ultimately am responsible for this loss.

My location situation was so bad that long term patients came right out and said they could not come to my current location until I relocated. It had moved from challenging to downright dangerous. We searched in earnest for a new location. We drew up plans and the business deal fell apart. We could have a beautiful office in a high rise but no one would find us there.

Luanne started working at the office. Having a background in accounting, one of her first questions was "Why are you writing off large amounts of these insurance checks before posting the actual payment?" I said, "We are under contract with an agreement to provide services." She said, "You are writing off too much of your fees, time to do something different."

She reduced office hours from over 50 to 35 by working more efficiently. We double booked hygiene and had two hygienists come in from a temp agency twice a week. We scheduled only what I now know as class II and III patients with Dave with the exception of dental exams. We scheduled patients who paid their bills. We dismissed - with cause - chronic "chair-sitters". We updated the fee schedule. We began the daunting task of severing our relationship with most of the insurance plans.

At a Chicago Midwinter meeting, I took technical classes and Luanne took one with Dr. Blatchford called, "Know Your Numbers." Joining the Blatchford Coaching, we gained a renewed confidence and clearer direction, how to put together a team, and pushing our imaginations to the limit. We had just five short months on our lease.

On the Internet, we found a practice in our perfect town of Homer. Bill contacted his friend, the listing broker. We flew to Alaska and sealed the deal. In the next few months, the Milwaukee practice's patient base was sold to a dentist with an office in a safer location and we were off.

Through Dr. Blatchford's sturdy coaching, we have a real team. Attitude is everything. You can teach most people basic dental skills but you can't turn them into caring individuals with a conscience. Our team overhead is at 12%, as we do not have a dental hygienist. Per the Homer Chamber of Commerce, Homer is home to 5,454 year round residents in the city limits and another 9,000 additional year round residents or so in the surrounding communities. The area welcomes around an additional 150,000 visitors annually.

We have had over 750 new patients since we opened the new office. We have a booth at the annual Health Fair, advertise on radio and newspaper, belong to Rotary and Luanne is a photographer who exhibits at the local Art Gallery. We belong to the Pratt Museum, sponsor the Halibut Derby as members of Chamber of Commerce, are very active in our Church and participate in fund-raising raffles, usually offering Zoom whitening. We include patient photos (with permission) in our ads and website. Amazing to us, patients call us and WANT to be in our ads. We have become very visible in a very short time here in Homer.

Most of our new patients are from Homer and the surrounding area, although we do take care of some of the tourists. Since Dave is on staff at South Peninsula Hospital, we have gathered many patients from the people who work there, too. We have had some patients travel to us from California, finding us on our website on the Internet. (www.davidnelsondds.com). Homer is filled with people from the lower 48, and a few of our new patients have encouraged their families to come to us for their dental work. Some do! Many of the fishermen come here now, one gifting us a huge fresh King Salmon straight from the sea.

We are very grateful to Dr. Blatchford for opening our eyes to the real possibilities. Our Blatchford consultant, Nanci Granahan worked with us too in our transition to a successful practice result. My plan for the future is to do my best with my ear to the ground and my eyes to heaven married to my loving wife and in the capable hands of the best coach on the planet.

www.davidnelsondds.com

David Nelson and Luanne moving from Wisconsin to Alaska.

Even for skilled David, it is a challenge to do your own hygiene.

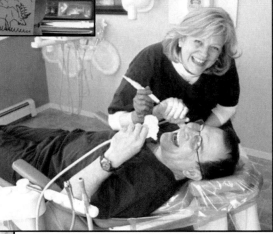

Part of Homer's moose population.

The great adventrue on the Kenai continues for the Nelsons.

FINDING BALANCE

We are caught up in the electronic age, never really having a full vacation or taking time for an original thought. There are Internet kiosks on the ski slopes, at the beach and we have email on our phones 24/7. If we allow it, someone can reach us every minute. We can even be tracked on this earth and never seem to escape. We love it, we hate it; we can't seem to escape it. We use our practice and work as the excuse to be so involved.

What are we really accomplishing by being a slave or servant to the Internet, to our cell phones, and constantly on the dental forums? Who are WE, anymore? Are we really forwarding the action or filling in time because we feel we must answer when someone calls? Are we real or becoming robots and automatons?

In a simpler time, L.D. Pankey spoke of the importance of finding your balance to make life worthwhile. He knew dentistry could be all consuming if you allowed it. The Cross of Life he espoused, with happiness at the core, is a balance between love and worship, work and play. His inference and warning is our work can erode and corrupt all other endeavors, leaving us out of balance. In most instances we find, the practice rules the roost. We let our work and preparation for work interfere with our family time, our vacations and our spiritual pursuits.

In these changing times, the first impulse is "spend more time at the office which will bring in more income." Unless you are turning people away and simply can't treat them, spending more time at the office is a fallacy. Especially during challenging times, we need balance to be refreshed and ready for a full day at the office.

How do we live in today's world and keep it balanced? There needs to be motivation to make a change to better balance. We are in control of our time. We make the choices. Some people say I wouldn't know what to do with free time or I need to be more successful so I can take time off or I don't feel comfortable unless I am working or how can working less create more income or I feel guilty taking time off? We actually sabotage ourselves from being balanced. We are choosing to work instead, out of guilt, fear or the unknown. We are choosing imbalance.

Dr. Evelyn Teague of Birmingham, AL has been a goal setting and high achiever all her life. As a dentist, she continued to work exclusively on her practice, forsaking her personal time. "After my Summit with the Blatchfords, I have been making every effort to concentrate on living and not just working. Now I have blocked several weeks off. The idea is not how much time you are in the office, but how productive you are when there. To be honest, this has caused me much stress. I have been racking my brain trying to figure out what I will do with my time off. It feels like I am not being productive if I am not working. I have to learn how to live."

If I could share with you how free days, buffer days and work days can actually increase your income, would you willing to listen? You increase your income when you are sharp, focused and well-rested. You need time away to have original thoughts, ideas and preparation for work. You need total relaxation time, free from work, to be excited and filled with passion about your work when you do return. This is a real challenge as I am working on it also.

Let's define the days:

- **Work days** are when the dentist is totally engaged at work with patient care. As Dr. Kevin Rykard of Oklahoma City says, "hands in the mouth."
- **Buffer days** are preparation to work days when you network, cross train, create systems, study numbers, make big decisions, communicate, read.
- **Free days** are free of work and preparation so as to refresh and return stimulated. A free day is 24 hours. You do not have to go anywhere but you cannot go to the office, turn on PC Anywhere, answer business emails, or return calls.

We are so out of the habit of absolute free time. Isn't that a shame! Finding real balance is a challenge. If you could increase your income and your happiness, are you up to the challenge of finding balance?

"Know the true value of time; snatch, seize and enjoy every moment of it." —Philip Dormer Stanhope

Dost thou love life? Do not squander it, for this is the stuff life is made of." —Ben Franklin

"Time is the coin of your life. It is the only coin you have, and only you can determine how it will be spent. Be careful lest you let others spend it for you." —Carl Sandburg

Bill Blatchford DDS

BALANCE AND A NEW LIFE

Dr. Evelyn Teague of Birmingham, AL

Dr. Teague has been a determined goal setter and hard worker all her life. She just joined Blatchford Coaching several months ago to help grow her practice but more importantly, she recognized she has allowed her practice to consume her life. She saw she did not have a real life and now wants a balance. Dentistry had consumed her young life!

"I think the most impactful thing since starting with Blatchford has been personal. After my Summit with the Blatchfords, I have been making an effort to concentrate on living, not just working. For so long, everything has been centered around my dental practice. I have actually blocked off several weeks for vacation. The idea is not how much time I am in the office but how productive I am when I am there. To be honest, this has caused me much stress. I have been racking my brain trying to figure out what I will do with my time off. It feels like I am not being productive if I am not working. It is one of the main reasons I joined Blatchford Solutions. Their coaching is in line with how I want my life to be. Therefore, I am learning to live."

In the practice, she has made changes in three months of coaching. They are block scheduling to be more efficient for patients as well. Dr. Teague now works 3.5 patient days and has half a day of administrative and preparation work. This allows her "to be off on my off days." Previously, Dr. Teague was known to stay late, arrive early, work through lunch and shuffle papers on her Fridays. She even checked her Blackberry for emails several times a day on weekends and had PC Anywhere at home. She was tied in tightly, feeling the sky would fall is she stepped away.

Her team, with a temporary assistant, is reading books on sales and marketing monthly. They role-play their phone scripts and sales conversations. Dr. Teague had a bonus system before based on her expenditures or overhead. They only made bonus once. Since joining Blatchford in December, the team has already bonused.

Dr. Teague is terminating her relationship with one insurance company by having a personal conversation with each guest about her changing relationship and has had a positive response so far. They are instituting a financial arrangement of "will that be check, cash or credit card?" and are finding it is working well with general procedures. With blocks held in the schedule, they are allowing patients to pay for their portion in advance but find they really need to collect all in advance so that patients will be accountable for holding that large block of time.

Their marketing is quite effective. She is in a high rise downtown with restrictions on advertising in the building. She has been in several spreads of Birmingham Magazine and now has a second billboard up. "This is face and name recognition with this repetitive form of marketing. I went into a local restaurant and paid with credit card. The owner saw my name and stated, "I saw your billboard." Now, Dr. Teague, invite them to become patients. Complete the sale.

"I hope to continue my studies at LVI and Neuromuscular Dentistry to help me address more difficult cases." She recently purchased a soft tissue diode laser for aesthetics and now realizes the many applications. She wants to take the LANAP perio laser course.

"On a personal level, I mix in the community with Middle Eastern Dance and I have been appointed to the Board of Directors for the Birmingham Museum of Art Sankofa Society which provides opportunities for travel, museum events and art education. I am continuing with my charitable donations to organizations and attending fundraisers, balls and galas to raise funds for medical centers. I have blocked off four weeks of vacation and an additional two weeks for continuing education. I need to plan those four weeks! I am now more excited about life and all its possibilities! To be honest, I never have dreamed…even as a child, I was very logical and really didn't play make believe. But now I think I should learn to dream the impossible and experience life to the fullest, making dreams become reality. I don't want to take everything so seriously. Even with all these changes, I am still working through lunch. I am in the process of correcting this and want to take advantage of my membership in the private dining club right across the street. I am actually making calls to schedule lunches with colleagues."

www.parkplacedentistrylonline.com

Dr. Evelyn Teague in her modeling days.

Her effective billboard in Birmingham.

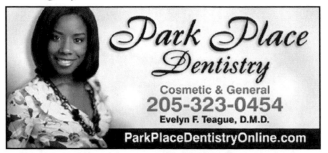

We are suggesting Evelyn be photographed periodically wearing a dental lab coat to affirm SHE is the dentist, not a model.

GUIDING PRINCIPLES FOR REAL LEADERS

- If you demand quality and excellence from your team, you must find the quality and excellence in your life
- Move to paperless now
- Don't let insurance run your office
- Dentistry needs to distance itself from medicine so we are not included in a national health care plan
- Do not invest in anything that needs paint or breathes
- Have a current copy of state/provincial statutes, know them and comply
- Have your practice evaluated every two years even if you are not planning to sell
- Your accountant's role is one of impeccable history. Don't play games. Give them all the information in a timely fashion
- Develop a "yes, I can" attitude with your team
- Don't play favorites on your team.
- Gain your team's respect. They don't have to like you but they must respect you. What is your plan to gain that respect?
- Make the tough decisions—that ones you have been avoiding
- Throw out the bad apples before they spoil the whole team

14

MARKETING

MARKETING—CREATING A PLAN

Relatively new to marketing, dentists are still mystified by the nuances of the marketing crowd. Many questions arise, the most important being, WHAT REALLY WORKS?

That is the mystery. We know we need to get our name out there. We know we can't just rely on our clinical skills to build a huge practice. We must do something but WHAT?

My feeling is to create a plan, a marketing plan. If you are going to advertise, what would you be saying that would differentiate your practice from all the others? What do you do that makes you special or attractive? Why would someone call you for their dental care?

While you are thinking of all these ideas, find out what is available in your community. Do some demographic studies on your own. Lots of information is available on the Internet. Perhaps you already know all the answers. Things move pretty fast in an area and we suggest you do this demographic study every year.

Answer questions like:
- What is the population of the drawing area?

- What industries support your area?
- What is currently the status of these industries and services?
- What is your competition for discretionary spending (no one needs teeth, remember?)
- What services do you offer that is different from others?
- What is the Internet usage in your area?
- What is the medium home price?
- What is the dental insurance coverage in your area?
- On education, is there a junior college, university, graduation rate in town?
- What is the medium income
- What is the average drive time to work?
- What is the average television usage vs. American average?

When working with a marketing firm, either they will do a demographic study or ask you the information. The more information you have on your own practice and vision, the better.

The marketing firm should also analyze your present practice composite. You have been in practice for a period of time. Who have you already attracted? Do you want more of the same or are you changing directions? To what are you changing and how is that going to work? See the article on Pareto's Law on the 80/20 application.

In a well devised marketing plan, all aspects must be examined and established. One of the essentials is strong internal systems used daily to create consistent service and efficiency. Business systems which result from strong leadership are a must. Real team must be in place, rather than individual team members who have no central theme or function in place.

Why spend money on external marketing if the advertisements show something special and your physical facility or staff is not matching your marketing efforts? It won't take long for the word of mismatch in your office to reach rumor level.

Be prepared internally so your external marketing efforts and money spent will produce the results you desire.

PARETO PRINCIPLE—THE 80/20 RULE

Pareto's Law (the 80/20 Rule) has been effectively used for years by big business in marketing and sales. The 80/20 Rule is a fascinating percentage which applies to so many areas of our lives and which nobody can explain why it continues to occur. It really is the secret to success by achieving more with less. As Mort Zuckerman said, "Before you build a better mousetrap, it helps to know if there are any mice out there."

Team and doctors acknowledge the existence of the 80/20 principle and find it fascinating but stop short of applying it for successful results in their own practice. It is a basic business principle that should be on the top of your list for success.

We coach our Doctors and teams in sales to ask questions so your guest or patient speaks 80% of the time. Conversely, if staff and Doctor are "educating" 80% of the conversation, you will talk your way out of a sale 80% of the time.

We receive 80% of our headaches, complaints and cancellations from 20% of our patients. These are patients who don't see value in what we have to offer. We create "office policy" for all because of the problem few. Your worst patients have then helped you create a pessimistic practice, rather than one of optimism and trust.

A computer survey will show you produce 80% of your production from 20% of the patients. Look carefully at the top 20% of those patients last year. Who are they? What did they elect to purchase in your office? Why are they attracted to you? What can you learn from this exercise? Be curious and study this magic 20%. Focus and concentrate on replicating that behavior.

The 80/20 rule of marketplace consumption is in every industry. Airlines know they make 80% of profit from 20% of fliers. These business travelers and frequent fliers are awarded with extra perks, bigger seats, upgrades and service. Airlines know they do not make their profits from a family traveling to Disneyland once a year.

Dentists tend to ignore the 80/20 rule because we are trying to please everybody all the time. Our percentages are reversed. We want patients to accept what we feel they need. We work hard to reverse the thinking of the emergency patient who is demanding of our time every three years.

We struggle to diagnose above insurance maximums. Frustrated, we quit trying. We fill our hygiene schedule with any "meat in the seat." Upon cancellation, we give them other immediate choices. We devalue our own work to cater to the 80% who are not our best patients.

In our Coaching Program, we designate patients as A, B and C. The majority of your patients are "A" patients who faithfully remember your birthday, bring tomatoes from their garden, keep their appointments, pay on time and refer people just like them. Conversely, "C" patients are the unfaithful who have no tomatoes, only come when it is convenient and refer friends just like them. These are the bottom 20% who create practice pain.

"B" patients just take up space. Their attention is sporadic. We want all "A" patients but tend to create policies and treat people as if they are "C's".

Watch for indications you and your staff may be catering to the B and C patients.

- Is insurance mentioned by you in the initial phone conversation?
- Health history in mail prior to first appointment relationship opportunity?
- Is money mentioned in the initial phone call?
- Is respect for time a problem in your office?
- Does a new patient sit alone in "waiting room" completing forms?
- Is one of your first questions, "do you have any concerns today?"

- Is finding insurance information a priority before Doctor sees a patient?
- Are you insurance experts on codes, fee structures and maximums?

If you answered yes to above, you have geared your practice for average. In order to cater to the top 20%, a clear sense of leadership and passion for change must be communicated and demonstrated. Stop doing the things that make you average and shift to being extraordinary. Attitude is a big factor. If you see yourself in the average 80%, unable to break out, stuck in a scheduling quagmire and insurance diagnosis paralysis, you will stay in the 80%.

Find yourself a coach who can turn that attitude into winning. As Lou Holtz says in a commercial, "Son, there is no such thing as just a sales call. You need a fight song."

*Another way to discover the top 20% of your patients is to ask each staff member to list their 100 favorite patients based on attitude, relationship, fun, commitment, etc. Then merge the list into the team's 100 top patients. Check this 100 list against your computer survey of the top 20% who are account for 80% of your income. There will be a great correlation of the two lists. Then study those people. Who are they? Where do they work and live? Why do they see value in your services? These are the top 20% of people who make your life wonderful. How can you thank them and honor them? Also, how can you duplicate them? How can we attract more of them?

Bill Blatchford, DDS

MAKING PARETO'S PRINCIPLE COME TO LIFE

It is very exciting to see the 80/20 applied to your practice and to make decisions which move you forward. The major application of Pareto's law and which every business uses is to track and analyze their customer base.

You have a solid customer base. Some people you like and they like you. Some you don't like and they still seem to like you. All are worthy of analysis as they create value in some way.

A practice is very fluid and dynamic. On the average, 20% of America moves because of transfers, better job opportunities or to be closer to their families. This is a natural occurrence and is even higher in some very desirable places like Scottsdale, Newport Beach, Hinsdale, Greenwich, Charlotte and many others. During economic downturns, Americans move even more.

What does this mean to your practice and Pareto's Law? You need to do this study to your practice at least every year. Since 20% of your practice moves each year, who are you attracting as new patients, where did they come from, what value are they contributing to our practice?

We apply the 80/20 principle by listing every patient in the last 12 months who has had treatment in our office. Some computer software will do this for you. In most cases, you need to do it by hand but what a study it is. It will help you make marketing decisions as to where to spend your dollars, it will emphasize for you and your team the value of duplicating the top 20% of your patients, and it will demonstrate the bottom 20% and leave clear decisions on the table.

Each guest will have a total money amount of treatment in your office. List it by the name. Once you find the top 20%, you investigate them more. For now, here is the Blatchford 80/20 spreadsheet.

MARKETING CLUE—20/60/20

You already have a group of patients you enjoy who are your fans. Have you ever really studied your fan base? Conversely, you have people scheduled for care and at the very mention of the name cause eyes to roll and boots to quake. Have you ever studied this group? Have you ever taken action on either end of the spectrum? By knowing intimately your own special 80/20 ratio, or 20/60/20, you can make much better marketing decisions.

Other businesses in America know and use their 80/20 rule, which Pareto studied in the 16th Century. Airlines and hotels know who is their top 20% and airlines honor them with free miles, better amenities, upgrades, special offers, priority luggage and seating. They know that 80% of their revenue comes from this top 20%. They need this group to be loyal to them. They have their eye on you and you are high on their list.

The opposite end of the spectrum is the family of five who only travel for spring break every other year and want the lowest fare possible where changes and refunds are not available. Their experience on the airline is very frustrating, food is minimal and their luggage doesn't make it. The airline knows who these people are, no amenities are offered and further trips are only encouraged by using that airline more which adds to their revenue.

This study of your practice is such a valuable tool. We encourage our Doctors to survey and take action every year. It is more than knowledge. Action must be applied to create a better practice. With an Excel spreadsheet (some dental software programs will do this for you), find these patients and numbers. Note also who is insurance based, how they entered your practice, who referred them, who are they referring and what factors you feel allow them to continue in your fan club.

We find an elaboration of the basic 80/20 rule to be alive in dentistry and that is the 20/60/20 rule. We know that 20% of your patients create 80% of your profits. The next 60% of your practice produce another 30% of your profit. Whoa, that is 110%. Hold the phone because the bottom 20% of your patients actually create a loss of 10% of your revenue thus, we now total 100%.

We are urging action now when you know the configuration of your practice base. Action is necessary because this bottom 20% keeps you from being more productive, more creative and enthusiastic. Do you feel you are destined to take care of people who don't see value in your work and consequently, show themselves poorly in your practice? Eighty percent of your problems, grief and frustration come from the bottom 20%. If you are losing money on the bottom 20% of your patients, what do you think would be a prudent thing to do?

- Quit appointing them in hygiene
- If they call for a hygiene appointment, ask for their credit card to hold the appointment
- Accept the fact this patient either has had the treatment they want or won't be accepting your work

As you carefully study the top 20% of your fan base, you will find the majority of your 80% production comes actually from the top 10%. When you identify these patients by name, it becomes very clear your priority needs to be on them. It is all about them. Create with your team a program of nurturing your top guests. Spend money and time acknowledging their interests, uniqueness and strengths. What systems will you implement which will allow them to always think of you when outside conversations are about time, value, relationships and focus? You want to be enthusiastically endorsed in these conversations. Knowing and analyzing your top 20% of clients will allow you to make confident marketing choices.

It may seem heartless to not encourage all your patients to excellence. Think of it as a gift you are giving that bottom 20% in your practice. They will eventually find a place with similar values and systems which will make them more comfortable. By allowing people to go elsewhere, you are creating an environment for more top clients and be more focused, enthusiastic and patient for them, the people who feed you and your family.

Bill Blatchford DDS

BLATCHFORD MARKETING MUSTS

Marketing is a mystery in dentistry. It is a new phenomenon and Doctors know they should do something. Marketing is a dynamic, always changing and on the cutting edge of ideas. In terms of DISC personalities, marketers are the true opposite (I) of the technical dentist who is a C. Marketers have an idea a minute and build upon those ideas. Dentists think marketers appear to be flighty and disorganized according to the precision and perfection of a dentist.

Marketing is such a mystery for dentists, inertia sets in and it is easier to do nothing or order a larger Yellow Page ad. When we do not know what to do, we do nothing because we are afraid to make a mistake. Marketers will tell you to go ahead, jump in, and make a few mistakes. You are in a perfect position when you do not know what to do. From Lao-Tzu, "He who knows, yet thinks that he doesn't know has great wisdom. He who does not know but thinks he knows is diseased."

Define your purpose in marketing. What do you want to accomplish and with whom? You can see the direct correlation between the office purpose and your marketing efforts. If your stated purpose reads, "We want to be known for quality and compassion," it helps in defining your marketing direction. The more you can know about yourself and your practice, the more successful will be your marketing efforts.

Have a map of your area in your office and ask your guests to place a red pin where they work and a blue pin where they live. How could this information help you in marketing?

Here is some motivating information to start a marketing campaign. New patients entering should be 15 to 20 adults a month. If you currently have four days of hygiene, you have 800 active patients. You may have more charts but these are the numbers. Twenty percent of America moves every year. You are naturally going to lose 160 patients this year through no fault of your own. At 15 new patients a month, you are gaining 30 a year. Less than 15 new patients a month is pathologic and you are shrinking. **Move forward with marketing.**

Marketing Musts:

- Your team must be skilled and knowledgeable about your marketing efforts as the phone will ring or your website will be examined. Are you prepared to make your marketing dollars count? Have you practiced scripts and ready for conversations with results?
- Is your smile ideal? How about your team members? Because we count everything we do at full production/full collection, schedule team days once a quarter where we all volunteer to keep our smiles bright.
- You and your team need to be known in the community. Each of you can belong and be active in different organizations which are meaningful for you. Examples are the Chamber of Commerce, Toastmasters, Business Women, Bible Studies, yoga or dog training. Each of you find something that interests you and participate fully.
- Create a program of meeting every business within a half mile of your office. Every six months, meet in person, give a gift basket, invite them to to be a guest. Make it easy for them to come in.
- Have you maximized your signage? Is it readable in third gear? Do you list phone and web info? Could it be improved? **Do it now.**
- Rid of all magazines and newspapers in your welcome room and replace with hardbacks of local history, manufacturing, cookbooks, or humor instead of competing ads for vacations, new kitchen flooring, etc.
- Provide a complete "juice bar" for your guests
- Beautifully framed after smiles of your guests should be very visible in your office. All ages, genders and ethnic groups are present
- Make a well-being call in the evening to your patients that day.
- Create a program of gifting in your office. Remember birthdays, referrals, specialists who send you new patients.
- Spa amenities are available. www.yourcomfortsolutions.com
- Is there a dentist retiring near you?

THE INVISIBLE DENTIST

You can't see the dentist because they are wearing "camouflage clothing" by choice, enter the back door of the dental office under the cover of darkness, have their lunch in the staff lounge or their own office then leave after dark so no one will see them. They exhibit this behavior so they do not have to mix with anyone new or be uncomfortable. We label them, "the invisible dentist." Seldom seen or heard in their community, they make great effort to be alone and comfortable.

A dental office can consume your life, if you let it. You could use the practice as your excuse to avoid mixing with others or meeting new people. Whether conscious or unconscious, it is a consistent behavior. How is that working for you? You may not be cognizant of this detrimental choice yet, we see it frequently in dental circles.

We know new patients are the lifeblood of a practice. You may boast of your triple hygiene but the real production comes from new patients. Unless you are redoing the dentistry on your hygiene patients, dentists must make an effort to reach out and meet new possibilities.

Every dentist wants and needs new patients, saying "If I just had more new people coming to me, I know I could do 50% better." Invisible dentists would much rather spend money and hire someone else to do their visibility for them. Realize your choice of behavior actually creates a negative situation for meeting new people, it hurts your practice.

Other situations showing you as the invisible dentist could be:

- Working out in your home gym
- Choosing to eat breakfast at a drive-thru
- Spending your down time in your big cluttered office working on your Game Boy.

- Spending every free moment on your computer in a solitary situation, either in dental chat rooms or thinking you are a day trader in stocks.
- Working on charts, billing, shuffling papers during non-patient days.
- Looking at your calendar and realizing weeks have gone by without a lunch appointment with a specialist, friend or community organization
- Living in a different community than your practice, a distance of more than half an hour.
- Not knowing or pretending you do not know of community events like farmer's markets, art strolls, community theatre, fund drives, school events, etc.
- Have no intention of meeting others so are not carrying business cards
- Your vision of yourself is one of a technical person rather than a business man providing a service. You do not see yourself as a business person.
- At social gatherings and continuing ed courses, you choose the empty table for lunch and don't introduce yourself when others join you.

The remedy? You have to hurt bad enough and want new patients in a significant way before you will really change your solitary behavior. Moving from the invisible dentist to visible will be a bold step for you, one which will result in a more interesting life, a more profitable life.

Here is what I suggest:

- Shed your invisible outfits and burn them. Never again can you retreat to being in camouflage.
- Join a Toastmaster's Club to relearn some social skills and participate in the challenges and joys of being with other people
- Make an assessment of your hobbies and activities. Is there a way to turn that solo activity into one of participation? For example, if you like to swim laps, consider the Masters Swim Program in your community? If you like to bike, find a group on Saturday which schedules a longer ride?

- Work out in an athletic club with people. If you participate regularly in a class, you will become part of the group and meet people
- Eat out at least three times a week. Meet a friend for breakfast, a dental colleague for lunch and take your team to lunch once a month in a busy restaurant.
- Announce to your team you want to change your behavior to be with people. They will encourage you to be visible.
- Join a networking group like Chamber of Commerce, Rotary or service group and attend at least two of their events a month.
- Be active in your Church. Go beyond being an independent lump of "do little."
- In addition to spending marketing dollars, do your part by hosting lunch and learns with specialists, physicians and other dentists. Yes, you can!

Being visible is a behavior choice. Make that choice. You'll be a happier person for reaching out.

Bill Blatchford DDS

ENRICHING THE HUMAN EXPERIENCE

The success of Starbucks is one to emulate in dentistry. Leadership and vision, marketing, staffing, and training create the Starbucks experience which is a commitment to the shared good for all employees and customers, according to Seth Godin, author of *The Purple Cow: Transforming Your Business By Being Remarkable.*

What if we empowered our team to be "partners" committed to the practice profitability, so essential to everyone's future success? What if we could provide a great work environment and treat each other with respect and dignity? There are still dental offices where one position is called "front desk" and another is denoted as "the back." What would it take for dentistry to move from staff to team and finally to partner?

The leader with vision can change a culture of team and patient interaction from an ordinary experience to an emotional connection with others. Starbucks makes a real point of **marketing to its employees** these principles. Founder Howard Schultz says, "We are not in the coffee business serving people but in the people business serving coffee."

To achieve enhancing the human experience at Starbucks, the partners know this is a result of building an emotional connection with customers. Have your team share those small and special things Starbucks partners make a point of doing to make you feel connected.

Can that be duplicated in a dental practice? Remember, the human experience is not about coffee or teeth.

In *The Starbucks Experience: 5 Principles for Turning Ordinary to Extraordinary.* author Joseph Michelli observes the five ways of being:

- Be welcoming
- Be genuine
- Be considerate
- Be knowledgeable
- Be involved

With strong and passionate vision, teams can be part of something bigger than themselves. They want to be part of something that touches their heart. Starbucks success is not about coffee but a force to enrich the human experience. The partners want to make a difference because leaders encourage involvement and sharing of ideas and are given opportunities to be more engaged and effective.

Howard Schultz is fond of saying "retail is detail." The environment is always warm, comfortable and pleasurable. They wouldn't even have to sell coffee to be attractive. They could charge an entrance fee, serve nothing but a room with music and people would still come. Partners are encouraged to take music to another level. They have checklists. Though dentistry is filled with perfection clinically, how much attention do we pay to the things our clients might notice? They notice changing, updated and clean décor, checklists before procedures, or solid systems to ensure a positive experience. By paying attention to detail, a business offers comfort, routine, and reliability. And in Starbucks world, it actually offers a sense of community.

Starbucks pays attention to feedback from customers. Even without a survey, you and your team could name three things that detract from your service. How can you improve or change?

In dentistry, you have naysayers bleating "I wouldn't do it that way." Ask yourself, "Why not? Why wouldn't it work? How willing are you to listen to the criticisms of others?

Howard Schultz, Starbucks leader, was interviewed on Larry King recently and shared the average Starbucks customer enters Starbucks 19 times a month and spends over $900 a year. Starbucks tracks their numbers, knows the numbers and owns them. How do you use the numbers you have?

Most dentists and teams are blissfully unaware of numbers. What if you did an 80/20 spreadsheet on all your patients of 2008, listed each by name and how much was spent in your office? When the total reaches 80% of your production, you have now discovered the real numbers of who constitutes your best patients, your top 20%. Study the top 20%—who are they, where did they come from? How can you duplicate quality patients like these? You will also discover your bottom 20% who give you 80% of your headaches.

To achieve the Starbucks mantra of wanting to enhance the human experience, they know their partner's motivation and feelings are critical. Starbucks essentially markets to their partners to create an experience, connect with people and be accountable for that exchange.

Talk with your team about enriching the human experience at your office. Starbucks has intentionally created a magic Wow! from customers. How will you uniquely enrich the human experience in your interactions and relationships?

BLUEPRINTS FOR SUCCESSFULLY MARKETING YOUR PRACTICE

Whether you are just starting or have been practicing for years, there are key steps in marketing and building your brand that will ensure success over the life of your practice. Starting with a **strategy** that clearly defines your vision is critical; from this strategy you **develop a unique brand** that is "YOU", and **define your audience**. Finally, using all of these components, you will need to **craft a mix of marketing materials** and campaigns to ensure that your brand is seen by the right kinds of potential patients.

This mix may include traditional marketing solutions, such as advertising in the newspaper, lifestyle magazines, and direct mail campaigns. We encourage clients to include several online pieces in their marketing mix and use more than one way to promote their specialty services. For example: email marketing, and a Search Engine Marketed (SEM) Web site. Making it easy for current and potential patients to find information is critical to your success.

By following these steps you'll ensure that your practice really stands apart from a "ho-hum" practice. A consistent brand message with a great look and feel is king. With so many options for consumers today, it is extremely important to have a clear and concise message about how your practice is different, and what makes your brand special. Is it the types of services you offer? Individual patient care? The latest in technology? Your credentials and training?

Starting with a strong strategy

A solid marketing strategy is like the blueprint for your house or office. It defines your practice vision and identity and provides mechanisms for enhancing and measuring the impact of that identity on your marketplace, customers, and team members. This is the first step in developing a successful practice. When you work with a marketing agency to help create the physical elements of your brand, they will ask you for these key elements to get started. It will be the cornerstone that all marketing pieces are measured against.

When we work with clients to develop winning brands there are five key elements that comprise the strategy phase:

- Defining and documenting the brand position and promise
- Creating a series of brand traits and values that make your practice unique
- Creating your brand story
- Designing your brand elements such as a logo, letterhead, business cards, and other practice identity materials
- Defining the ideal patient - where do they live? where do they work? what's important to them? who are they?

This phase may seem like a lot of work especially if you have never gone through a branding exercise before, but trust me it will all be worth it. By going through this exercise, you will now have the building blocks you need for a stable and successful marketing strategy.

Creating the Brand. Who are you? What do you do? For whom do you do it?

Now that the strategy phase is complete, you will want to start creating the look and feel of your brand and crafting your message. We work with clients to help them understand that branding is much more than just a logo - it is a lot larger than that. The brand is your practice's promise. A brand is built over time, by everything a practice does—everyday. Every time you support your brand strategy you are helping to build a strong brand for your practice.

For example, we created an advertising campaign for Dr. April Ziegele, with the headline "I am 50 years old and I still believe in the tooth fairy— her name is Dr. April Ziegele". We encouraged the practice to see how they could start living the brand by incorporating the concept of the "tooth fairy" into their everyday interaction with patients. They took this idea and imple-

mented it into their phone greeting when someone called the practice. "Thank you for calling Dr. Ziegele's office where we still believe in the tooth fairy— her name is Dr. April Ziegele." It was a huge success and started an engaging conversation with new patients. Hats off to the Ziegele team! They really understand how unique and consistent marketing really makes a difference.

Think about your brand like you think about yourself as a person. Your "brand" is composed of everything that is "YOU". It's not just your clothes (your logo, colors, imagery, fonts), which can change with the styles of the decade. It's your character or personality (your brand traits) and the core of who you are (your promise). Your logo, your 'look-and-feel', and other graphical elements are important to reflecting your "brand" to the world, but they are not the brand itself.

One of the keys to successfully building a great brand is the "buy in" or as we like to call it "living the brand". Everyone on your team must start living the brand-—from the person up front answering the phones, to the hygienist in the back. All employees must work together as ambassadors for the brand—this means being consistent in how they present the brand to each other, as well as to patients. By representing your practice in a consistent and meaningful way, you establish a promise and create an expectation for the quality of your products and services. A successful brand creates a positive expectation that builds awareness, loyalty, and overall equity. Understanding this concept BEFORE you spend money on marketing activities is imperative to your success.

Dr. James Birrell, who has been a client of ours for almost a decade now is probably the living embodiment of his brand. He just gets it. When you meet Jim, he immediately introduces himself as "Dr. James Birrell, Natural Beauty - Brilliant Smiles." This is the positioning statement we developed for him that really signifies how he feels about the dentistry he provides. His goal is to create beautiful, natural looking smiles that get the same reaction every time—"your smile is amazing!"

Define Your Target Markets

When working with a marketing agency one of the initial projects will be to define your target audience. The process will start by taking a look at your existing patients and finding common elements (i.e. how far from the practice do they live, what kinds of cars do they drive, where do they shop, etc.), then categorize them into specific segments. Be sure to think of target markets as customer group categories and be very specific in your definitions.

Next think of and evaluate similar markets that might be new potentials for you to draw patients from. By choosing markets that are similar, you can leverage your experience and credibility within Market #1 to break into Market #2 more successfully and cost effectively. By creating the messaging that addresses specific "points of interest" you will make sure your materials are more effective.

For example, if you are offering a service such as Sleep Apnea, you will want to create materials that answer specific questions for the patients: how much does it cost? how many times do I need to visit the office? etc.

Crafting the perfect mix of marketing materials

Now that you have put a strategy in place, developed a unique brand promise, and defined your audience, it is time to start the process of creating a suite of marketing materials that will be used to attract the types of patients you want. This process should be unique for each practice—just because radio works for one office, does not mean it will work for you. This is where working with an agency that understands the right questions to ask really starts to pay for itself. As Bill likes to ask, "Are you an average dentist, doing average dentistry, charging an average fee? Or are you a great dentist that is delivering the best possible treatment to your patients?" Your practice is unique. Your marketing approach should be too. By working with an agency you can create materials designed to reflect who "YOU" are. Conveying what makes your practice special and whom you are is a very important part of your marketing success. This process usually starts with a custom logo and suite of business papers, then moves onto the marketing elements every practice needs: a Web site, an advertising campaign, an email marketing program, direct mail campaign, and maybe some additional elements like TV or Radio spots.

So where should you start? In today's world the Internet is an extremely popular marketing tool - one that should not be overlooked when promoting your practice. We feel there are several key factors in making sure the Web is doing the best job it can for you. Start with a Web site that reflects the kind of practice you want to be known for – from the design to the message. Make sure your smile gallery shows your best work and has a range of people with varying age groups and ethnicities. You should show your skills by displaying a variety of different types of dental treatments. Once your site best represents you and your practice you need to make sure it can be found. Be wary of the firms or services that promise a #1 spot in Search Engines, they often have little or no effect. Search Engines are constantly changing the way they display results, so keeping you at the top of search listings requires someone to check in on your site and its placement on a very regular basis.

Another great online source for new patients is by implementing an email-marketing program. These kinds of solutions are very effective in tracking who visits your site, who actually read your email and did they forward it on to a friend. Direct mail usually gets between a 1%-2% return, meaning 1%-2% of people who get your direct mail piece actually do something with it. With email the return can be somewhere between 10%-15%. And it can all be tracked.

Dr. Rhys Spoor in Seattle is a great example of how we have implemented a consistent, multi-pronged marketing program that has paid for itself over and over again. As you can see from the images below, Dr. Rhys Spoor is presented as a premier dental practice that delivers the best dentistry has to offer. The consistency of look and feel between the ads and the Web site insures that any potential patients have no confusion on who Dr. Spoor is.

Whether you are just starting a dental career or have been practicing for years, a clear vision is one of the keys to success. As one of the pivotal steps in the Blatchford Solutions process, a clear vision greatly increases the potential for successfully marketing your practice. At RocketDog Dental, we have found that over our decade of delivering successful marketing solutions for dental practices across the country, an office that has a clear vision and internal systems in place is the blueprint for a more effective and more efficient marketing program.

Following these steps for marketing success will ensure success over the life of your practice: start with a strategy that clearly defines your vision, develop a unique brand that is "YOU", and define your audience. Next you will need to create a mix of marketing materials and campaigns to ensure that your brand is seen by the right kind of potential patients. Constantly monitoring your campaigns is also important. You will need to know where your successes are coming from as marketing IS all about testing.

What's next

With the latest development of Web 2.0 technologies, the Web is becoming a more "user generated content" kind of place. For example, sites like Facebook, MySpace, Twitter, and Flicker are all sites that only exist because users are generating the content. To ensure your practice continues to be relevant to the marketplace you will want to take advantage of this technology on a more regular basis.

MARKETING GUIDELINES

- If you chose a location 20 years ago which is no longer great, do not hesitate to move. Location, location, location
- Collect email addresses of your guests
- Become known in your community by eating out for lunch, working out regularly, becoming involved in your cause.
- Ask for referrals. Practice in front of a video camera until you are comfortable. Don't miss an opportunity.
- Why would people choose to have dental care in your office rather than buy a cruise, a new stereo or motorcycle? This is your competition, not other dentists.
- When a new person calls, do not ask about insurance or how long it has been since they have had their teeth cleaned
- No amount of flowers will make up for an error which could have been avoided. Do it right the first time.
- Have health history, post-op instructions and entry forms on your website.
- Post easy driving directions to your office on your website
- If you add a new skill, add it to your website
- With today's modern families, be certain who belongs to whom or not.
- Create a protocol for responding to your web hits in a timely manner. What is your goal for conversion rate?
- Take before and after pictures of team dentistry. You won't believe how often their conversations will involve showing the photos
- Never burn any bridges. Thank families for being patients and welcome them back
- Watch for guest compliments. They can be subtle and learn to say "thank you."
- At the initial phone call, hear their name the first time and repeat it during the call
- Send Valentines or Thanksgiving cards and be noticed
- Smile when you speak on the phone
- Send birthday cards. It may be their only acknowledgement
- Do not come to the office on your day off in your old clothes
- Do not run errands in your sweaty paint clothes
- Always be reading a book on marketing
- Give generously of your dental skills to your community.

- Ask every time, "how was your visit today?" If it was great, they will tell their 200 family and friends. If it was not great, they will also tell 200 of their family and friends.
- Be prepared. You never have a second chance at a first impression
- Don't rely on personalized refrigerator magnets, coffee mugs or t-shirts to create a successful practice
- Give generously to your dental school. Select an area of special interest to you and specify how you want funds spent
- Shop local, support local artists on your walls
- Establish a health science scholarship at your high school
- Remember people's names
- When encountering patients or people who you might not recognize, quickly introduce yourself rather than avoid the situation. Don't assume people remember you
- Avoid nametags or logos with cute extracted teeth
- When you advertise "24 hour emergency care," that is exactly what you will receive
- Be proud of your community by attending and participating in art strolls, musical events, sports events, fund raisers, antique fairs
- Make arrangements with a taxi to transport your guests when necessary
- Never compromise your integrity
- Show respect for all those who serve your practice by sending thank you notes, sending digital pictures back to the laboratory tech, holidays and birthdays
- Give Christmas gifts from local industries
- Avoid coupons or any semblance thereof
- Make arrangements with a local car repair to take care of flat tires, dead batteries or other car unknowns for your guests
- Label yourself as the "On Time" dentist. Become an expert in time management
- Keep your guest restroom stocked with every amenity you would desire. Be generous
- Never talk about a guest, team player, fellow dentist or your family in a gossiping manner
- Have a working lunch with your referring Doctors at least once a month
- Take care of your reputation. It is your most valuable asset.

15

FINDING BALANCE

ANONYMOUS

When I was approaching mid-life, I had a crisis. I was attempting to restart my life after a divorce from a 32 year marriage filled with continued emotional abuse. It was suggested I would never own a home or anything else, if I divorced. I chose freedom.

After the divorce, I had $21 left in my checking account. I would buy a few cans of tuna, a small loaf of bread and a box of animal crackers. Each day I ate 1/2 a sandwich for lunch and 1/2 for dinner and 6 animal crackers. This continued for three months or more. However, I gained a sleek figure! I was determined not to fail.

I prayed for God to put someone in my life to help me and weeks later, I met Dr. Bill Blatchford speaking at the Las Vegas Institute. Now, I am not saying Dr. Blatchford is GOD, but he was in my life by direction, not mine or his, either. At first, I struggled with some of his concepts about team accountability and ownership.

The ironic thing is I was an assistant at the time. I went to work at 7 AM, watched my watch until 6 PM and ran out the door as though the building were on fire! I felt like a glorified janitor picking up what the doctor and patient left behind, including spit! Since taking Blatchford Custom Coaching, I developed ownership mentality. I started owning the concept of the only way to increase my income, was to increase the doctor's income. What an idea? This meant I could somewhat control what I made as a business partner, not a janitor.

I worked hard to develop my own systems and be involved in team cross-training. These became office systems and team started to appear. We were moving from staff to a TEAM. Was it all a bed of roses? NO! Many people do not like change, in fact, they fear change. It grabbed me and I just knew it was a great start to a new plan for the dental office. I increased my income dramatically. I worked only short weeks, mostly three days a week. I began to work with Dr. Blatchford part-time speaking to doctors and teams and supporting him at conventions.

In the short period of two years, I bought my own home and, later a new car. I had financial freedom and I could control my destiny. I have learned from my own mistakes and have rejoiced in my own successes.

Several years ago, I heard Sheila Sheinberg in Houston share the "Pie of Life."

- First piece of the pie is to develop your skills to make a living.
- Second piece of the pie was to work hard at the skills you developed, have a family and live your life,
- Last piece was to give back to those who so richly gave to you.

Funny, how we remember pearls from each meeting. Doctors, this is learn one, do one, teach one mentality.

In September of 2008, I retired from a practice of 20 years. I loved my leader like a brother. I was struggling with the change. Yet, I believe GOD does speak to us. I was struggling because GOD had a bigger plan for me. HE has to take you out of where you are to take you where HE wants you to go. I resigned my position and assisted the transition for one of our team to fill my place which she did beautifully.

Living the third piece of pie at 58 years old, I wanted other teams and doctors to have what I had. The only way to accomplish that was to work full time for the company who gave me my life back. I am not advocating for a team member to come work for Blatchford but believe it was my calling in this part of my life. This program gave us the tools to not only the life of the practice but my life as well.

More than 55% of young women with children will raise them for all or part of their life as a single parent. With Blatchford principals, they can choose a life partner. Choices can be made for love and forever after instead of putting a roof over their children's heads. They can partner for success not fall to abuse to protect their children or themselves.

Blatchford creates leaders!

Thank you Bill and Carolyn.   I love you both.

P.S. A special thank you for being some of my first successful doctors. You believed in me enough to enroll in Blatchford Coaching. I visited an office prior to Christmas last year and a team member proudly showed me her Dooney bag, purchased with her bonus. She was gleaming with the success. Others spoke of being out on time and family fun now that they have time. Dr. Phil Davis, thank you for being my Star. Thank you to Dr. Brant Crisp for sharing your life, which without knowing it changed mine. Your dedication to success is second to none. Dr. John Vinings, you are what every practice stands for. Your practice is so beautiful and richly deserves the success it has achieved. My doctors and teams are all extensions of my family now. What a gift!

I WANT MORE TIME

The biggest question I hear from clients is," how can I find a balance in my life?" Balancing a successful professional life with all the other things we want to do in the rest of our life is a challenge. Successful dentists love their profession and the practice of dentistry. It is too easy for a dentist to work many hours, to be consumed by the practice and allow other parts of life to take the leftovers. We all know dentists with very successful practices yet, they end up with broken marriages, family problems, health issues, substance addictions, or just unhappiness. I do not believe that we have a corner on these problems as they seem to be prevalent every where you look today.

Dentistry has the potential to be one of the most rewarding and satisfying professions. It also allows one to have a full, rich, and balanced life. It does however; take some planning to accomplish this balance. L.D. Pankey spoke of the importance of finding balance to make life worthwhile. He knew dentistry could be all consuming, if you allow it. I believe it is a result of failing to plan otherwise. He developed his Cross of Life with happiness at the core. His cross was a balance of work and play, love and worship. I believe many never really visualize what balance looks like to them. If you do not know what you are looking for, it is very difficult to find it.

Here is what I have found works for me and the premise from which I coach our Doctors who are struggling to find more time and a balance in life. Design your life first. Do not be content to take what is left over. What would you like to be known for? What is the reputation you want to have 20 years from now? How would you want to spend your free time? Where would you like to have traveled? What skills would you like to acquire? How do you want to spend your family time? How do you want to give back to the community? How much money do you need to support your lifestyle and how much money will it take to retire? Or do you want to retire?

Read the books *One Hundred Places To Go Before You Die* by Schultz, *50 Places to Fly Fish Before You Die, How To Get Control Of Your Time and Your Life* by Alan Lakein, *Life Launch: A Passionate Guide To The Rest of Your Life* by Hudson, *500 of the World's Greatest Trips* by National Geographic.

Once you have answered the lifestyle questions, design a practice to support it. There are many models of practice to choose. What will work for you?

There are many practice models to choose from which could work for you. Locations, city versus small town, part of the country, near recreation, travel to recreation, type of facility, type of treatment, how much continuing education, net income, overhead, size of staff, gross production, type of marketing, time spent in the office, time spent on vacation, CE choices and offerings.

In creating your practice, understand the concept of capacity / demand. More time does not create more demand. Unless you are turning patients away, more time does not equate to more income.

Time and effort/results. As a dentist you are paid for results. This is production, not time spent at the office or with patients. Many dentists never understand this concept. They will not go on a vacation if production goals are not met, believing by staying in the office more hours or more days production will increase.

Some dentists have the ability to produce large amounts of treatment while others struggle to reach a survival level. My observation is the large producers spend fewer hours in the office. How can this be? Yes, large producers have learned to use their time wisely.

There are three types of time in the year. **Focus time** is you doing what you do to earn a living. Focus time for dentists, means hands in the mouth. In every office the dentist spends much time doing tasks that someone else could do or are not even necessary. **Buffer time** is getting ready for focus time and is administrative, continuing education, staff meetings, networking etc. And the glorious **Free time** is free time away from the office. Free time is doing anything but business.

Each period is 24 hours long. That means that your free days are absolutely free of business with no emails, journals, continuing education or anything to do with your practice.

Dentists who can discipline themselves this way are far more productive than the ones that mix focus, buffer and free days all into everyday of the week. It is easy to mix these activities or to say 'I enjoy working.' That just means you have not learned any skills except working. You have not learned to play. You are more comfortable working so it seems unnatural not to be working. Some even develop a sense of guilt over spending any time not working. That is because you believe that working and making money is more important than anything else. You have bragging rights about how hard you work. Many set artificial deadlines for projects as an excuse to work all the time. You may even notice you are always behind on these projects which just puts stress on you and lowers your productivity. Effective dentists recognize the difference between urgent work and important work. Low producers have a lot of 'urgent work' to do all the time. Urgent work exhausts us. Important work energizes us.

Many dentists cannot stand to have staff being paid if the dentist is not in the office working. High producers would rather reward the staff to produce an effective schedule with less time required of the dentist. If you pay by the hour, you encourage your staff to have you working longer hours. Many think they have to be more successful to take more free days. This type of thinking will prevent you from ever taking free days. You will notice when you start taking free days you will be more successful and it is more enjoyable. Many think their patients will miss them. Your patients will follow any rules you establish.

One step further is the concept of taking more frequent vacations. After a vacation, we are recharged and much more productive. This is especially true if we develop some skills for activities on vacation. This may be physical which means you must stay in good physical shape or you will return exhausted. Perhaps it is just sitting and reading a book. Do you allow time for yourself to just be entertained or do you take your workaholic habits with you on vacation? Do you allow yourself to be disconnected from the Internet and phone or do you have to just get a little fix? The alcoholic who just needs a little drink never becomes sober. You may be traveling to an interesting place. This adds to your interest in life. You see a vacation requires discipline to be an effective rejuvenating time.

After the productive phase we can enter into a mechanical phase. We are just going through the motions. We think we are being productive but are irritable, constantly allowing ourselves to be interrupted while working. We are easily distracted and end up working on many urgent projects even though they are not important. We become poor managers of our time.

The last phase is the burn out stage. We are always tired. There is never enough time to complete things. We spend time day dreaming about being somewhere else. This is the phase that many dentist turn to addictive behavior. In this phase work and personal time all blend together. Family suffers. No matter what this phase is destructive.

Why not avoid the last two phases completely. One must view vacation as preparation for productive time rather than a reward for hard and long hours.

Plan your whole life rather than just your practice life. Your values and desires in life should form your practice, not the other way around. You are always at choice in every given moment. To make these vital changes, many times it takes an outsider to coach you to balance.